THE DEVIL'S GARDEN

Related Titles from Potomac Books

Getting Away with Torture: Secret Government, War Crimes, and the Rule of Law, by Christopher H. Pyle

The Secrets of Abu Ghraib Revealed: American Soldiers on Trial, by Christopher Graveline and Michael Clemens

Harvest in the Snow: My Crusade to Rescue the Lost Children of Bosnia, by Ellen Blackman

THE
DEVIL'S
GARDEN

A WAR CRIMES INVESTIGATOR'S STORY

JOHN R. CENCICH, SPECIAL AGENT, USAF (RET.)

Foreword by Christian Chartier

Potomac Books
Washington, D.C.

Potomac Books is an imprint of the University of Nebraska Press

Library of Congress Cataloging-in-Publication Data
Cencich, John R., 1957-
  The devil's garden : a war crimes investigator's story / John R. Cencich, Special Agent,
USAF (Ret.).
    pages cm
  Includes bibliographical references and index.
  ISBN 978-1-61234-172-9 (hardcover : alk. paper)
  ISBN 978-1-61234-173-6 (electronic)
  1. Miloevic, Slobodan, 1941-2006—Trials, litigation, etc. 2. International Tribunal
for the Prosecution of Persons Responsible for Serious Violations of International
Humanitarian Law Committed in the Territory of the Former Yugoslavia since 1991. 3.
Criminal investigation—International cooperation. 4. Yugoslav War Crime Trials, Hague,
Netherlands, 1994- 5. Yugoslav War, 1991-1995—Atrocities. I. Title.
  KZ1203.M55C46 2013
  341.6'90268–dc23
                                                                            2013003489

Printed in the United States of America on acid-free paper that meets the American
National Standards Institute Z39-48 Standard.

Potomac Books
22841 Quicksilver Drive
Dulles, Virginia 20166

First Edition

10 9 8 7 6 5 4 3 2 1

To war crimes investigators throughout the world,
"Let justice be done though the heavens fall."

From the Latin maxim
Fiat justitia ruat caelum

CONTENTS

Foreword by Christian Chartier   xiii

Preface   xvii

Author's Note   xxi

List of Abbreviations   xxiii

Cast of Key Characters   xxvii

Introduction   1

1. The Hague   5

2. Bosnia   15

3. Wooden Rifles   29

4. A Policeman's Murder   45

5. Two Spanish Legionnaires   59

6. Kosovo   69

7. Team Four   79

8. The Conspirators   109

9. Inside the Shadows   123

10. Indictment of a President   143

11. Mala Jaska   163

Epilogue: The Hague Crucible   171

Acknowledgments   191

Appendix I. Cenčići Jerbićevi   193

Appendix II. Cases and Related Legal Documents   207

Notes   209

Bibliography   213

Index   215

About the Author   225

Political map of Yugoslavia following World War II. *Reprinted from* The Palgrave Concise Historical Atlas of the Balkans *by Dennis P. Hupchick and Harold E. Cox*

Political map of the successor states of the former Yugoslavia. *Reprinted from The Palgrave Concise Historical Atlas of the Balkans by Dennis P. Hupchick and Harold E. Cox*

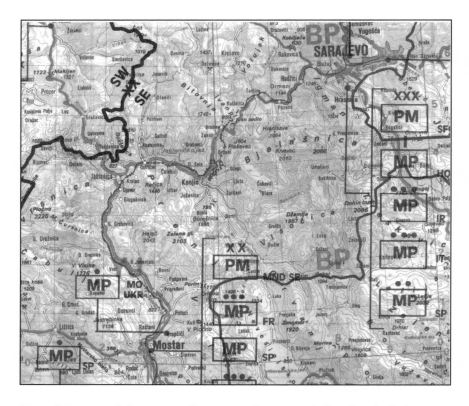

Map of Mostar and the surrounding area in Bosnia, including Sovići, Doljani, and Raštani. *Source:* NATO

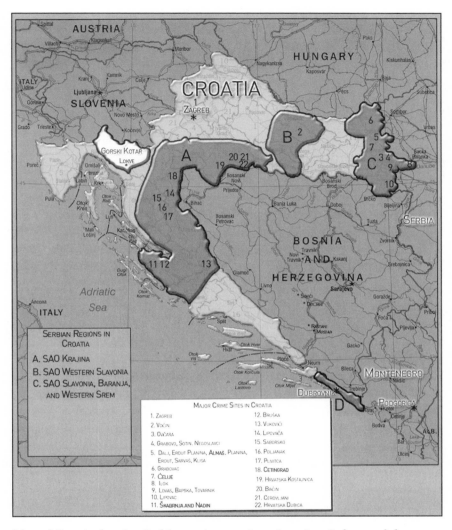

Map of Croatia showing Serbian regions, major crime sites, Lokve, and the Gorski Kotar region. *Base map courtesy of the University of Texas Libraries, The University of Texas at Austin; additions and modifications by S. C. Spangler*

FOREWORD

In the summer of 1992, TV reports were broadcast across the globe that showed pictures, reminiscent of the Holocaust, of emaciated prisoners behind barbed wire in concentration-like makeshift camps. These were followed by the graphic images of the shelling of the jam-packed central market in Sarajevo, a city under siege. Other reports of mass killings, "ethnic cleansing," and systematic rape and torture were widespread, including the abduction and murder of more than two hundred wounded hospital patients in Vukovar, Croatia. Outraged Western public opinions eventually pushed the international community into action—the International Criminal Tribunal for the former Yugoslavia (ICTY) was born, the first ever really international criminal tribunal.

Help was needed to investigate and pursue war criminals, and it quickly came from the White House. Like the establishment of the landmark trials of the major Nazi and Japanese war criminals in Nuremberg and Tokyo in the wake of World War II, the U.S. government was a driving force behind the ICTY. The UN Security Council exercised its powers under Chapter VII of the Charter of the United Nations, which authorized the Council to take measures to "maintain or restore international peace and security." Consequently, the ICTY was officially established in 1993. All of this was done under the sound and clear pressure of strong diplomats. This included the then U.S. ambassador to the United Nations Madeleine Albright, who solemnly avowed to the Security Council and the world, "There is an echo in this chamber today. The Nuremberg principles have been reaffirmed. The lesson that we are all accountable to international law may finally have taken hold in our collective memory."

These were the diplomatic and political efforts that brought about this truly historical event. Yet politicians don't bring criminals to the dock, and help was needed to commence the investigations that would eventually result in war crimes trials. From that day on, the Clinton administration, followed by the Bush administration, spared no effort to assist this completely new court of law in many ways. One of its main contributions was to make available skilled prosecutors, expert investigators, and experienced law enforcement officers. The U.S. government immediately seconded staff to the tribunal and promoted UN recruitment efforts through the State Department.

I remember quite well when, in the autumn of 1998, American investigator John Cencich, the author of *The Devil's Garden*, arrived in The Hague in the Netherlands to work in a new venue. It is one that he describes quite accurately in his book as the true "end game" for "war, violent crime, and espionage," and a place where "the masks were taken off the men who committed crimes that shocked the conscious of humanity." As an international civil servant and UN appointee, John was precisely one of these gems who worked day and night on missions throughout the Balkans and in many other parts of the world in order to expose the atrocities and bring those responsible to justice.

At the time perceived by many as a "fig-leaf" or a "toothless tiger," the ICTY progressively became a feared investigative and prosecution body. There is no mistaking that John Cencich is one of these determined experts who, always working tirelessly and frequently under dangerous conditions, made this happen. You will see this through *The Devil's Garden*, a one-of-a-kind legal thriller. And while respecting the confidentiality demanded of UN appointees, it is a stunning revelation of their everyday work, both at the ICTY's seat in The Hague and on various locations throughout Yugoslavia.

John's ultimate goal, and that of his fellow international war crimes investigators coming from no less than fifty different countries, was to link senior political and military figures with the many crimes committed throughout the former Yugoslavia. A once solid, multi-ethnic federation, which in the 1990s was torn apart by brutal inter-ethnic conflicts, became the scene of atrocities at a level not seen in Europe since World War II. I need not list them. *The Devil's Garden* provides a nailing account of the "crimes against humanity" that were committed by regular military forces, paramilitary militias, police, and even by individuals who, all of a sudden, turned against their former friends and neighbors.

As the only non-member of the Office of the Prosecutor authorized to attend the daily morning briefings at the ICTY, I saw firsthand the hard work of the war crimes investigators, although operational matters were never discussed, for obvious reasons. But there is nothing like having actually been there. *The Devil's Garden* provides an inside look of the world of war crimes investigators and their genuine investigative acumen, diplomatic skills, resilience, imagination, and above all else their unsurpassed compassion for the victims and their families.

The Devil's Garden helped me gain a better understanding of why the ICTY's pioneering investigative and prosecutorial work has become a blueprint for all subsequent international courts, such as the International Criminal Court and the Special Tribunal for Lebanon. This is what makes reading this book fascinating! As John so eloquently says, war crimes investigators' work allowed them to "look inside the spirits of the dead and expose the hearts of the killers." His tremendous account of the missions and the intricate undertakings of war crimes investigators fully captures this essence through a breathlessly written book that reads like a novel, although there is no fiction here!

By sharing, with full honesty, his own experiences as an international crimes expert, John provides *unprecedented* insight into what investigating war crimes actually means and takes. You will be flabbergasted and fascinated! You will see how complex cases made their way from the "killing fields" to the courtroom as the result of the incredibly patient and determined efforts of UN war crimes investigators.

In addition to paying one of the best services ever rendered to the ICTY in particular, and international criminal justice at large, this page-turner provides a compelling professional perspective that helps vindicate the need for international criminal tribunals and their fight to bring war criminals to justice. In addition, the harmonious manner by which John intertwines his own ancestral background in the narrative provides a unique human dimension to this story, which leaves the reader with the profound universal awareness that we are all part of a much larger world.

However, moving beyond his personal experiences, it is fittingly conspicuous that John gives credit to the many wonderful and dedicated war crimes investigators, international prosecutors, analysts, and other colleagues who worked together for the noble cause of international justice, peace, and security.

As one of his many colleagues and friends, I am privileged and honored to have been extended such confidence to write this foreword to a must-read book that tells an exceptional and unique "War Crimes Investigator's Story."

Christian Chartier
Chief Spokesperson (1994–1998)
Chief, Public Information (1998–2010)
United Nations–Nations Unies
International Criminal Tribunal for the Former Yugoslavia
Tribunal Pénal International pour l'ex-Yougoslavie

PREFACE

In 1945, with the close of World War II, man's inhumanity to man was to have come to an end. Atrocities such as those committed by the Third Reich were never to happen again. But they did. Almost fifty years later, in Yugoslavia, hundreds of thousands of innocent people were killed, tortured, forcibly transferred, or otherwise persecuted.

These people didn't suffer as the direct or collateral consequences of warfare. They were victims of an international criminal conspiracy masterminded by Slobodan Milošević, then the president of Serbia and later the president of the Federal Republic of Yugoslavia. The crimes that were perpetrated as part of this conspiracy, or as a direct consequence of the overall plan to form a "Greater Serbia," were so horrendous and widespread that they rose to the level of crimes against all humanity.

In the aftermath of the bloody Yugoslav war of the 1990s came one of the largest international criminal investigations ever undertaken. It differed substantially from the World War II war crimes investigations and subsequent trials, including those at Nuremberg. This time criminal investigators ensured the rights of suspects were respected and used modern criminal investigative techniques to bring the accused to justice. This time teams of international war crimes investigators assembled from national police agencies from around the world undertook the investigations. It was a job for experienced criminal investigators, not soldiers and army legal officers, as had been the case five decades earlier.

This is the inside story of what went on behind the scenes of the investigations into some of the world's worst crimes—mass murders, serial rapes, torture, extermination, and persecution almost beyond human comprehension. This answers the questions, so often asked, about how the investigators put the cases together, protected witnesses, and tracked down mercenaries, assassins, and other killers around the world.

As the senior American investigator at The Hague–based United Nations war crimes tribunal and the lead investigator on the case against Milošević and fifteen high-level coperpetrators, I want to tell a story that goes beyond the crimes alleged to have been committed throughout Croatia. I want readers to see what it takes to investigate international war crimes. I want to show the political influences that affected the case each day. And I want readers to know how we formulated the prosecution theory that ultimately brought Milošević to The Hague—an approach that would have an impact on almost every subsequent major international criminal indictment for crimes ranging from war crimes to international terrorism.

Nowhere in this book will I disclose protected or confidential information. In fact, at various points in my story I make it plain that I am intentionally omitting confidential, classified, or otherwise protected facts. In many instances I have changed the tribunal-assigned pseudonyms for protected witnesses, thus providing a double measure of protection. Sometimes I have created new aliases for witnesses who testified openly. Unless noted otherwise, all relevant dialogue, biographies of suspects and accused persons, descriptions of the crimes, and related information came directly from transcripts, indictments, trial judgments, appellate proceedings, and other public and open sources.

Some locations, dates, and names, including official code names, have been changed to ensure that the work of the war crimes tribunal is not compromised and to maintain the safety of all concerned. In most instances, the names and identities of war crimes investigation team members have not been included, save again for those who have already been disclosed publicly.

It also should be noted that I identify only those war crimes suspects who have been publicly identified, indicted, or named as unindicted coperpetrators by the tribunal. Even then, every individual named in the book is presumed innocent unless and until proven guilty.

Throughout this book, I have tried to explain the complexities of writing about inside sources and protected witnesses, secret intelligence services such as the Central Intelligence Agency (CIA) and the British Secret Intelligence Service (MI6), and elite special operations units such as the

British Special Air Service (SAS), Delta Force, and U.S. Navy SEALs. I have documented the events at the heart of my story through my personal experiences investigating these crimes, my own research, and my travels to Europe, where I gained intimate knowledge of people and events from long before the Yugoslav war broke out.

To be sure, this is a war crimes investigator's story. It is a story about life, and often death, on the streets and in the darkest corners of the earth.

AUTHOR'S NOTE

At the International Criminal Tribunal for the Former Yugoslavia, the language spoken throughout the region is referred to as B/C/S, or Bosnian, Croatian, and Serbian. In its Latin form, there are few letters in B/C/S that are different from those in English. To avoid the difficulties of pronunciation, some writers use the process of transliteration. For example, the surname Milošević may be transliterated as Miloshevich or Miloshevitch in order to reflect its pronunciation. However, I have chosen to retain the original spellings. Accordingly, the following key offers some assistance with the pronunciations.

> C: ts as in wince
> Ć: ch as in fetch
> Č: ch as in chuck
> Đ: g as in ginger
> J: Y as in Yugoslavia
> Š: sh as in shove
> Ž: z as in azure or s as in pleasure

ABBREVIATIONS

2IC	second officer
ABiH	Army of Bosnia and Herzegovina
AID	Agency for Information and Documentation (Bosnia)
APC	armored personnel carrier
ATG	antiterrorist group
CFU	Croatian Fraternal Union
CIA	Central Intelligence Agency, headquartered at Langley, Virginia
CPD	common purpose doctrine
DB	State Security Service of Serbia, a component of the Serbian Ministry of Internal Affairs (MUP)
DevGru	U.S. Naval Special Warfare Development Group, a.k.a. Navy SEAL Team Six, one of four tier-one U.S. special mission units*
ETA	estimated time of arrival
FBI	Federal Bureau of Investigation, headquartered in Washington, D.C.
FIST	Fugitive Investigative Support Team
FRY	Federal Republic of Yugoslavia, successor state of the Socialist Federal Republic of Yugoslavia (SFRY), originally consisting of the republics of Serbia and Montenegro but later reconstituted as the State Union of Serbia and Montenegro
GPS	global positioning system

---

* The four U.S. special mission units are (1) Delta Force (U.S. Army); (2) SEAL Team Six, a.k.a. DevGru (U.S. Navy); (3) Twenty-Fourth Special Tactics Squadron (U.S. Air Force); and (4) Intelligence Support Activity (U.S. Army).

HIS	Croatian Intelligence Service
HOS	military arm of the Croatian Party of Rights
HUMINT	human intelligence
HVO	military arm of the Bosnian-Croatian Defense Council
ICRC	International Committee for the Red Cross
ICTY	International Criminal Tribunal for the Former Yugoslavia, United Nations agency headquartered at The Hague, Netherlands
IPTF	International Police Task Force
IRA	Irish Republican Army
ISA	Intelligence Support Activity, top-secret tier-one U.S. special operations team that specializes in clandestine signals intelligence (SIGINT)
JA	Yugoslav Army
JATD	special operations component of the State Security Service (DB) of Serbia, also referred to at different times as Red Berets and JSO
JNA	Yugoslav People's Army, successor of the Yugoslav Army (JA)
JSO	See JATD
JSOC	Joint Special Operations Command
KB	Convicts Battalion, special-purposes sabotage unit of the Croatian Defense Council (HVO) responsible for war crimes in Bosnia and Herzegovina
KFOR	Kosovo Force
KGB	Committee for State Security, a Soviet-era spy agency
KLA	Kosovo Liberation Army
KOG	Counterintelligence Group of the Yugoslav People's Army Security Administration (UB)
KOS	Counterintelligence Service of the Yugoslav People's Army; former name of the UB/KOG
MI5	British Security Service; protects the United Kingdom, its citizens, and its interests within the country and abroad against threats to national security
MI6	British Secret Intelligence Service; collects intelligence abroad and provides a global covert capability for national security
MND	Multinational Division

MSS	Ministry of State Security (China)
MSU	multinational specialized unit
MUP	Ministry of Internal Affairs (uniformed, investigative, and state security) in the former Yugoslav republics, such as Serbia and current independent states
NATO	North Atlantic Treaty Organization
NCO	noncommissioned officer
NGO	nongovernmental organization
OHR	Office of the High Representative (UN)
OPORD	operational order
OSCE	Organization for Security and Co-operation in Europe
OSI	Office of Special Investigations (U.S. Air Force); investigative branch for serious crimes with major responsibilities for counterintelligence, counterespionage, and counterterrorism, headquartered at Quantico, Virginia
OSS	Office of Strategic Services; U.S. military counterintelligence, special operations, and spy agency during World War II, predecessor to the Central Intelligence Agency (CIA)
OTP	Office of the Prosecutor of the International Criminal Tribunal for the Former Yugoslavia (ICTY)
PIFWC	person indicted for war crimes
PJP	special police units (Kosovo)
PLO	Palestine Liberation Organization
RPG	rocket-propelled grenade
RSK	Republic of Serbian Krajina, an area within Croatia that was declared an independent state by Croatian-Serbs
SAJ	special antiterrorist units (Kosovo)
SAO	Serbian autonomous district; regions within Croatia that were declared autonomous and independent by Croatian-Serbs
SAS	Special Air Service, a component of British Special Forces (UKSF) with elite tier-one stature equal to but predating the U.S. Navy SEALs and U.S. Delta Force
SATCOM	satellite communications
SBWS	Slavonia, Baranja, and Western Srem, an area in eastern Croatia

SCI	sensitive compartmented information
SČP	Serbian Četnik Movement
SDB	Yugoslav federal State Security Service within the Secretariat for Internal Affairs (SUP)
SDG	Serbian Volunteer Guard
SDS	Serbian Democratic Party
SFOR	Stabilization Force
SFRY	Socialist Federal Republic of Yugoslavia, formed following World War II with Josip Broz "Tito" as its longtime leader
SIGINT	signals intelligence
SITREP	situation report
SNB	Serbian National Security
SPABAT	Spanish Battalion
SPS	Socialist Party of Serbia
SRS	Serbian Radical Party
SSNO	Federal Secretariat for People's Defense
STA	senior trial attorney of the Office of the Prosecutor (OTP)
TO	territorial defense forces in the former republics of Yugoslavia, which, under total-war military doctrine, formed part of the Yugoslav People's Army (JNA)
UB	Yugoslav People's Army Security Administration; responsible for security and counterintelligence services
UDBA	State Security Administration (secret police) of the Socialist Federal Republic of Yugoslavia (SFRY)
UKSF	United Kingdom Special Forces
UN	United Nations
UNESCO	United Nations Educational, Scientific, and Cultural Organization
UNHRC	United Nations Human Rights Council
VPS	Military Naval Sector (Yugoslav People's Army)
VRS	Bosnian-Serb Army
WARNORD	warning order
ZNG	Croatian National Guard

CAST OF KEY CHARACTERS

Adžić, Blagoje—Yugoslav People's Army (JNA) colonel general; chief of staff of the JNA and later federal secretary for national defense of the Socialist Federal Republic of Yugoslavia (SFRY)

Andabak, Ivan—Croatian Defense Council (HVO) general who served as deputy commander of the Convicts Battalion (KB)

Arbour, Louise—former chief prosecutor of the International Criminal Tribunal for the Former Yugoslavia (ICTY) and the International Criminal Tribunal for Rwanda (ICTR) at The Hague; former justice of the Ontario Court of Appeal and the Supreme Court of Canada; former UN High Commissioner for Human Rights

Arshad, Azim—war crimes investigator on Team Four; deputy inspector general of police in Pakistan

Babić, Milan—Croatian-Serb dentist who became the first president of the Republic of Serbian Krajina (RSK); committed suicide in prison after cooperating with the war crimes tribunal

Blewitt, Graham—deputy prosecutor at the ICTY, from Australia

Bulatović, Momir—former president of Montenegro

Cenčić, Josip—Great-grandfather of Special Agent John Cencich; immigrated to the United States from Austria-Hungary (Croatia) in 1892

Cencich, John—war crimes investigator on Team Ten; later promoted to head Team Four; retired special agent—superintendent—(reserve) with the U.S. Air Force Office of Special Investigations (OSI); and retired special agent in charge with the Commonwealth of Virginia

Curtis, Kevin—investigations team leader for Team Eleven (responsible for Kosovo); previous Team Four member; former police officer in the United Kingdom

Del Ponte, Carla—chief prosecutor at the ICTY (succeeding Louise Arbour); former attorney general of Switzerland

Đinđić, Zoran—prime minister of Serbia; assassinated in 2003

Driguet, Catherine—Team Ten war crimes investigator from the French National Police with the rank of commandant (major)

Dzuro, Vladimir—Team Four war crimes investigator; former police captain from the Czech Republic

Groome, Dermot—legal adviser for Team Five; codeveloped the prosecution theory of the joint criminal enterprise; former assistant district attorney in Manhattan

Hadžić, Goran—former president of the Serbian Autonomous District (SAO) Slavonia, Baranja, and Western Srem (SBWS); later president of the RSK

Hardin, Bill—war crimes investigator on Team Four; retired supervisory special agent with the Drug Enforcement Administration and former Oakland, California, police officer

Jokić, Miodrag—vice admiral in the JNA navy; commander of the Ninth (Boka Kotorska) Military Naval Sector (VPS) during the unlawful assault on Dubrovnik

Jović, Borisav—member of the Presidency of the SFRY from Serbia; vice president and later president of the Presidency

Kadijević, Veljko—JNA general; federal secretary for national defense of the SFRY

Kostić, Branko—member of the Presidency of the SFRY from Montenegro; vice president and later acting president of the Presidency

Kovačević, Vladimir "Rambo"—captain first class and commander of the Third Battalion of the JNA, Trebinje Brigade, during the unlawful attack on Dubrovnik

Martić, Milan—Croatian-Serb police inspector; later became minister of internal affairs for the Krajina and president of the RSK

Martinović, Vinko "Štela"—commander of the Vinko Skrobo (a.k.a. Mrmak) antiterrorist group (ATG), a subunit of the KB

Milošević, Slobodan—former president of Serbia; later president of the Federal Republic of Yugoslavia (FRY); died in prison while war crimes trial was ongoing

Mladić, Ratko—JNA colonel who commanded the JNA's Ninth Corps, which operated in Croatia; later colonel general who commanded the Bosnian-Serb Army (VRS); indicted for his alleged involvement in the massacre at Srebrenica

Mrkšić, Mile—JNA general found guilty for his involvement in the Vukovar Hospital (Ovčara) massacre

Murugan, Rajie—Team Four war crimes investigator; former police captain from South Africa

Naletilić, Mladen—"Tuta" commander of the KB

O'Donnell, Bernie—investigations team leader for Team Five (responsible for Bosnia); former supervisory federal agent for the Australian Federal Police

Pfundheller, Brent—Team Four war crimes investigator; retired detective sergeant with the Washington State Patrol

Radić, Miroslav—JNA captain ultimately acquitted of criminal charges related to his activities connected with the Vukovar Hospital (Ovčara) massacre

Ralston, John—former chief of investigations at the ICTY; former police supervisor with the New South Wales Police Service in Australia

Ražnatović, Željko "Arkan"—head of Serb paramilitary group known as Arkan's Tigers; assassinated in 2000

Šešelj, Vojislav—former president of the Serbian Radical Party (SRS)

Simatović, Franko "Frenki"—head of the special operations component of the State Security Service (DB) known as the Red Berets

Simović, Tomislav—JNA general; minister of defense of Serbia

Šljivančanin, Veselin—JNA officer (major, later lieutenant colonel) found guilty for his involvement in the Vukovar Hospital (Ovčara) massacre

Stambolić, Ivan—former president of Serbia; assassinated in 2000

Stanišić, Jovica—head of the DB

Stojičić, Radovan "Badža"—(Brutus) general in the Ministry of Internal Affairs (MUP) of Serbia; assassinated in 1997

Strugar, Pavle—JNA lieutenant general from Montenegro; commander of the Second Operation Group during the unlawful assault on Dubrovnik

Torkildsen, Morten—financial investigator on Team Four, from Norway

Uertz-Retzlaff, Hildegard—senior trial attorney (STA) assigned to the Milošević case for Croatia; attorney and judge from Germany

Ulemek, Milorad "Legija"—(Legionnaire) former commander of the special operations component of the DB (JSO); convicted for masterminding the assassination of the prime minister of Serbia, Zoran Đinđić

Van Hecke, Jan—senior Belgian police investigator (*commissaire principal*) and head of Team Ten

Vasiljević, Aleksandar—JNA major general; commander of the UB, which includes the Counterintelligence Group (KOG)

Vasiljković, Dragan—(a.k.a. Daniel Sneddon) operated under the nom de guerre "Captain Dragan" in conjunction with the DB and the Red Berets

Williamson, Clint—legal adviser for Team Four; later U.S. ambassador at large for war crimes

Zec, Milan—battleship captain and chief of staff of the Ninth VPS during the unlawful attack on Dubrovnik; charges against him were later withdrawn by the prosecutor

INTRODUCTION

I WAS UNDER SURVEILLANCE JUST MINUTES AFTER MY PLANE LANDED IN Zagreb. It was 2007, and I had returned to Croatia five years after my experiences working international war crimes. As soon as I left customs and immigration, I was bird-dogged all the way to a forested park just outside the village of Lokve, which rests in the mountainous Gorski Kotar region of Croatia. I'm not exactly sure who the dark-clothed men in the black BMW were, but after all these years I'd grown accustomed to seeing them. It was the nature of my business.

My oldest son, Jonathan, was with me as we joined about thirty members of the Cenčić clan (Cenčić is the Croatian spelling of our surname). The villagers were there to welcome me not only as an American descendent of Josip Cenčić, a local Croat who had immigrated to America in 1892, but also as the person who had led the investigation into the murders, torture, and persecution of the Croatian people during the Yugoslav war of the 1990s.

A lamb cooked on a slow-turning spit, and the *šljivovica* and Croatian wine flowed. These people and this get-together reminded me of my early teenage years in Detroit. My great-grandfather, Josip, lived on Newbern Street in the city's Eastside neighborhood, near Hamtramck, and my father grew up in Centerline, just a few miles north over the Detroit city line. I remember the Croatian-American Fourth of July picnics we attended, hearing the distinctive mix of English and the Slavic language my relatives spoke. Many of my relatives were married to Serbs. There was laughter and children getting into mischief. There were people with heavy lines on their sun-darkened faces.

The people of my past spoke passionately about the old country and often kindly of a man they referred to as Tito. Others seemed troubled by the situation in Yugoslavia. As a child, I had absolutely no idea what was going on in that part of the world. It was all a puzzle to me, and I never imagined that one day I would be there, right in the middle of it all.

With me in Lokve was Mirjana Pleše, the principal of the local school. Mirjana took me to the school, where she showed me the original logbooks with entries for my great-grandfather, his brothers and sisters, and even his father. She took me to St. Katarina's, the church where my great-grandparents were married and a place that World War II occupying forces later used for clandestine operations. I entered the train station where Josip had purchased his ticket for Naples, the first stop on his voyage to the New World, and I crawled inside bunkers that had been used by Nazis and Italian Fascists during World War II. I saw where Josip's house had stood before it burned to the ground.

I traced the steps of generation after generation of the Cenčić clan in this lovely village. Mirjana took my arm as we walked through the town in the rain, dodging puddles in the dirt roads. We walked up the steep steps to Kalvarija, where the Crosses of Rejection, Repentance, and Redemption stand, and then to the local cemetery, where the Cenčić family members who stayed behind were buried. We spent several days together—days that have become some of my fondest memories. Mirjana never spoke a word of English to me, but many of the messages she conveyed needed no translation.

When we left the forest, Mirjana gently began to sing a song to me. My cousin Boris translated. It is a song about the people from Gorski Kotar who left and longed to come home one day:

> *Snowflakes were gently falling*
> *On a lonely Christmas night.*
> *My forests kept calling,*
> *But I had to leave.*
> *The paths of my childhood*
> *Were weeping after me.*
> *At that moment I promised myself*
> *That I would come home.*
>
> *Come home to you, my dearest Gorski Kotar.*
> *Come home to you, the most beautiful country of mine.*
> *There is nothing like your sunshine,*

No place else that shines so bright,
And the only ones who know it
Are your inhabitants.

Many long years have passed,
But I still remember it all.
My heart longs to go back
To your spring of old.
The paths of my childhood
Were weeping after me.
At that moment I promised myself
That I would come home.

("My Gorski Kotar" by Gordana Brkić Žagar)

"Josip has finally come home, through you, Ivan," Mirjana said, using the Croatian translation of John.

I had come home. But it was through an ironic twist of circumstances. Gorski Kotar, I learned, was once called Hortus Diabolicus, or the Devil's Garden, by the Romans who drew the first Slavic blood in a never-ending series of wars that still haunt the people of this beautiful land. As a U.S. federal agent, I ended up serving a four-year appointment with the United Nations (UN) International Criminal Tribunal for the Former Yugoslavia (ICTY) at The Hague, Netherlands, leading one of the largest international criminal investigations undertaken in history. It was a case that took me and a dedicated international investigative team of senior police officers throughout the entire world.

As I listened to Mirjana's gentle song, I could see the faces of the hundreds of thousands of innocent people who had been forced from their homes; the civilians who were raped and murdered; the prisoners of war who were beaten, tortured, and executed without a trial; and the many women, children, and elderly, some of whom couldn't leave their beds or their wheelchairs, who had been exterminated by cold-blooded murderers.

There have been many books written about the turbulent history of the region, the latest war in the Balkans, and international war crimes trials. This book is about what it takes to bring some of the mass murderers and serial rapists to justice. This is not a soldier's story, a court-room scene, or an academic essay. It is the real world of war crimes investigations.

And *these* are the events that caused me to be followed in Croatia years after my work had been finished.

1

The Hague

I FIRST SAW THE PRISON NOT LONG AFTER I ARRIVED IN THE HAGUE, the international city of peace and justice in the Netherlands. It was September 1998. With the sound of the crashing waves from the North Sea and the tall walls and Gothic architecture, the premises seemed more like a castle than a place for serial rapists, torturers, and mass murderers.

I knew it had been used to hold Dutch resistance fighters during World War II. I could imagine the guards removing more than three hundred of the prisoners, including those held in the infamous "Death Cell 601," and executing them in the nearby dunes. For the Nazis, it was one final crime of war, committed in a place where my job was just beginning. A special wing of the prison, under the command of the UN, now housed war crimes suspects awaiting trial for atrocities committed in Yugoslavia.

It was almost dark, and my thoughts about the Germans took me back momentarily to twenty-two years earlier, in East Berlin. I recalled a cold Sunday afternoon walking past the many gray and gloomy buildings that still bore heavy scars from World War II. In the distance I could see the graffiti-covered Berlin Wall, which served not only as a symbol of the then-ongoing Cold War but also as the demarcation between where I stood and a place where I didn't have to fear being arrested or, worse yet, shot.

But first I had to get past the Volkspolizei, the Soviet officers, and the East German sentries, both on the ground and in their observation posts, to return to West Berlin, where I was stationed in the U.S. Air Force. Land mines were on either side of the seemingly endless walkway that took me back through Checkpoint Charlie. I was just barely eighteen, and this surreal experience provided a quick lesson, both in history and in life. I never imagined that two decades later I would be back in Europe, this time leading an international investigation of the president of a country for war crimes and crimes against humanity.

The next day I reported to my new job at the ICTY. I took the tram from the Carlton Beach hotel in Scheveningen, listening to the mixed voices of Dutch-, French-, and English-speaking passengers along the way. Through the window I could see well-dressed children, many of whom were boys with spiked hair, as well as adults, riding their bicycles. I disembarked in front of the tribunal headquarters and took a short walk into another world.

Inside the headquarters building, everyone seemed to have a sense of purpose, of urgency. I was escorted to the investigations wing of the Office of the Prosecutor (OTP), where I met senior members of police forces from Italy, South Africa, Belgium, France, Canada, and many other nations. Most were multilingual. They spoke various languages when it suited them; English when it was necessary. In this environment the most serious levels of major-crimes investigation, military intelligence, and juridical operations were combined. There was no other place quite like it. Here the masks were taken off the men who committed crimes that shocked the conscience of humanity. For war, violent crime, and espionage, it is the true endgame—full stop.

The countdown for one such war crimes suspect was under way just as I entered the highly secure premises for the first time. Operation Ensue was in full force. The target: Stevan Todorović, a former Bosnian-Serb police chief who had been involved in the brutal rapes and murders of Bosnian-Croats and Bosnian-Muslims. Just days after my arrival at headquarters, Todorović had been outside of Bosnia, beyond the reach of the war crimes tribunal—or so he thought.[1]

I later learned that British Special Air Service (SAS) operators, armed with sealed indictments issued by the tribunal, had captured Todorović in a log cabin hideout some eighty kilometers over the Bosnian border, just inside of Serbia. Evading and eluding Serb military and security forces, the SAS smuggled Todorović back into Bosnia by way of the River Drina in an inflatable, high-speed rubber boat designed specifically for clandestine military operations such as this. Next, they took him by helicopter to Tuzla Air Base in Bosnia, where he was turned over to war crimes investigators.[2] Fighter jets escorted him to a secret airstrip in the Netherlands. The final stop on Todorović's nocturnal journey was the castlelike prison in the Scheveningen area of The Hague that I had just recently reflected upon.

This was just one example of how special operations units were assisting the tribunal in the capture of war crimes suspects. Soon after I arrived at The Hague, U.S. Navy SEAL Team Six, also known as "DevGru," snatched another one of our suspects—individuals the military called persons indicted for war crimes (PIFWCs). SEALs, operating as part of the Joint Special Operations Command (JSOC) under an overall operation code-named "Amber Star," were engaged in low-intensity, yet high-risk, operations.[3]

Hidden deep inside Amber Star was a highly secret intelligence service that formed part of the U.S. special operations community. It operated under the code name "Torn Victor" and captured real-time, top-secret intelligence, which was then provided to other elite tier-one U.S. and British special operations units, such as Delta Force, SEAL Team Six, and SAS. The Dutch 108th Special Operations Corps (Commando Troepen) was there too. Together, they were working aggressively to help the tribunal capture violent war criminals. Torn Victor was additionally known for having twice provided key human intelligence (HUMINT) and signals intelligence (SIGINT) that enabled the capture of Colombian drug lord Pablo Escobar.[4] These operators knew what they were doing.

The world of war crimes investigations is an environment with absolutely no margin of error. These weren't just "snatch and grab" jobs; long before the capture of war criminals came the delicate work of international war crimes investigators, who had to deal with spies, intelligence agencies, elite special operations units, and issues relating to sovereignty and national security.

We worked with information and evidence that was highly classified. My top-secret U.S. security clearance, with sensitive compartmented information (SCI) privileges, couldn't even begin to touch the information I now had my hands on. As a UN officer, I had to undergo a special security check, and in no way could I share the protected information with anyone, including my own government. Even the slightest breach of security could result in a situation where politicians, diplomats, and ordinary witnesses could be murdered in a heartbeat, assassinated on orders issued secretly from deep inside prison walls. In some instances, they were. As international criminal investigators, we understood that our job was unlike any other, due to the seriousness of crimes, the complexity of the cases, and the deadly consequences for mistakes.

The man who set the stage for these high-speed and incredibly interesting cases was my new boss, John Ralston, the chief of investigations. Some say Ralston, a former Australian cop, came from the "old school." We were fortunate that he did. Few others at the tribunal could have forged the relationships (or continued associations previously cultivated by others) with Western governments, including intelligence agencies, than Ralston could. He was an unassuming man, but he commanded great respect. Colleagues at The Hague viewed Ralston, as well as Chief Prosecutor Louise Arbour and Deputy Prosecutor Graham Blewitt, as confident, competent, and fair-minded.

"Welcome, John, we've been looking forward to your arrival," Ralston said when we met.

An experienced copper, no doubt, I thought.

"We've got you on Team Ten, that's the Convicts Battalion inquiry. We'll have someone take you down there after we talk a bit more. You'll like the case, John."

Did he say Convicts Battalion? Did I hear him correctly?

"But first, take care of your family. Get your flat, bank account, your mobile, and anything else you need. Once you have that sorted, we have a lot of work for you."

The message was clear: Get your personal business in order and out of the way. There was serious work to be done.

I was soon the second officer (2IC) on the investigations team working the case of the notorious Convicts Battalion (KB), a subordinate unit of the military arm of the Bosnian-Croatian Defense Council (HVO). These men had committed atrocities against Bosnian-Muslims in the ancient city of Mostar, in western Bosnia, not far from the Adriatic, about 130 kilometers from Sarajevo.

Many members of the KB had been involved in racketeering in Eastern and Central Europe before the war. Others had been in exile because of their political beliefs. The battalion also included foreign mercenaries, for example, including a former East German soldier who had twice attempted to escape over the wall precisely during the time

I had been in West Berlin. To add to his repertoire, he had served two sentences in Stasi prisons for his crimes against the state before he became a killer for hire.

Other battalion members came right off a page of E. M. Nathanson's *The Dirty Dozen*: they were convicts who had been released from prison simply for the fight. And as I came to know more about the case, it became clear to me that these prisoners were far more deadly than their cinematic counterparts. They enjoyed what they were doing, and the murders of innocent civilians meant nothing to them. They were cold-blooded murderers who, I later learned through interviews and interrogations, often fantasized about raping, torturing, and killing their victims, even before committing these acts.

I often wondered what caused these men to do what they did. Was it psychopathy, hatred, or a twisted sense of ultranationalism? Through the next four years, I came to the conclusion that it was most likely several combinations of these and other causes. For members of the KB, it was all of the above.

Ralston had put me on the KB investigations team because of my background in leading conspiracy and organized crime cases for the Commonwealth of Virginia, which included time spent as a special agent with the Bureau of Law Enforcement for the Department of Alcoholic Beverage Control. It is the oldest law enforcement agency in Virginia, with full statewide police powers and investigative responsibility over a wide range of criminal activities, from bootlegging and drug dealing to organized gambling and money laundering.

I also had experience working violent crimes, counterintelligence, and national security investigations as a special agent with the U.S. Air Force Office of Special Investigations (OSI). As a federal agent, I was accustomed to operating outside of the traditional military chain of command while working serious crimes and counterintelligence operations. I was well prepared for the KB, but I knew I would need every bit of my experience and training.

Like all the other cases at the tribunal, these investigations were not ordinary homicide or sexual assault matters. For one thing, the elements of the crimes (specific factors that must be proved in order to establish the commission of a crime) were stricter under international law. And while we surely had to demonstrate who the principal offenders were, the more difficult task was putting together the evidence showing military, police, and political chains of command and conspiratorial relationships. Imagine working the Lindbergh kidnapping and homicide case and also proving—hypothetically—that the child's murder was committed by state police and federal agents, aided by the Central Intelligence Agency (CIA), and authorized by the president. Even then, the "Crime of the Century" would have been nothing more than a single page in a much more complex and voluminous investigation.

To work our way up from the rapists and killers to the generals, chiefs of secret police, cabinet-level officials, and even presidents, we conducted ourselves like any national-level task force working major crimes. Major components of our portfolio included the analysis of intercepted wire and signal communications, reconstruction of clandestine records, financial search warrants, analyses of military and criminal intelligence, witness interviews, cultivation of informants, witness protection, crime scene analysis, DNA and forensic science, and my specialty, interviews and interrogations of suspects. In the world of war crimes investigations, this is what we did every day.

To be clear, war crimes investigators and prosecutors at The Hague sought to prove the individual criminal responsibility of serious offenders for the purposes of criminal conviction and appropriate sentencing and incarceration. These investigative efforts were by no means akin to national immigration cases, which typically seek, at most, the deportation of war criminals. We did, however, make requests to national law enforcement agencies for forensic laboratory assistance, to help locate witnesses in their countries, or to run relatively minor leads on our behalf.

To help ensure our success, the UN Security Council established the tribunal with provisions for both diplomatic immunity and primacy over national courts and law enforcement agencies. We had jurisdiction over the most serious crimes occurring in the territory of the former Yugoslavia in four basic categories: violations of the laws and customs of war, grave breaches of the Geneva Conventions of 1949, crimes against humanity, and genocide. Offenses that fell under one or more of these categories included rape, torture, murder, extermination, forced deportation, and many other serious crimes relating to the treatment of civilians and prisoners of war. And after some basic introduction to the unique elements of the crimes that constitute violations of international criminal law, I was ready to proceed with my job.

The team chief was Jan Van Hecke, a senior commissioned Belgian police detective—a *commissaire principal*, the rough equivalent to my rank as special agent in charge in the United States. By then he was a veteran war crimes investigator, having received his baptism of fire just three years earlier while working the siege of Sarajevo and the shelling of Tuzla. Those experiences placed him in a perfect position to lead the investigation of the KB.

Van Hecke sat me down and gave me a brief overview of the case. "In principle, we are working two major suspects, but there could, of course, be more," he said in gruff yet excellent English. The two principal targets of our investigation were Mladen Naletilić, a.k.a. "Tuta," and Vinko Martinović, a.k.a. "Štela." They were the commander of the KB and the commander of a subordinate so-called antiterrorist group (ATG), respectively.

I needed to learn about the suspects, to get inside their minds, so I began to read the case files page by page. Tuta's background information was thorough. He was a Bosnian-Croat, born in Široki Brijeg, Bosnia and Herzegovina, in 1946. A Croatian nationalist, he fled Yugoslavia for Germany, where he owned and operated two casinos. Known for his love of gambling, liquor, and beautiful women, he was involved in a number of terrorist activities throughout the years, many of which involved subversive Croatian nationalist organizations. He was linked to Ilich Ramírez Sánchez, the Venezuelan terrorist who operated under the nom de guerre "Carlos," a.k.a. Carlos the Jackal. Carlos was the Palestine Liberation Organization (PLO)–paid assassin who was once released from a Belgrade prison on Tito's personal orders, but who is now serving a life sentence in France for the assassinations of two French secret agents.[5] We knew that Tuta was also associated with the Red Faction Army, a.k.a. the Baader-Meinhof Gang, and was linked to the Irish Republican Army (IRA).[6]

Next I opened Štela's file. Like many of the other documents I read, it was written in slightly broken English, but after a little adjustment, I was able to drill deeply into Štela's background. He was also a Bosnian-Croat, born in Mostar in 1963. He was not much of a step up from a street thug. Before the war, Štela was a taxi driver and racketeer who extorted and shook down residents and smuggled cigarettes, liquor, and anything else that could make him a profit. His was exactly the kind of criminal I had so often worked in the United States.

Eventually I met Tuta and Štela face to face. I also met another key player in the KB: Ivan Andabak. A Bosnian-Croat, he was born in 1953 to a father who had served as a member of the Ustaše, the World War II Croatian Fascist soldiers headed by Ante Pavelić and aligned with Adolf Hitler and Benito Mussolini.[7]

Andabak avoided imprisonment for his ultranationalistic views by escaping to West Germany in 1970 at age seventeen and receiving political asylum there. Just a few months later, he joined the Canadian army, but that type of discipline wasn't for him. He deserted and then began a violent life as a terrorist and unrepentant killer. By age eighteen he'd been arrested for arson in connection with a terrorist firebombing of the Yugoslav Airlines office in Frankfurt, and in 1972 he was involved in a shootout with police.[8]

After a relatively short stint in prison, he hooked up with Tuta, which eventually led to his involvement with the IRA. Under the alias "Patrick," he often went to Belfast, where he is alleged to have obtained caches of weapons.[9] There was a clear connection between the IRA and Croatian revolutionary groups, but it had little to do with the Catholic faith. It was about weapons, power, and terror. Andabak is said to have later repaid the IRA for this weapons cache in kind.

Andabak traveled the world using other aliases and false passports.[10] In 1978, the year I graduated from the police academy, Andabak went to Konstanz, Germany, near the Swiss border on a mission to assassinate the Yugoslav consul. Unbeknown to him at the time, he had actually been double-crossed by an informant for the Yugoslav secret police, and the diplomat never arrived as planned. Others showed up in his stead, and lying in wait until just before midnight with his gun under the table of the smoky nightclub, Andabak shot two other men dead and fled the scene.[11] Hardly any jurisdiction at all was immune from the reaches of Andabak and his band of terrorists and killers. The national authorities didn't always know it, but Andabak left a trail of bodies everywhere he went. Nevertheless, as UN investigators, we didn't focus on domestic crimes, even murders, unless they helped lead us to killers whose activities rose to the level of international atrocities.

With this background, I was ready to hit the streets of Sarajevo, and in December 1998 it was wheels down and boots on the ground in Bosnia. The snow was knee deep, and I was definitely in for a new experience.

I was in the Balkans, the land of my ancestors. Just a little more than one hundred years earlier my great-grandfather, Josip Cenčić, had left this area of the world at the spirited age of eighteen and immigrated to America. In fact, the Cenčić clan had made its home in Bosnia until the sixteenth century.

Like many other Christians, they fled Bosnia to escape the persecution of the Ottoman Empire. And now, ironically, I was in the land of my forebears investigating a new era of oppression, brutality, and murder.

2

━━●《◉》●━━

Bosnia

I WOKE AS THE SUN BEGAN TO PEEK ABOVE THE HORIZON ON MY FIRST
morning in Sarajevo, a Bohemian-looking city of about 300,000. From
the window of my apartment I could see minarets and hear the muezzin
call the Muslim faithful to prayer. The echoing calls sound spiritual to some
people, mystical to others. The sound grabbed me in an eerie, hypnotic
way. I thought that Sarajevo had probably been very much like this on that
deadly St. Vitus Day in 1914, when, under Serbia's Black Hand, the Archduke Franz Ferdinand was assassinated. That murder sparked World War I
and, to a great extent, began a chain of events that ultimately led me to this
smoky patch more than three-quarters of a century later.

In the city with me were Van Hecke, Catherine Driguet from the
French National Police, and colleagues from the Royal Canadian
Mounted Police and the Portuguese police. We spent the first couple of
days becoming acclimated to Sarajevo, obtaining UN driver's licenses,
and receiving briefings on land mines and areas with active hostilities
and security checkpoints.

Next, I went to the site of the 1984 Winter Olympics. Commingled
with the thousands upon thousands of grave markers of the war victims,
I could see the tattered image of the five Olympic rings that had once
made Sarajevans so proud. Most were Muslim victims, but there were
many Bosnian-Croats and Bosnian-Serbs who had died together with
their Muslim neighbors while defending their homes and neighborhoods
from the Serb forces who had held them under siege.

With these images in my mind, I passed through the NATO-run security checkpoints on our way to Mostar.

15

Over the next two years, I would come to take the winding roads from Sarajevo to Mostar many times. On one particular occasion, we couldn't get through the vehicle checkpoint, despite our diplomatic documents. I decided to switch tactics and take a different approach. I exited the marked UN vehicle and approached the noncommissioned officer (NCO) in charge of the security detail. Within a couple of minutes, the sergeant presented me with a sharp salute, and we were on our way. Being a U.S. federal agent often had its advantages.

From the moment I first set foot in Bosnia, I was under constant surveillance. My training and experience in counterintelligence for the U.S. government helped me to pick up on this straightaway, and my background as a police investigator allowed me to work confidently in this shadowy atmosphere. Van Hecke's experience in Belgium's gritty underworld and Driguet's years of streetwise know-how, acquired as she worked her way up the ranks to commandant (major) of a serious crimes unit in Paris, made us a team that wouldn't easily be taken by surprise. We knew that appearances were deceptive and that anyone could be a double agent playing both sides of the street.

In Mostar, the first order of business was to meet with case officers of the Bosnian Agency for Information and Documentation (AID). This was the Bosnian national intelligence agency that was charged, among other things, with gathering evidence of war crimes. The operatives were there to assist us in any way they could. They also kept a watchful eye on us. Sometimes they provided security, keeping us safe from war criminals, organized crime, and even other intelligence agencies, some of which had previously been affiliated with the Soviet Committee for State Security (KGB). At other times, AID was there to spy on us. We couldn't fully trust them, but then again, we couldn't afford to trust anyone. Too much was at stake.

Our local AID point-of-contact was Ahmet (I've purposely omitted his last name). When he was introduced to me, I noticed he reacted slightly when he heard my surname.

"*Govorite li Bosanski?*" he asked me.

"I beg your pardon?"

"Do you speak Bosnian?" my interpreter translated.

I had understood what Ahmet had said on my own, but I didn't want to let on. Some of the words from my boyhood had stuck with me, despite my youthful attempts to ignore them. The Bosnian language was essentially the same as Croatian and Serbian.

"No. I am sorry, but I don't."

A Muslim, Ahmet was about my age, forty. He had lost many family members during the war, and he had lost his home. In fact, his whole village had been destroyed. Despite everything he and his people had been through, I never heard Ahmet say a single bad word about the Serbs, Croats, or any ethnic group for that matter, even though men of such ethnicities were responsible for the pain he still endures. I came to admire Ahmet for that. Sometimes in the evenings when we had dinner, I could see his eyes go glassy as he reminisced about the time when Serbs, Croats, and Muslims all lived together harmoniously in Bosnia. It tormented his heart to see how his country and his neighbors had been torn apart.

Now it was time for my colleagues and me to begin putting the pieces back together. It was time to build a case so our prosecutors could successfully present evidence before the Trial Chamber at The Hague. I interviewed intelligence agents, police officers, and survivors. Witnesses also included international observers, UN officers, and members of the foreign services of many countries.

To help build the case, I went on dozens of investigative missions around the world. I interviewed the former commandant of the British Royal Marines and the national security adviser of a European country. I even walked into a president's office. I particularly liked cities, such as Paris, London, Stockholm, Edinburgh, and New York, but the remote areas, including an island in the Black Sea where I interviewed a foreign mercenary, were also quite interesting. Working war crimes investigations, I gained an entirely new perspective on Washington, D.C. There was no continent, save Antarctica, that we did not set foot on as investigators. And we would have gone there too, had it been necessary.

On one mission to Switzerland, I arrived in Geneva without my national passport. I was quite surprised to learn that because the Confoederatio Helvetica was neither a member of the UN nor a signatory to the Schengen Agreement at the time, my UN laissez-passer was unacceptable. Immigration officers told me in unequivocal terms that I would have to turn around and go back to The Hague. I had to think quick on my feet and resorted to what I knew would work. I asked to speak to the highest ranking police officer on the detail. After a few minutes of a private conversation, I had the unique privilege of entering Switzerland with a bright red cross prominently displayed in the Swiss visa just placed in my diplomatic passport.

Even with diplomatic immunity and the primacy of the tribunal, we still had to respect national sovereignty when entering countries on official UN business. This involved notifying the country through the proper diplomatic channels before embarking on the mission. We weren't required to explain the nature of our investigation but simply to give appropriate diplomatic notification. I even had to alert the U.S. State Department when I entered the United States to conduct a criminal investigation that included obtaining documents, interviewing suspects, and tracking down witnesses.

The witnesses I interviewed and the documents I read provided me with background on the crimes I was investigating. Upon the death of Josip Broz "Tito," president of the Socialist Federal Republic of Yugoslavia (SFRY), national rivalries had emerged. Eventually, Slovenia and Croatia declared their independence from the SFRY. This didn't sit well with the Serbs for many complicated reasons, and the Yugoslav People's Army (JNA), which consisted mostly of Serbs, particularly at the senior officer level, took action to prevent the republics from seceding. The war in Slovenia lasted only ten days. Croatia was entirely another matter, and I will give a more detailed account of the conflict there later on.

Bosnia, which had been a harmonious, multiethnic state consisting of Serbs, Croats, and Muslims, the latter calling themselves Bosniaks, also declared its independence from the SFRY in 1992. What happened next shocked the world. I had seen images of the fierce fighting, ethnic cleansing, and civilian casualties on television back in the United States, where I worked both as a special agent and as an adjunct professor at Virginia Commonwealth University. Up until that time, many people believed that the atrocities of World War II had closed the book on crimes against humanity. We were all wrong.

In 1992 Bosnia was attacked by land, air, and sea. Serb forces encircled Sarajevo and lay siege to the city. Innocent civilians, including children, were shot at as they walked through what became known as "snipers' alley" in search of food and water. The UN Security Council imposed an arms embargo on all the republics in the former Yugoslavia, but this effort hurt the Bosniaks the most. They needed help defending themselves, and thus mujahideen—Muslim guerrilla fighters—and members of the Iranian Revolutionary Guard were brought in. The North Atlantic Treaty Organization (NATO) eventually stepped in, but not before most of the death and devastation had already occurred.

Serb forces also attacked other areas of Bosnia, and with a strong ring of truth to the Arab proverb that "the enemy of my enemy is my friend," the Bosnian-Croats and the Bosnian-Muslims fought together in and around Mostar as part of the HVO defense force against the Bosnian-Serbs. The alliance was successful, and the Serbs fled Mostar.

But not long afterward, the partnership turned to perfidy. With the Serbs gone, the Bosniaks had become a majority, and the local Bosnian-Croats were not happy about the situation. Soon the Muslims in Mostar and relatively nearby areas, such as Sovići, Doljani, and Raštani, saw their neighbors turn on them in unconscionable and unprecedented fashion.

More than five years later, on a blistering hot summer day, I walked into what had once been the primary schoolhouse in the village of Sovići. The windows were all gone, part of the roof was missing, and it looked as though it was all that remained after an apocalyptic war. The survivors provided me with similar characterizations.

Surrounded by a personal protection team from the NATO-led Stabilization Force (SFOR), including Ukrainian soldiers who once were commandos with a former Soviet Union Spetsnaz unit, I began to direct the processing of various crime scenes. As the mission leader, I was responsible for collecting relevant evidence that eventually would be used in court.

As I stood there at the *locus delecti*, I knew I needed to gain a complete understanding of the events that had taken place on that very spot. I needed to sift carefully through the physical evidence, including the actions of the perpetrators, but I also needed to see things from the perspective of the victims. My training in equivocal death and violent crime analysis would definitely come in handy. In many instances, the detailed analyses of the offenders' behavior served to prove the motive for the crime—that is, the discriminatory intent necessary to elevate a murder or series of murders to the next step: crimes against humanity. The same held true for torture and rape as part of a pattern of evidence that demonstrated an overall scheme of persecution.

The premeditation was evident. One witness described to me how checkpoints had been set up before the attack to prevent Bosnian-Muslims from leaving the village. Sovići had a population of about eight hundred. Most residents were Muslim, and the Bosnian-Croats had been their neighbors and dear friends. This is why they were so completely taken by surprise. They never suspected the treachery that lurked, quite literally, right around the corner.

During the early morning hours on a spring day in 1993, the entire KB and two ATGs under Tuta's command began their shock attack. The tiny villages of Sovići and Doljani and their nearby hamlets, nestled in a valley just fifty kilometers north of Mostar, were hit hard.

Numerous witnesses told me how the KB targeted only Muslim homes. As I looked down on Sovići from atop a mountain ridge, with a Dutch police video camera capturing the view, it was evident that they were correct. Another witness described how the different designs of the houses, particularly the roofs, made it easy for the perpetrators to engage in discriminatory fire against Muslim homes, leaving the Bosnian-Croat residences unharmed.

Many Muslims were killed on the spot. Others fled to the mountains and the woods. Some couldn't leave their homes quickly enough, and others were physically incapable of doing so. Witnesses told me, quite graphically, that it was a living nightmare. One witness described what it was like as the forces came closer to her home. Her son was hiding in the woods, but he couldn't elude the KB. The attackers—Tuta's men—yelled for those in the woods to come out. If they didn't, the women and children would be killed.

"What else could they do?" the witness asked.

She went on to describe how the KB took all the Bosnian-Muslim men away to the schoolhouse I had been standing in. There they were detained and processed. Like other wives and mothers, the witness went to the schoolhouse to confirm that her husband and son were being held there. Although her suspicions were correct, she was sent away empty-handed. Her emotional pleas for their release went unanswered.

There were cries from within as well. The schoolhouse was the scene of torture and interrogation, and the anguish went on for three consecutive days. The men were beaten, whipped, and brutalized. They were threatened: if they didn't talk, their wives and children would be raped, killed, or both. These were the types of horrific crimes that had brought the investigators here. Years later, we were finally putting this case together.

Those three days had been difficult for our witness too. Tuta's men came to her house. When they took her outside, she could see other women, children, and elderly people being "escorted" to the schoolhouse. Along the way, she saw what remained of the Muslim homes in Sović.

"They had all been set on fire. I could see that they had all burned down."

At the school, almost four hundred civilians were packed in like sardines, and a line was beginning to form outside. By this time, the men had been taken to another detention center. I interviewed some of the survivors, but many were never again seen alive.

I could read the excruciating pain on the witness's face as she described what happened to her next: "Women and children and elderly in that group of ours went to the school, but there were many more people. As a matter of fact, we simply couldn't fit in. There wasn't room enough for us. So we didn't stay there long."

She was taken to an adjoining hamlet, where she was held with more than seventy other civilians in a house built to accommodate a family of five. It was a place where innocence was instantly transformed to terror.

This scene was repeated over and over throughout the area. In fact, scores of overfilled houses held elderly men, women, and children, shoved against one another so closely that they felt as though they were suffocating. Again, Tuta's men were there, perpetrators in the first degree. They even had Tuta's picture affixed to some of their vehicles. The witness and the other civilians eventually were loaded into freight cars and trucks and deported to other areas of Bosnia, many to a common detention center.

Tuta's headquarters in this area was a wooden shed at a fish farm in nearby Doljani, only about six kilometers from Sović. Doljani also had been attacked. The mosque and most of the Muslim homes were destroyed. Those Muslims who were not killed or able to escape, including women and children, were captured.

At the fish farm, Tuta and Andabak tortured and interrogated detainees. We obtained evidence of this not only from surviving victims but also from two German mercenaries who had fought with the KB. We even acquired a diary that detailed many of the crimes from one of the perpetrators. The testimonies of several other witnesses remain confidential today; only summaries have been made known to the public.

One witness, protected under the alias "Baseball," was scarcely a teenager at the time. He was abducted in Doljani and taken to the Sovići school. There his captors cut his hair off with a knife, beat him, threw him to the ground, and bound his hands. One of them sliced the young boy's face with a knife. He had committed no wrong—except that he was Muslim.

One of our inside witnesses was a foreign mercenary who had fought with the KB. He told us how the special subversive-duty unit drove Bosnian Muslims from their homes, rounded them up like cattle, and transported them to detention facilities. He told us how Tuta, who was considered a general officer, personally issued the order of "no quarter" for Doljani.

"Complete cleansing and no prisoners to be taken!" Tuta instructed.

But, as we know, some people were taken prisoner. The mercenary and other members of the KB beat them as they made their way on all fours through the mud.

"They had to crawl on their knees and hands to the shed. There they were kicked with the feet, and they were beaten with the butts of rifles in their backs," the hired killer told us.

Next, Tuta and Andabak interrogated and tortured the prisoners at the fish farm. Before long, though, members of the KB led the detainees to the woods. The mercenary didn't see what happened, but the circumstantial evidence said it all: "I heard shooting, firings . . . from that place in the woods where the prisoners were taken to. The only people who emerged from the woods were our people from the unit. When they came out, they replenished their magazines."

Less than a month later, the HVO targeted the civilian Bosniak population of Mostar, a city of about 125,000. It was approximately 5 a.m. on May 9, 1993, just before sunrise, when armed HVO units surrounded apartment buildings and houses, rounding up Muslim civilians. In many blocks of apartments where both Bosniaks and Bosnian-Croats lived, only the Muslims were forced to leave. Devastated, and in fear for their lives, women, children, and elderly were unlawfully forced out of their homes.

On one occasion, nine armed men, dressed all in black and calling themselves Štelići, or "Štela's men," entered a Muslim woman's apartment searching for cash, gold, and other valuables. Her family and others were evicted, and the men were separated from the women and children. The latter were placed aboard trucks, taken to the Health Center, and lined up. The armed men opened fire, but by this time the woman had somehow, miraculously, escaped. Not everyone was so fortunate.

Chain-smoking, witness after witness explained to me the terror that Štela and his so-called ATG inflicted on the Muslim residents of Mostar. Sometimes the KB shook down the civilians, promising they would be freed or left alone upon proper payment. The extortion racket was successful for Štela, but it did nothing for those who gave up the money. Soon they were either dead or expelled to the east with nothing but the clothes on their backs.

So that I could begin to piece together what had occurred in Mostar, I was strapped into a French SFOR helicopter flying over the city. Outfitted with a radio headset, I was able to direct the pilot and Dutch police photographers to the specific areas where I needed aerial crime scene photos. For protection, I was accompanied by two French gendarmes deployed from a predominately French Multinational Division (MND) military installation not far from Mostar. Heavy machine guns provided additional air support.

Supporting our air mission from the ground were scores of military and police personnel, including the Italian Carabinieri and a special long-range reconnaissance platoon from the Spanish marines. They were providing counterintelligence and countersurveillance support because a number of foreign intelligence services and racketeers were in the area—with us as their specific targets. A special unit of the Spanish Legion, las Canarias, also assisted us, and its members were definitely on top of their game.

From the air, the view reminded me of an old World War II movie depicting London or Berlin after those cities had been bombed. I could easily see the confrontation line with its hollowed-out buildings along the Bulevar, one of the main thoroughfares in Mostar, where once-beautiful structures had been reduced to ruins. The street separated the Bosnian-Croats to the west and the Bosnian-Muslims to the east.

I could see the areas where large numbers of Bosnian-Muslims had been expelled to the eastern side of the city. Thousands of innocent, helpless civilians had been corralled into an area where they faced unimaginable terror. The Bosniaks were completely under siege, surrounded by snipers.

In the meantime, the village of Raštani was the next target for the KB. It is situated north of Mostar on the west bank of the Neretva, a river into which blood has poured for centuries. Raštani consists of several small hamlets of houses and decrepit buildings. I walked every inch of these areas. Countersnipers and heavily armed NATO riot police provided cover as I stepped into the ruins of homes where families had been murdered. I entered the silos and hydroelectric facilities where crime victims had been tortured and interrogated before they were killed.

As a result of all the attacks, thousands of Muslim civilians were forced to leave their homes in Sovići, Doljani, Raštani, and West Mostar. In addition, large numbers of people, both prisoners of war and civilian detainees, were held at detention centers in the area. The main detention center was the Heliodrom, which at times held thousands of prisoners, including civilians.

The HVO tried to claim that civilians were held at the Heliodrom for security reasons, to protect them. But the evidence indicated otherwise. They had been "arrested" without being given a reason and did not know why they were detained. These abductions of civilians violated the laws and customs of war and were also considered crimes against humanity.

As my colleagues and I continued to interview witnesses, I began to understand how intolerable life at the Heliodrom had been. Inside, the Bosniak defenders and civilians often were not fed for days. There was hardly any running water, and dysentery was rampant. The premises were overcrowded and smelled of urine and feces. Armed, drunken criminals beat many of the emaciated detainees.

The personal accounts of the detainees were deeply affecting. The Heliodrom was a place where victims felt they had lost their souls. They had been stripped of all dignity. How a man or woman could live through such horror, I do not know. Often they didn't.

Outside the Heliodrom, wives pleaded feverishly for the release of their husbands; mothers wept for their sons. The women often knew the abductors by name. After all, many had been their neighbors before the conflict broke out. Sometimes the wives and mothers were successful, but mostly their cries and prayers went unanswered.

Some of the prisoners, defenders and civilians, were taken from the Heliodrom to perform forced labor at or near the confrontation line and to serve as human shields for Štela and his henchmen. One might imagine that temporary release from the detention center would offer some relief, but in truth it did nothing of the sort. I personally interviewed a number of witnesses who had "volunteered" for these dangerous and often deadly excursions. What happened outside the Heliodrom was far worse than even the living hell within.

My colleagues and I were searching for additional inside witnesses to help corroborate Tuta's command authority and his individual criminal responsibility for the crimes committed by him and members of the KB. Sound investigative procedures are the same anywhere: We developed a network of informants from around the world, and through these contacts we learned about another foreign mercenary. This man was believed to have the valuable evidence we sought, so after evaluating the credibility of the initial informer through our premission intelligence, an operational order (OPORD) was issued. The mission: to interrogate another German foreign mercenary being held in a prison deep in Eastern Europe.

On a bitterly cold day I arrived at the prison to conduct the interrogation of the killer, code-named "Glock-1."* The prison was located in a dirty, industrial area, and its inmates reputedly faced some of the worst living conditions in any of the former communist countries. Even the prison's psychiatric department was cited as being terrible. Official statistics indicated that the prison also had the highest number of recorded cases of violence among prisoners. I definitely didn't want to spend any more time here than necessary.

I was guided through a maze of dark, damp, and foul-smelling hallways by two prison guards whose pallor suggested they had spent as much time in this dungeon as some of their charges. Soon I found myself sitting in an unventilated, airless room, two stories below ground level. The walls of this windowless, concrete pillbox had a dried blood paint job and a floor made of hard-packed, mildewed dirt. This was the interview room.

---

* Glock-1 is a composite of several war crimes suspects. Accordingly, the description of events here serves to provide an example of what my colleagues and I did on a regular basis without providing information that could be used to identify certain individuals who may continue to pose threats to international security.

Reticent at first, Glock-1 looked to be about thirty-five years of age. His head was shaved, and his face was heavily scarred. He'd been shot in the head and lost his right arm during combat. His intense eyes exposed the horror of the many people he had killed, which was intermingled with my own reflection. There was definitely a certain morbidity about him.

My first task as I began the interrogation was the rights advisement, or "caution." Without it, the questioning would have to cease immediately. The killer's eyes followed my every move with great intensity, trying to size me up. Then, without the slightest hint of trepidation, Glock-1 waived his rights and agreed to speak.

He laid out the details of his past violent criminal life, which included cases of armed robbery and kidnapping. Conveniently, as war was breaking out in the Balkans, he had decided to leave Germany to see what Yugoslavia could offer him. His connections were already in place.

First, he went to Budapest for a few days and received funds and documents for his cover. Once in the Balkans, he was provided with uniforms and weapons and assigned to a special unit. He was told that his existence was secret and that if anything happened to him, he would be "erased."

Glock-1 then began to lay out the background that I was looking for. He described his special unit as an ATG, but he looked me straight in the face and said they were not fighting terrorists—they themselves were committing the crimes against the Bosnian-Muslims. Glock-1 was now in a deadly league all of its own. The KB was extremely well-armed, he said, and there were other mercenaries in the unit too. He told me that many found their way from other countries by way of *Soldier of Fortune* magazine. There was more than one "Rambo" with a torn shirt, bandanna, and bandolier.

Interrogation is both art and science. The process is a combination of psychology, sociology, and experience on the street. Interrogating Glock-1 was not easy. A lot of preparation in understanding the killer's mind was necessary, and the dark, gloomy prison setting complicated matters. International investigators are required to videotape all suspect interviews—a good practice as long as the camera and recording equipment are not within the suspect's view. Visible cameras often serve as a psychological barrier to the communication process. Suspects are more reluctant to talk and often shut down altogether. In this case, the equipment was staring right at Glock-1, but despite these obstacles, I got what I was after.

I was making my way closer to Tuta and Štela. I had turned the dark corner on the path for information toward Štela's headquarters in Mostar, where preparations for the infamous "wooden rifles" incident had taken place. On this notorious day, four men were dressed to be killed. What happened next was not only a grave breach of the Geneva Conventions of 1949, but also a crime against all humanity.

3

Wooden Rifles

ON A BUSY DAY IN MOSTAR, I STEPPED INTO A GLOOMY BRICK STRUCture that once had been used as a battle fortification. It was almost completely black inside, but as my flashlight cut through the darkness, I could see remnants of the death dealt to the Bosniaks who had defended this place. Shattered glass, shell casings, spent rounds, and bullet holes were everywhere.

This was all that remained of the decrepit buildings on Mostar's Bulevar, the street that served as the confrontation line between the Bosnian-Croats and the Bosnian-Muslims. I stood on the side once held by the Army of Bosnia and Herzegovina (ABiH). Here, men had spilled their blood for the Bosniaks—the women, elderly, and children who were under siege and being persecuted by the HVO and the dreaded KB. I declared the area a crime scene.

Overhead, French SFOR helicopters armed with machine guns provided cover for my colleagues and me on the ground. As the mission leader, I had a personal protection team consisting of an elite, heavily armed special mission squad from the Italian Carabinieri. They were part of a multinational specialized unit (MSU) that had been deployed specifically to Bosnia pursuant to the General Framework Agreement for Peace in Bosnia and Herzegovina, better known as the Dayton Agreement. Spanish army and marine forces were there as well, providing cover and intelligence, and Spanish SFOR tanks blocked off the streets. War crimes investigations require this level of security.

As I looked through an embrasure—a small opening that had once been used as a firing port—the air all around me seemed to go silent. In the stillness, I detected the scent of fear. I could see what was left of the fountain in the center of the plaza, and the remains of the Health Center on Šantičeva Street, where members of the KB had lain in wait. I sensed the ghosts of the defenders standing next to me, and I pictured specters walking slowly through the field of fire and across the urban streets. The scene played out again in my mind's eye, the details drawn from the people I had interviewed, the statements I had taken and read, and the documents and photos I had so carefully reviewed.

I could almost see the olive-green, Soviet-built T-55 tank and the four men who had been dressed up by their enemy to be killed on that fateful day, September 17, 1993. I pictured the tank inching its way toward me, firing 100 mm rounds in my direction, hitting the wall of the building I stood inside. The men beside me would have been firing back with M2 .50-caliber machine guns, Yugoslav AK-47s, and whatever else they had. Caught in the crossfire were four Bosnian-Muslim detainees, placed next to the tank to draw ABiH fire so the HVO would know where to strike. Their silhouettes came alive for this moment in time.

There would have been a bright flash, mortar fire, and screams, with guns blazing and explosions coming from all directions. I could almost feel the ground quivering and thick smoke billowing in as a man was hit, his lifeless body seeping blood. Another, barely alive, was holding what was left of his stomach. The innocent Bosnian-Muslims were human shields falling dead to the ground, one by one, with bursts of machine-gun fire cutting several of them down while hand grenades and mortars took care of the rest.

Among them, I knew, were Aziz Čolaković, his cousin Hamdija Čolaković, and Enis Pajo. All three men had families. None of them had done anything wrong, but their killers considered them *balija*, a pejorative term for Bosnian-Muslims.

On that day Bosnian-Croats were also lying on the streets, the last words of the dying among them heard only by the disembodied souls of those who also were leaving this world. Many of the dead on both sides were simply young men caught up in the political machinations of the ultranationalists. The savage attack on the Muslims was not the act of the Bosnian-Croats as a people, but the depraved and malicious work of the HVO leaders and the men who made up the KB.

Through witnesses, I was able to put together what had happened at this crime scene. The tank continued to move slowly toward the building where I now stood, the four men still at port arms and keeping cadence alongside the tank. They were wearing camouflage uniforms bearing the red-and-white checkerboard patch of the HVO. From their vantage point—*my* vantage point—the ABiH defenders couldn't have seen that the four men weren't carrying real rifles but, instead, imitations made of wood, painted black, with army-green slings. The defenders couldn't tell that the four men's "Motorolas," a Yugoslav colloquialism for portable two-way radios, were actually plastic bottles painted black, just like their phony hand grenades.

All of a sudden, at least two of the "wooden-rifle men" began yelling and pleading. "We are one of you! Stop shooting! Stop shooting!"

The ABiH defenders who stood exactly at this location were indeed shooting at the tank, the four men, and anything else they viewed as a threat. Shrapnel and debris were flying both ways, striking some of the wooden-rifle men. It was about then that the ABiH soldiers began to understand their frantic words. These four terrified men were their own people—Bosniaks—who had been forced to dress like HVO soldiers.

To my mission team, it didn't matter whether the four detainees were civilians or prisoners of war. In either scenario the incident violated the laws and customs of war. Those four men had been required to serve as members of their enemy's armed forces, and they had been placed in imminent danger. Under the Geneva Conventions, negotiated in the aftermath of World War II, this never should have happened. But the rules of war were the least of the KB's worries. Tuta and Štela had long ago thrown that book out the window.

At a decisive moment under heavy fire, two brave members of the ABiH slipped through the openings in the wall, grabbed the wounded men, and dragged them back inside. They were dead weight, unconscious. Perhaps they lived so one day they could tell their stories.

I interviewed the wooden-rifle men and some of the defenders who had lived through that deadly day. It was a hell from which many others never returned.

The scene had been set five years before I arrived, in the autumn of 1993, at the Heliodrom Detention Center. The men held there had been captured in different areas in Bosnia, including Mostar, Doljani, Raštani, and Sovići. It is hard to imagine that anyone would ever be the same after experiencing the Heliodrom, where detainees were beaten, tortured, and sodomized. Yet something even more treacherous and deadly had come their way.

It began during the early morning hours of September 17, when Štela's driver showed up at the Heliodrom, at the wheel of a truck. He rounded up thirty-one male detainees, all Bosnian-Muslims, and took them to Štela's headquarters in Mostar.

The prisoners knew that something was wrong. More men than usual were being taken from the Heliodrom. Members of the KB routinely used the prisoners as forced labor. They made the detainees work, sometimes day and night, under threat of the stick, the butt of a rifle, or a bullet to the head. At gunpoint, they took them to the front line and forced them to fill sandbags, dig trenches, carry explosives, and recover injured or dead HVO combatants. Sometimes they did this work with machine guns blasting in both directions over their heads as they crawled on the ground. Even worse, Tuta, Štela, and their men, used the detainees, both civilians and combatants, as human shields.

On that September day in 1993, Štela was waiting for the prisoners at his headquarters on Kalemova Street. Most of them knew him by various names, including "Mr. Colonel" and "Commander." In any case, the mere sound of any of these names made even the most fearless detainees tremble. With his closely cut hair, large build, and hardened face, Štela looked like a boxer or a killer, the detainees said. He definitely had a deadly presence about him.

At Štela's headquarters the prisoners were lined up to be counted, to be killed. Some thought this was the usual modus operandi, a preparation for forced labor. But others suspected something more evil was coming. One witness later succinctly described the situation:

"Štela pointed his finger at four of us, and he said, 'You! You! You! And you!' and told us to go down to the cellar of the building."

Ernest Takač, a.k.a. "Beard," was with Štela at the time.

"Take them to the basement!" Štela ordered.

By the time Takač and the prisoners reached the basement, Štela was there waiting for them.

"There was a very large table there, and Štela was sitting at that table," the witness recalled. "He called the four of us, and he told us to get dressed. In one of the corners of the room there were some camouflage uniforms. At that moment, I asked—because I had a premonition of some sort that things were not going so well—so I asked him if we could do without [going through this mission]."

Štela told him to shut up. If he was to say anything, it would be only, "Yes, sir. Yes, Colonel." It was as simple as that.

Next, the men were issued their "arms" and other equipment—the wooden rifles and imitation portable radios and hand grenades. Their rucksacks were filled with rocks. Their mission, the men were told, was to climb down into trenches and retrieve weapons from dead combatants. If they were successful, they would be released in forty-eight hours.

But it was just one more subterfuge in an already deadly pack of lies. The stakes were too high, and the preparations were much too intense for something so simple. A major attack against the Bosnian-Muslims was planned for that day. Štela wanted human shields on one side of the confrontation line, and these four men to draw fire on the other.

By now, one of the Bosniak detainees who had been dressed up like an HVO soldier knew he was done for. He went pale and fell to the ground. Some observers thought he was having an epileptic seizure. Others believe he feigned the fit to avoid what he most certainly knew would be a fatal mission. The witness who provided me with some of these details was the new "fourth man." He was ordered to strip the uniform off the unconscious detainee and put it on. For both men, the situation went from bad to worse.

The four wooden-rifle men waited nervously until Takač arrived. He took them to the Health Center, a place used as a deployment point by the HVO and the KB. The four men remained there until the T-55 tank arrived shortly before noon. Not too much later they were escorted at gunpoint from the building through a side exit; they had the appearance of a small fire team ready to take out the enemy. The enormous T-55 tank pulled up in front of the Health Center. The hearts of the wooden-rifle men beat furiously.

The four men were reluctant to move. Members of Štela's ATG had to push them closer to the tank. Also providing a little motivation was the foursome's knowledge that HVO snipers positioned in the Health Center had their sights zeroed in on them. The tank would fire a few rounds, and the prisoners would have to take a position around it. Facing the ABiH, the mission of the wooden-rifle men was to draw fire from their fellow Bosniaks, who had no way of knowing they were not members of the

HVO. It was "reconnaissance by fire" for the HVO, and a lose-lose situation for the men bearing wooden arms.

"We held our rifles at the ready, soldiers' fashion, so the rifles were slung around our necks," one of the four men related.

The first time the tank fired, the concussion shook them violently.

"I was totally disoriented, and so were the others. . . . Can you imagine being right next to the tank's barrel, perhaps half a meter away?"

One of the riflemen looked over to where the other twenty-seven detainees had been lined up as human shields. Among them was the man who some believed had faked the epileptic seizure. Guns were blazing in both directions.

"I saw that there were many people dead, killed, HVO soldiers but also prisoners. I saw that people were panic-stricken, and they were hauling the bodies, removing them to a place behind the fountain. And I had already mentioned that behind that fountain, Štela's soldiers were standing, as well as inmates."

Another one of the riflemen described his last moments in the crossfire: "When I came 'round, when I regained consciousness, I was covered with rocks, rubble, plaster. I only remember that I was pulled inside the building. I was frozen. I don't remember if it was unconsciousness, but I was disoriented. My mind was not working properly."

Five years after the battle, I was on the scene where Bosniak defenders had pulled that detainee and the three other wooden-rifle men through the openings in a wall. Other members of the team—including Driguet, the French police commandant—took photographs and measurements. It was evidence that later would be shown to the witnesses in court as we built a case against Tuta and Štela.

Before nightfall, our mission was complete. The investigation team retreated to the security of the nearby French NATO base, where we were billeted in a special military compound, and retired for the night. I awoke every morning at reveille and to members of the French Foreign Legion chanting and singing as they marched through the post before dawn. The words "nous sommes tous des volontaires" were comforting—and so was the high level of security the base provided.

Not far away, just as the sun began to set at the edge of our base, a bomb was detonated in our operational mission area. Intelligence sources confirmed that organized crime members from Herzegovina had set it off as a warning, telling us not to come back. Two innocent people were injured in the bombing. Still, we had to return, and I met some of the mob guys face to face the very next day.

There is much more to an international war crimes investigation than proving that people were mistreated or killed. Typically, the prosecutor, who represents the "people of the world," must prove that the victim was a protected person under either the Third Geneva Convention of 1949, relating to prisoners of war, or the Fourth Convention, relating to the protection of civilians. Crimes against humanity bring the investigation to an even higher level.

Since our team went after only high-level suspects, we had to work our way up from the dead bodies on the street all the way to the top— the men who were most criminally responsible under international law. Often, Tuta and Štela didn't pull the trigger themselves. But like an organized crime boss who orders a hit, they were responsible for the crimes they planned and ordered to be carried out.

There were two traditional ways to build a "war crimes" or "Geneva Conventions" case against Tuta and Štela. First, we could prove they were the actual offenders, the individuals who committed, ordered, or in some way aided and abetted the crime. Sometimes surviving victims provided those details, but usually we needed inside sources, witnesses who had intimate knowledge of the planning and execution of the crimes. Even with that information, we also had to demonstrate that our witnesses were telling the truth.

As investigators, it was our job to corroborate minute details the witnesses provided. Sometimes that meant analyzing physical evidence or finding independent sources for the same information. We also analyzed records or obtained strategic pieces of information through interviews and interrogation. Often, the subjects of those interviews had no idea how valuable a seemingly meaningless piece of information could be.

The doctrine of "command responsibility" gave us the second approach to pursuing the top perpetrators. Under this theory of international law, Tuta and Štela could be held criminally liable because they either knew or had reason to know that crimes would be committed, yet they failed to prevent them from happening.

Alternatively, command responsibility can apply to situations in which a commander or superior officer has knowledge of crimes—or reasonably should have known about them—yet fails to punish the actor or to initiate appropriate action as required by law. To complicate matters, this notion applies only to military commanders or those who have military-type authority to control and punish their subordinates.

Before undertaking the mission, these factors were carefully contemplated and strategically laid out in the investigations plan. These were high-cost and high-stakes missions. Often there would be no second chance to obtain the evidence prosecutors would need to present their cases successfully in court. As investigators, we had to get it right the first time.

Our pursuit of evidence went well beyond the Mostar city limits. We found what we needed in unexpected corners of the world, where we tracked down foreign mercenaries who had fought with the KB and who were present at the scene of the crime.

I found the first gun-for-hire on an island in the Black Sea. He confirmed that on the day before the Mostar attack, he'd been informed that a special operation would take place. He had heard Štela tell soldiers that the aim was to take over two buildings on the other side of the front line—and that the operation would involve heavy artillery and the use of prisoners carrying wooden rifles and serving as human shields.

The Black Sea mercenary told me he was in the Health Center with a group of HVO soldiers and prisoners, waiting for the operation to start. This happened around 11 a.m., when a T-55 tank arrived and started to fire.

Another mercenary, whose identity remains confidential today, corroborated the other's story. This killer described how the soldiers and prisoners waited together before they were ordered to attack. The soldiers then moved from the Health Center to a small wall, with the prisoners running a few meters ahead of them. He remembered seeing three prisoners wearing camouflage jackets and carrying wooden rifles. In the course of the attack, a tank passed through a gap where sandbags had been removed, and then it started to fire. There were violent explosions from all sides, and the witness lost sight of the prisoners.

On one mission, I traveled by air, motor vehicle, and boat to locate and interview another mercenary. He was a tough man who had killed a number of people, but now he was concerned about his family. He told me he'd been recruited through *Soldier of Fortune* magazine.

Others were interested in our mission too. The next night, back on the mainland, we were followed by a man and a woman whom I believe were an intelligence team composed of agents from at least two different but allied countries. They might have had their eyes on us for any number of reasons, but I believe they were focused on a microcassette tape we were after. We never did obtain this particular piece of evidence, but our tail didn't know that.

Alternatively, the couple could have been trying to learn how the mercenaries were recruited or what we knew about their compatriots. In any event, the two-person team was on our heels, street after street, staying about one block away. Their surveillance methods were straight out of the Cold War—fieldcraft that was easily picked up on.

Before the end of that mission, we came up with a Bosniak who had fought on the side of the HVO—and who sang like a bird. We had this crime nailed down tight. Altogether, we were able to corroborate the circumstances surrounding the killings and abuse of many detainees on September 17, 1993. We could show that in order to protect attacking HVO soldiers, approximately fifteen prisoners and detainees had been deployed as human shields in an adjacent section of the Bulevar front line under Štela's command. At least ten of them, including the poor soul who feigned a seizure in an effort to avoid the wooden-rifle mission, had been killed. He had ended up being redeployed as a human shield.

This case also took me to England, where I interviewed Sir Martin Garrod, a retired lieutenant general and former commandant of the Royal Marines. After his military career, he had served in Bosnia in a number of international capacities.

In May 2000 I spent two days with General Garrod. We talked about many things, including the 1996 Provisional IRA attack on the barracks in Deal, where eleven Royal Marines were killed by a fifteen-pound time bomb. Garrod was a kind gentleman who would give a perfect stranger the proverbial shirt off his back. But as an officer who had led a Royal Marines commando unit on the volatile streets of West Belfast and other dangerous sectors of Northern Ireland, he was no one to fool around with. Tuta and Štela learned this the hard way.

Garrod was familiar with the two warlords. He knew about the killings and violence these thugs were a part of. So in October 1998, when he was a senior member of the UN Office of the High Representative (OHR) in Mostar, Garrod held a press conference. Describing Tuta and Štela as the notorious criminals they were, he demanded their arrests.

Media and political pressure grew until the Croatian authorities, acting pursuant to the notion of extraterritorial jurisdiction, finally came to Bosnia and arrested Tuta on racketeering charges, including narcotics, extortion, and incitement to murder. Štela was taken into custody separately on charges relating to a number of domestic murders and assassinations carried out at Tuta's behest. These didn't rise to the level of international war crimes, but at least Tuta and Štela were in custody. Before long, the two war criminals were transferred to the custody of international war crimes investigators.

Some of my other missions also took me to cities and rendezvous points straight out of a Sydney Pollack spy movie or a Tom Clancy novel. In one case my colleague and I entered an embassy in Paris that was serving as a pseudo safe house to interview a military officer who had been taken there secretly from a third-party country. From there, I had another mission. The next stop: Charles de Gaulle. Wheels up in sixteen hours.

Operation Goshawk involved the Croatian Presidential Archives, HVO files, and dossiers of the Croatian Intelligence Service (HIS). As UN investigators, we had unprecedented access that had been negotiated at the highest levels, through the president of Croatia and the UN tribunal's chief prosecutor. It allowed us to look deep into matters that spoke directly to the sovereignty of an independent nation.

I was the operational mission leader on the ground, responsible for coordinating with police and intelligence services to provide transport for our team of investigators, attorneys, political research officers, criminal intelligence analysts, military intelligence officers, and interpreters. I was also our liaison with all onsite officials, including representatives from the prime minister's office and the military, police, and intelligence services. I reported daily to the overall mission leader, who was staging the operation out of our field office in Zagreb. He, in turn, reported to the investigations commander in The Hague.

Every morning we left the Intercontinental Hotel in downtown Zagreb in a caravan of passenger vans. My first job of the day was getting people into those vehicles at precisely 7:30 each morning. I rode shotgun in the lead van, which took us to a safe house hidden in the hills somewhere well beyond the city limits.

There we examined volumes of well-organized documents that were of critical importance to the investigation. Although there was no way of knowing whether the documents before us were complete, they held some valuable information. On day one, as we were returning to our hotel from the safe house, I sat in the front seat with the driver of one of the primary escorts. These operatives had done a great job of sanitizing their identities, but I looked at the keychain hanging from the key in the ignition and saw the emblem of a particular governmental service. I couldn't resist pointing out that he had missed this minor detail, and I motioned to the keychain. The driver had no reaction—but the next day the emblem was gone. I hoped he would give it to me as a memento, but that never happened.

In addition to analyzing the documentation contained in the archives, we had plenty of work to do to make this a solid, prosecutable case. Numerous missions took us to both urban and rural areas of Bosnia. From my perspective as an outsider, the cities, such as Sarajevo, seemed gritty and fast-paced, with a blend of spirituality, sophistication, and sensuality. In contrast, the mountain homes of witnesses were isolated and hard to reach. Like the hollows of Virginia I had sometimes worked back in the United States, they held the distinctive aroma of illicit white liquor. All the places we visited held omnipresent threat.

On one occasion, in March 1999, Van Hecke and I missed a car explosion by ten minutes. Jozo Leutar, the deputy Bosnian-Croat member of the Federation Ministry of Interior, wasn't so lucky. He was murdered by a remotely detonated directional bomb. I didn't know it then, but before long I would interrogate the man who to this day is the suspected mastermind behind Leutar's assassination.

He is Ivan Andabak, the HVO general who served as Tuta's deputy—and who surely had a wealth of information that could be used against his former commander. Andabak also was believed to have been killing people all over the world.

Team Ten came up with the idea of having Andabak arrested and interviewed. At the time, Andabak was suspected of being back in Croatia, so we sought a warrant for his arrest for the sole purpose of interrogating him. We hoped that the Croatian authorities would follow through with their commitment of cooperation with the ICTY. Consequently, a judge from the tribunal signed a "material witness" warrant, which was sent through diplomatic channels to the government of the Republic of Croatia. Andabak was to be arrested and delivered to our field office in Zagreb.

Initially, the interrogation was to be undertaken by the team chief, but operational changes dictated otherwise. The execution of the mission was turned over to me, as the 2IC. Most of my colleagues believed that Andabak would never let himself be arrested, let alone consent to an interview. Nevertheless, I began my preparations immediately. I was confident that the Croatian police could find him and arrest him. I had even more confidence in my ability to get Andabak past the "caution" and talking.

On September 12, 2000, I flew to Zagreb accompanied by an attorney who was part of the team. We had an agreement: Only I would ask Andabak questions. If the attorney had some follow-up questions that needed to be asked, he would provide them to me during breaks.

These ground rules were important. In the past, I'd had problems with other legal officers who held the view that conducting interrogations was the same as taking depositions. For these reasons, I once almost completely lost a confession to multiple murders. I wasn't about to let the same thing happen again.

And so there we were in Zagreb. The telephone rang, and the deputy head of the office, speaking in near-perfect Croatian, took the call. When the short conversation was over, he gave me the sign: Andabak had been picked up by the Croatian police. His estimated time of arrival (ETA) was less than forty-five minutes away. I was ready.

A short while later the police caravan pulled up with its blue lights flashing. A crack team of young plainclothes Croatian police officers brought a handcuffed Andabak inside and turned him over to me. The police were professional, and I recognized their sense of pride in this high-profile capture.

Andabak's cuffs were removed, and he was taken into a room that had been set up with a camera to record the interview. Andabak sat down. He was clearly caught off guard.

"¿Como esta usted, señor General?"

"Bien, y usted," he answered with a nervous sort of smile.

Andabak had lived in Spain for a number of years, I knew, protecting the family of Ante Pavelić, the former Ustaše chief who had been shot by Tito's assassins in Argentina after he fled Croatia following World War II. Married to a Spanish woman, Andabak's Castilian was better than mine, but the idea was to make him feel more comfortable. It was working.

I told Andabak that when I was finished with him, he would be free to leave. Continuing in Spanish, I explained that once we went on the record, I would speak to him in English through an interpreter, and he would answer in Croatian.

"*Entiendo*," he replied.

I then read Andabak his formal rights to counsel and to remain completely silent. He waived his rights in both regards.

My first order of business was to break Tuta's lingering hold over Andabak. During the next several hours, Andabak and I took a metaphorical trip around the world. We talked about the past and the present, and gradually he relaxed. He trusted me. I told him that he had the right not to answer any particular question, and he knew that I would honor that agreement. He also realized that I knew what I was talking about. This is important when interviewing terrorists, war criminals, or anyone else who has committed crimes at this level. They can smell when you are afraid, and the interrogator reeks of ignorance when he doesn't know the case inside and out.

I am often asked about interviewing witnesses and suspects through interpreters: Is it even possible? In this case, my interpreter was top notch, and I firmly believe that this is the key to a successful foreign-language interrogation. No matter how good an interrogator may be, everything is lost if the interpreter isn't up to speed. In this case, we never missed a beat. The interrogation proceeded as though I were speaking fluent Croatian myself.

Several days after I returned from this interrogation, BBC News broke a major story in London. On September 20, 2000, at approximately 9:45 p.m. BST, a man believed to be connected to the Real IRA stood on the tracks near London's Waterloo Station and fired a man-portable, Russian-built Mark 22 rocket-propelled grenade (RPG) launcher. Witnesses saw the flash and heard the explosion as the deadly projectile soared through the sky and struck Babylon-on-Thames, headquarters of the British Secret Intelligence Service, a.k.a. MI6.[1] It was a direct attack on the queen and the sovereignty of the United Kingdom. It was an attack against all of us.

About a month later I was standing on a different set of railroad tracks when I received a cryptic phone call. I was on mission in Germany, and without a secure line I couldn't get all the details, but I was needed in The Hague right away. I later learned that several police and intelligence services wanted to talk to me about the Andabak interrogation. A special team composed of British Security Service (MI5), MI6, and Scotland Yard members was in The Hague.

This is what we knew: Just a couple of months prior to my interrogation of Andabak, the Croatian authorities had seized a cache of weapons destined for the IRA. The shipment included RPGs, plastic explosives, and machine guns—all purchased on the black market. Herein lay the intersection of war crimes, terrorism, and organized crime. Some say that's where Ivan Andabak stepped in.[2]

Describing it as one of their "most successful operations ever mounted against dissident Republicans," the Irish Garda said, as reported in the *Sunday Tribune*, that it had shut down one of the main arms supply routes for the Real IRA.[3] And in a special report from Northern Ireland on September 24, 2000, the UK's *Observer* reported, "The war crimes prosecutor's office in The Hague confirmed that investigators have interviewed Andabak. A spokesman said the general is believed to have received explosives training from Irish republicans in the 1990s and to have helped since to procure weapons for the dissident Real IRA."[4]

I don't believe anyone from the tribunal released this type of information. If they had leaked it, they should have been fired straightaway, whether the information was accurate or not. It was noted that the reports first appeared in the *Boston Globe*, located in a city that historically had small pockets of supporters of various IRA factions.

I arrived at a conference room in The Hague where two MI6 men, the Scotland Yard liaison officer to The Hague, and an MI5 operator were waiting for me. Naturally, they wanted to know what I had discussed with Andabak. Their request was a matter of Britain's national security. I surely wanted to help them in any way possible, but I needed authorization. After receiving clearance from senior officials with the OTP, I spoke with the British authorities strictly about matters related to the alleged supply of arms and Andabak's alleged relationship with the IRA. This is not meant to imply that there were indeed any substantive matters to relate in this regard, but only to point out that I shared with them no evidence related to ongoing war crimes investigations.

I often wondered whether Western intelligence services didn't know the real answers to these questions even before I returned Andabak to the

Croatian police on the day of the interrogation. At other times, I was convinced they didn't know. I've speculated that perhaps this was the reason I was followed throughout Europe, and even once to the United States. Shortly after this meeting with the British intelligence officers, I spotted a vehicle following me. I was driving through Germany on my way back to the Netherlands from Spangdahlem Air Base, a U.S. Air Force installation near Bitburg and Trier. I was able to pick up the tail easily. After just a couple of minor evasive maneuvers to see if I was being tailed, I recognized their surveillance tactics.

A switch-off (the number one or "command" surveillance vehicle replaced by a backup or layup vehicle in order to avoid detection of the surveillance) occurred once in Luxemburg and twice more in the Netherlands before I arrived at my residence in The Hague. I didn't know who was bird-dogging me, but when I went back to my office, I obtained an intercepted sixty-second communication between two apparent Brits. I can't disclose how it came into my possession, but at the beginning of the recording, there was a dial tone and some electronic beeps, and then I was able to discern that these guys were conducting a recce on someone in The Hague. A recce is a military term, which is short for reconnoiter or reconnaissance.

The British were not the only ones interested in my interrogation of Andabak. Minutes after I left the MI6 meeting at tribunal headquarters and walked into my office, I received a call on my mobile phone from a Western embassy. I recognized the number as soon as it flashed across my Nokia's screen. I was invited to meet with an intelligence officer at the embassy. These men too wanted to know what had happened during those few hours in Zagreb.

Back home, if the government had tried to interfere with a criminal investigation, I would have shut them down in a heartbeat. But here I needed to be more diplomatic in my response. In fact, I had more important things to do than satisfy someone's curiosity on a subject over which they had no jurisdiction. I had to investigate the murder of a policeman.

4

A Policeman's Murder

THE TIME HAD COME TO EXECUTE A SEARCH WARRANT AT ŠTELA'S headquarters. I knew from our intelligence that the premises, bearing the large, bold letters "HVO" over the entrance, would be covered by members of the Herzegovina mafia. And there they were, all dressed in black, with dark sunglasses that served to mask their eyes and accentuate their menacing faces. I arrived with an international search warrant and served it to the reluctantly cooperative mobster in charge, who was surrounded by a small group of thick-necked lackeys.

I had my backup too. Two French SFOR choppers hovered overhead, one with thermal imagery to detect surreptitious threats and the other with machine gunners just waiting for a chance. My close protection team, an elite squad of the Carabinieri, never left my side. Scores of Spanish legionnaires and marines, Guardia Civil, and members of the International Police Task Force (IPTF) were also on the scene, each playing a carefully coordinated role. And just to make sure nothing went wrong, I had two Spanish M-60 tanks level off on Štela's headquarters.

The planning paid off. The search warrant was executed without incident, and the crime-scene processing began. Some of the worst crimes in Mostar had been perpetrated, planned, or staged on this site. Among other things, we were looking for evidence relating to the wooden-rifles incident and the murder of police officer Nenad Harmandžić.

Just two hours earlier I'd showed up without notice at the office of the canton's minister of interior, a powerful office in Bosnia. I showed my credentials and asked to speak to the minister.

45

"I am sorry, but the minister is occupied in a meeting. He is not receiving anyone at this time."

"Madam, you don't understand. Please interrupt the meeting and tell him that investigators from The Hague are here on a matter of the utmost urgency." In less than a minute I was in the minister's office, looking up at a Bosnian-Croat, who was about 195 centimeters tall and dressed entirely in black.

"I have a search warrant that needs to be served within your jurisdiction, and I have been instructed by the prosecutor to request from you the assistance of local police in executing it," I said.

Technically, we didn't need one ounce of assistance from either the operational or the legal perspective. The decision to make the request was a tactical one: My colleagues had another case in Bosnia in which the defendants and government representatives argued that in spite of our broad authority under UN Security Council resolutions and the Dayton Agreement, whatever was seized should be excluded as evidence if national authorities were not present at the time of the search. The Trial Chamber and the Appeal Chamber of the ICTY both ultimately agreed with the prosecutor's position, which was that we had the legal authority to act unilaterally in such matters.

In the meantime, the minister made it abundantly clear that he was in no mood to help.

"Sorry. I have no one available to assist you. Perhaps you come back in hour or two."

"Are you saying that out of all of the police in the entire city, there is no one available?"

"*Da*," he said in a contemptuous whisper as he leaned forward.

"Sir, I am only going to ask one more time. We will conduct the search with or without your help, but I must inform you that if you do not provide the requested assistance, I will promptly inform the prosecutor, who will in turn report the matter to the Security Council. It is your call."

This was part of the strategy. If he declined to assist, it would negate any future argument for the suppression of evidence on the sole basis of having no Bosnian police with us at the time of the search.

It was as though he could read my mind. With a pissed-off look he picked up the phone and arranged to have a small number of uniformed officers meet my team just minutes before we deployed and executed the warrant.

I had experience doing business this way back home. There were occasions when some local police or sheriff's deputies couldn't be trusted. As special agents working bootlegging, narcotics, and organized gambling cases for the Commonwealth of Virginia, we sometimes arranged to have them meet us nearby just minutes before converging on the raid location, leaving them little or no time to tip anyone off.

Before I left the minister's office, he turned and glanced inquiringly at me: "So, where you from?"

"The United States."

"I mean your family, your surname."

"I'm not sure exactly. Somewhere in the Balkans, I understand."

"Mmm. I had a police chief who reported to me once with the name Cenčić."

"Interesting."

I wasn't going to go down that road with him. And to the best of my recollection, this was as bold as anyone in the former Yugoslavia had been about my ancestry. Presumably, the police chief to whom the minister referred was a Cenčić who had not fled Herzegovina when the Ottomans razed Christian towns and tortured and murdered their residents. Now, in many ways, the tide had turned. I was there investigating a horrific persecution, this time with Muslims as the victims.

Alone in my room, I sometimes wondered whether any of my distant relatives were either the victims or the actors in the conflicts fought in this desperate land. I prayed they were neither. I don't know if this Bosnian policeman who shared my surname was Catholic or Muslim, and if the latter, whether his direct ancestors had been converted to Islam against their will. I also don't know what role he might have played in the war.

Fortunately, these thoughts never stayed with me for long. I had work to do, and it made absolutely no difference to me which ethnic groups committed which crimes. I was thankful for the extraordinary privilege of being charged to pursue evidence of grave crimes and, when necessary, to speak on behalf of the dead. For those of us who work homicide cases, particularly at this level, the task before us puts everything else into its proper perspective.

I entered Štela's headquarters, where police officer Nenad Harmandžić had been tortured and then carried away to be executed with a single shot to his head. I wanted detailed crime-scene sketches and photographs. Live witnesses would present this evidence to the court, and I wanted to show that their stories were true.

Sketches and photos would corroborate the veracity of those witnesses who claimed they observed specific details of Harmandžić's torture, the mistreatment of the wooden-rifle men, and other serious violations of the laws and customs of war. If their statements about the layout of the premises matched the photos and sketches, we could verify events that were material to the case, including Harmandžić's abduction, torture, and murder. I had used this technique many times in the past, albeit never on this scale.

I hadn't arrived in Mostar with the search warrant by happenstance. Obtaining it had been a protracted, difficult struggle. A number of OTP legal advisers held the view that a case couldn't be made on the murder of Nenad Harmandžić. And from their perspective, the murder of only one person didn't necessarily warrant the time, money, and dedication the case required. They made some good points, but I saw this as the murder of a fellow police officer. And I was convinced that what had happened to Harmandžić some five years earlier formed part of a larger scheme of persecution of the Bosnian-Muslims. I believed it would be relevant to the overall investigation and indictment.

At a meeting of the entire team, including investigators, legal officers, and crime analysts, I distinctly recall saying, "Harmandžić was murdered while in the custody of Štela, who was committing a series of serious crimes, including forced labor and the use of detainees as human shields. We can build a circumstantial case to prove who physically murdered Harmandžić under Štela's leadership or command authority, and we can hold Štela individually criminally responsible." In some respects, it was as simple as that. In others, this was just the beginning of a complex undertaking. My colleagues paused for a moment and looked at me. Some nodded with approval. Van Hecke, as head of the team, spoke up. He agreed with my assessment and gave me the green light. The case was mine.

For Harmandžić, the barbarity of war began on May 9, 1993, when the Bosniaks in West Mostar came under attack by the HVO. Like thousands of others during those early morning hours, the entire Harmandžić family awoke to the sound of shells exploding all around their house.

People were being killed and their homes destroyed. They all were afraid, but the Harmandžić family felt fortunate that they had survived the initial attack. For a short while they felt relieved, but all hell had broken loose by noon the very next day. Wearing black uniforms and firing weapons, paramilitary forces rushed into Harmandžić's home and seized him. He was taken by force to the Heliodrom.

I spent many days and nights on the streets of Mostar, and finally I was able to locate a witness who knew what had happened to Harmandžić in the filthy bowels of the Heliodrom. The man, code-named "Falcon," was able to describe the events in specific detail; he also had been abducted and held in the detention center against his will. For ten long, terrifying days he shared a corner of the hard floor with Harmandžić. He witnessed the police officer being viciously beaten by his brutal and notorious captors. Harmandžić was beaten so badly during those ten days that he urinated blood and suffered broken ribs and two black eyes. On one occasion he was dragged away by his feet as his frightened fellow detainees ignored his calls for help. He was beaten again and again.

I was never able to ascertain the precise motive for Harmandžić's release from the Heliodrom. After ten days he returned to his home, where he lived with his family until the end of June 1993. Harmandžić was a marked man, and he knew it. Within days of his release he saw Štela, who verbally abused and threatened him. Harmandžić suspected he would be arrested again. The next time, he thought, he would surely be killed. He was right on both counts.

On June 30 Harmandžić again was taken by force to the Heliodrom Detention Center. This time, he wasn't concerned only about the HVO or the KB but also about criminals he had arrested—and who now were detained along with him. They had an opportunity for revenge, and some seized the moment.

Not long after Harmandžić arrived at the Heliodrom, two men, the Stempf brothers, came there looking for him. Not knowing the purpose of their visit, Harmandžić attempted to hide. It remains unclear whether he was given up by a frightened detainee or one who was seeking revenge, but soon Harmandžić was in the hands of ruthless men who transported him to Štela's headquarters with a group of twenty-four other prisoners.

There, a witness who knew Harmandžić well saw him wearing a dark blue T-shirt, blue jeans, and burgundy moccasins. The witness was certain it was Harmandžić, who at that point was surrounded by armed men. One of his eyes was blackened and swollen shut.

It became evident that Štela had targeted Harmandžić specifically. In fact, he made it known that Harmandžić was designated as "game," meaning he could be mistreated at will. The opportunity arose when Ernest Takač, the same despicable man who had helped Štela organize the wooden-rifles incident, walked into Štela's office and gave the racketeer-turned-warlord the news that Harmandžić had been captured after he'd tried to escape from the Heliodrom.

"It's not true, Štela. I didn't do it," the police officer said.

Štela didn't believe Harmandžić. There was evidence of his attempted escape. But whether he believed Harmandžić or not likely would not have mattered anyway. In fact, our investigation revealed that Štela had seen Harmandžić on the street even before the May 9 attack and warned the policeman, telling him that his day would come. Now Štela showed no mercy.

"Take him to the basement!" Štela ordered.

Even before Harmandžić was led away, Takač and another man began to strike him in the groin, repeatedly and brutally, until the police officer fell to the ground in excruciating pain. Harmandžić appealed for mercy, but his pleas meant nothing to Štela. Takač took Harmandžić down the stairs.

Some minutes later another witness heard a loud scream and saw a number of soldiers on the basement stairway. This witness too was taken to the basement, where he was ordered to beat Harmandžić or suffer the officer's fate. Harmandžić had arrested this witness a number of times in the past. But although he felt a certain amount of ill will toward Harmandžić, the witness couldn't bring himself to lift a finger against the helpless man.

Later, there were allegations that the "Muslim secret police" had paid this witness to provide evidence to the tribunal. In an attempt to discredit him even further, some claimed he was psychotic. But whatever the case, once the witness saw Harmandžić covered in blood, he simply couldn't beat the helpless officer. He was as sane as that.

Harmandžić may have surprised some people—but not me—when, without regard for his own well-being, he told the witness to go ahead and strike him. Harmandžić knew that the witness, a fellow Bosniak, had many children—and he considered himself done for, anyway. The soldiers mocked both Harmandžić and our witness. They taunted both men as the witness was allowed to go back upstairs. With every step he took, he could hear Harmandžić's screams.

Finally, the cries in the darkness ended. Harmandžić was barely alive. His severely battered body was carried out of the building, thrown into a pit in the garage, and covered with boards.

I can only imagine the sheer horror he must have felt as the soldiers, still taunting him, started pouring buckets of water over him through the boards. Harmandžić was bleeding from the nose, ears, and mouth and was in unbearable pain. Štela's men urinated into empty beer cans and forced Harmandžić to drink the piss. One of perpetrators pulled out his penis and forced it into Harmandžić's bruised and bleeding mouth, asking him whether he liked it. The torturers were sadists, indeed.

Nevertheless, Harmandžić maintained his dignity until the bitter end. The witness saw the near-dead policeman for the last time shortly before he was transported back to the Heliodrom with the group of detainees. Before the group—minus one—was sent back, Štela lined them up and addressed them: "Twenty-four of you will return, and what you saw, you did not see. What you heard, you have not heard. He tried to escape, so he will remain here."

I will never forget what the witness said next. Speaking nearly in a whisper, with fear on his face, he related Štela's now infamous remark: "*Sam pao, sam se ubio.*" He fell himself—he got himself killed.

There were tears in the witness's eyes as he repeated Štela's deadly words, which included a warning to each of the detainees that they too could share the same fate.

Upon Štela's orders, the remaining detainees were transported back to the Heliodrom. Štela instructed the driver to inform the men in charge there that Harmandžić had tried to escape and had been left behind. This contradictory and inculpatory statement would later prove critical to the court. But, even with that, the investigation was far from over. I needed to find out what had happened to Harmandžić next.

I sat down with Falcon and went over a series of events in slow motion, minute by minute. He told me that for some time following his release from the Heliodrom, he had been hiding in the attic of his girlfriend's house, which was near Štela's headquarters. One night Štela,

Takač, and two other men entered the house to speak to the girl's father about Falcon's whereabouts. Without making a sound, the terrified Falcon slowly unscrewed the lightbulb in the attic. It was pitch black. Lying there motionless, he overheard one of the men say that they already had killed Harmandžić, and it was their intention to kill Falcon just as soon as they found him. Then there was a creak in the attic. Fortunately, Falcon's pounding heart was heard only by his protectors.

There was still more work to be done on the case, and our team of investigators located two other witnesses who had held a conversation with one of the cooks at the Heliodrom. Hearsay evidence is admissible at the tribunal, so I took note of every word the cook had told them about Harmandžić. The officer had actually been killed at Štela's headquarters, the cook said, although those in charge at the Heliodrom had been given a different story.

Serving to further corroborate what had happened, one of Štela's soldiers, who went by the nickname Dinko, told Falcon that Harmandžić had been killed, adding that the "times were such that the roles were reversed." I took it to mean that the policeman, once the hunter of criminals, in the end had become the hunted.

In the meantime, the investigation took me closer to Harmandžić's body, a critical element in the case. I learned about another man who had helped to bury a corpse that was believed to be Harmandžić. Štela ordered the dead body to be picked up from the area of the Health Center, where it had been lying for a while, and taken to Liska Park in Mostar, where it was buried. Witnesses provided me with details of the exact location: It was in the second row from the sidewalk.

Falcon told me he was convinced the corpse was Harmandžić. A number of factors contributed to his conclusion; among them were the height, graying hair, weight, and overall appearance of the body, which was wrapped in a dark blue blanket. The man who had helped to bury the corpse also knew the victim by the nickname "Neno," the name Harmandžić's friends and family called him, something Falcon became aware of.

Another witness told us that on the same morning that Harmandžić had been taken from the Heliodrom to Štela's base, he had been transported there too in a group of thirty to forty detainees. Takač, who was in charge of the detainees, lined them up, made a gesture, and asked, "Who is strong enough to carry fifty kilograms?"

Takač selected two detainees and took them behind the Health Center. The eyewitness and the other detainees were then locked inside a garage. When Takač returned, he selected three more detainees, gave them shovels, and took them behind the garage to a garden. Takač instructed the men to dig a hole—a shallow grave—quickly. Soon the two detainees who had been taken to the Health Center returned, carrying a body in a dark blue or black blanket. It was the body of a big man who fit Harmandžić's general description. One of the men who carried the body also talked to us: Štela had told him that a detainee had been killed while trying to escape. Štela directed the prisoners to go and pick up the body at the Health Center.

The corpse first was brought to the gravesite in the garden, but that location was abandoned after a soldier approached the men and told them to bury it somewhere else. It is important to note that we had another witness who told us that before long, Štela came to their location and instructed Takač to clean up the evidence that had been left behind. The detainees then transported the body to Liska Park, where they buried it. The corpse was put in a grave. The witness noted the exact location on a piece of paper, which he later handed over to the exhumation team. It was subsequently provided to the investigative team as well.

The witness told me that the body was badly damaged in the area of the head, the chest, and the stomach. Decomposition had begun. The stench was so bad that the witness knew the victim must have been dead for a while. He had been a big, well-developed man who weighed over one hundred kilos, the witness said. He wore a bloodstained summer T-shirt and had some kind of a sport shoe on one foot. The other shoe was missing.

When the witness returned from the burial, he talked about the incident with other detainees in the Heliodrom. He described the body to some of the detainees—locals from Mostar—who told him the dead man was a former police officer from that city.

Yet another witness described in detail what it was like at the pit. Surrounded by murderous soldiers, he arrived at the spot in the dark of night, around 3 a.m. The soldiers used flashlights to light up the area. That's when they saw two bodies with bloodied clothes in the hellish hole.

The two detainees were under orders to remove the bodies from the pit, wrap them in blankets, take them to Liska Park, and bury them. It was easier said than done. The bodies were stiff and heavy. One of them was an exceptionally large man who was very difficult to carry. Indeed, the pair had to drag the body through the streets for about two hundred meters before reaching Liska Park.

Forensic evidence is extremely important, particularly in a circumstantial case. As in any homicide investigation, particularly a cold case, I sought out the pathologists who had examined the remains of the body we believed to be that of Officer Harmandžić. I learned that on March 30, 1998, almost five years after Harmandžić had been murdered, an exhumation team from the Institute for Forensic Medicine at the University of Sarajevo had exhumed the completely skeletonized body of a man about forty-five years old. Uncovered in Liska Park in Mostar, the body initially was labeled "Working Number 05."

Other members of the medical team were on the scene, along with police and prosecutors. An investigating judge was there to lead the inquiry, performing a function similar to that of a senior investigating police officer in a common-law country. Falcon was there too. He had known Harmandžić before the war, spent time with him at the Heliodrom, and now he was present as his friend's body was being touched by humans for the very last time. It was closure for Falcon. It was evidence for us.

By medical calculations, the victim was between 182 and 183 centimeters tall. His height and age were consistent with Harmandžić's. But that wasn't enough. I asked the pathologist about DNA testing. He told me no DNA analysis had been performed; they had no doubt about the identification of Nenad Harmandžić. Investigators had the victim's belt buckle, with its distinctive rectangular shape and three diamond symbols. A piece of the victim's trousers was consistent with what Harmandžić had been wearing. The shoes were size forty-five, the size worn by Harmandžić, and the color and characteristics were the same as what he had worn. We even had a positive identification by yet another witness, who had given Harmandžić those shoes. The victim's teeth were missing, but we knew that Harmandžić had a full set of false teeth.

There had been some question about a bullet injury to the dead man's leg, since none of the witnesses had told me or any of the other investigators working on the case that Harmandžić had been shot in the leg. In fact, one legal officer at the OTP stated that the unexplained leg wound might undermine the credibility of the entire case.

I located a witness who solved the matter on the spot. He told me that years before his death, Harmandžić had accidentally shot himself in the leg with his 6.35 mm pistol. He related this fact to the pathologists and said the bullet had never been removed. The pathologist corroborated the witness's story, informing me that a 6.35 mm bullet had been found in the region of the corpse's right upper leg, in soft tissues decayed from the skeleton.

According to the exhumation report, the body displayed premortem injuries, including fractures of the right shin bone, the pelvic bones, the right ulna, the left shoulder blade, the collarbone, and the left and right jawbones—all caused by blunt force trauma. The report also noted that defensive wounds were present.

The cause of death was a single bullet to the head, which entered the left cheekbone and exited at the mouth, ripping the victim's face apart. The report noted, however, that the bone fractures found on the body were so serious that, even in the absence of a fatal bullet injury to the head, they could have led to a traumatic shock that likely would have been fatal. The pathologist concluded that Harmandžić first was severely beaten and then was shot to death.

To finalize the investigation, I needed to authenticate certain documents. These were issued by the Security Services Center, which by then was known as the MUP. Organizationally, the MUP houses and oversees the police. I sat down with the official keeper of the records to go over every detail. In order to prove a murder, I first had to prove the existence of a life. Nenad Harmandžić was born on February 19, 1947, in Sarajevo. His name will be forever recorded in the *Book of Deaths*, he having left this world by violent means on or about July 14, 1993.

———

With Tuta in the custody of the Croatian authorities on domestic charges of narcotics, extortion, and incitement to murder, our next mission was to transport him to The Hague. Štela initially escaped capture, but several days after Tuta's arrest, he too was arrested. Charges against Štela ran the gamut of organized crime activities and murder committed on Tuta's orders.

In April 1999 I traveled to Zagreb to sit in on extradition hearings for Tuta and Štela in district court. This was my first time in Zagreb—or Croatia, for that matter. I had been prepared for the worst, and I was a bit apprehensive. But I found the Croatian authorities were as cooperative and professional as anyone else I had met during my missions to the former Yugoslavia.

The issue before the court: under Croatia's constitution, was it lawful to extradite Croatian nationals, which both Štela and Tuta were deemed to be, to the Netherlands? The Supreme Court of Croatia eventually agreed that the extradition was indeed lawful. From an international law perspective, it wasn't technically considered an extradition to another state but rather a transfer from one venue to another under orders of the tribunal.

Less than four months later, on August 9, 1999, Štela was in the air and on his way from Croatia to The Hague. I was waiting for him.

To prepare for the international arrest, I had arrived at Schipol Airport several hours earlier with Van Hecke and our interpreter. We met members of the Marechaussee, the Royal Dutch police who, although part of the military, are responsible for law enforcement and security at civil airports in the Netherlands.

We arranged to meet Štela and the Croatian police escorts in the wind tunnel once all the other passengers and crew had disembarked the Air Croatia jet. Soon he was there, hands cuffed in front of him, accompanied by Croatian police and other authorities.

As the head of the investigation, Van Hecke took over: "Mr. Martinović, you are under arrest by the Office of the Prosecutor." Van Hecke served Štela with a copy of the indictment and read all the charges aloud.

Now it was my turn: "I am John Cencich. I am an investigator with the International Criminal Tribunal at The Hague. . . ."

"Ja sam John Cencich, istražitelj međunarodnog suda u Haagu," my interpreter echoed in Croatian.

"You have heard the charges, including murder as a crime against humanity," I began. "You have the right to remain silent. . . . You have the right to legal counsel. . . . Anything you say can be used as evidence against you in a proceeding before the tribunal. . . . You cannot be compelled to testify against yourself or to confess your guilt."

I had repeated similar words many times throughout my career, but there was nothing like saying them to an international war criminal. For me, it added a new layer of meaning to the Miranda rights police officers read to suspects in the United States. It was the thrill of the collar on one hand and ensuring the rule of law on the other.

Štela looked straight into my eyes. He indicated that he understood his rights. I nodded to the Croatian police officers; they nodded back. I knew who they were, and there was no question in their minds about who I was. It was a matter of professional courtesy.

To conceal his identity during the transport, a full-face motorcycle helmet was then placed over Štela's head. At our request, the Marechaussee whisked the accused war criminal away to the UN detention wing at Scheveningen Prison.

Harmandžić's murderer was now in the custody of the International Criminal Tribunal. Štela, however, was responsible for much more. He was also charged specifically with the wooden-rifles incident; with the mistreatment and torture of prisoners of war and civilian detainees at the Heliodrom detention center; with attacks against Bosnian-Muslim civilians; and with destroying homes, looting, unlawful evictions, forced expulsions, forced labor, unlawful detentions, and the use of civilians and prisoners of war as human shields. All this constituted grave breaches of the Geneva Conventions of 1949, violations of the laws and customs of war, and crimes against humanity.

We still needed Tuta in our grip, but the Croatian government claimed he was too ill to be transported abroad. A request for assistance to the Office of Legal Counsel at the U.S. embassy at The Hague was met with an immediate response. Within days a U.S. Air Force air ambulance left Zagreb with Tuta on board.

I was waiting at a remote Dutch naval air base, and officials from the U.S. embassy soon joined me. Within moments I received a message on my mobile: "Wheels down in ten mikes [minutes]."

Precisely ten minutes later, a U.S. Air Force C-17 Globemaster touched down. It was a magnificent sight. First to disembark was a formidable U.S. Air Force Security Forces fire team. They immediately took their places, surrounding the aircraft to provide 360-degree protection.

There was good reason for their tactics. Herzegovina mob guys and right-wing paramilitaries had made direct threats: they would kill anyone who obstructed the freedom of Tuta, who had previously ordered the assassination of the head of the military arm of the Croatian Party of Rights (HOS) and eight of his soldiers.

As a U.S. federal agent, I took a special pride in the way our "package" was delivered, particularly since I had served on just such a team as a young airman more than twenty years earlier. Soon my colleagues Van Hecke and Driguet escorted Tuta down the aircraft's steps to the tarmac. Handcuffed, with his head hanging low and his long, gray hair blowing in the wind, the once-powerful warlord was turned over to a special team of high-risk Dutch transport police, who swiftly took him to our detention facility in The Hague. The Dutch police were on high alert for this mission.

The men and women of Investigations Team Ten knew that another major violent criminal had been taken into custody. Now Tuta and Štela both were charged with war crimes and crimes against humanity, ranging from torture and cruel treatment to willful killing and murder.

As to the Harmandžić murder, the court eventually rendered a decision. The Trial Chamber held that while it had not been definitely established who pulled the trigger to kill Nenad Harmandžić, "the chain of circumstantial evidence established by the Prosecution allows only one reasonable conclusion, namely that Vinko Martinović at least participated in the murder of Nenad Harmandžić." Moreover, the court held that "the sum of all evidence adduced excludes any reasonable possibility that Vinko Martinović could *not* have participated in the murder."[1] This was international criminal justice at its best.

5

Two Spanish Legionnaires

FROM A SNIPER'S DEN IN AN HVO-CONTROLLED AREA OF MOSTAR, the killer lay in wait, his Yugoslav 7.62 mm rifle aimed to the east. With a single glance, a coup d'oeil, he carefully selected his target. The crosshairs on the scope were dead on.

For a moment, perhaps, he wondered if he would be punished for what he was about to do. He likely had no real understanding of the legal concept of "superior orders." The triggerman may have been a psychopath, but more than likely he was just a confused young man who was following illegal orders.

Ever since World War II, international law has been clear that superior orders are no defense when the act itself is manifestly unlawful. The law can place a soldier in a difficult position, but under the laws and customs of war, it is nevertheless his or her duty to disobey an illegal order. In particular, superior orders can never be a complete defense in a criminal proceeding when the directive in question is to kill a UN peacekeeper— even if the soldier is under duress and threatened with his own imminent death. Regardless of the legal system, the law views with distain the taking of an innocent life in order to save one's own.

This case involved more than the trade-off of one life for another. When one murders a UN peacekeeper under the circumstances of war, it is a crime against humanity. It is as if thousands upon thousands of innocent lives are taken with the firing of a single shot.

None of this mattered to the sniper. He relaxed his muscles and maintained his measured breathing as he slowly squeezed the trigger. The gunpowder exploded. The harmonics of the barrel echoed as the bullet rushed down the bore and out the muzzle.

The projectile found its mark. An aerodynamically precise round with a velocity of more than seven hundred meters per second struck 1st Lt. Francisco Aguilar Fernandez. The legionnaire was standing in his armored personnel carrier about seven hundred or eight hundred meters from the sniper. The bullet pierced his flak jacket, entered his body at the left shoulder blade, and crushed his spinal cord. He died instantly.

As I had done in the case of Bosniak police officer Nenad Harmandžić, I convinced my superiors to allow to me to investigate the deaths of this Spanish peacekeeper and one other. For me, killing a legionnaire wasn't just another crime. It was an unlawful attack on a Blue Helmet serving international peace.

To help build the case, I needed a better understanding of what had occurred at the fatal moment. My inquiry took me back to the events of June 11, 1993, and to the streets of Mostar. The fighting had been fierce that day. Many people were dead and many more wounded. To save as many lives as possible, the International Committee for the Red Cross (ICRC) had a load of blood plasma and medicine delivered to the HVO hospital. But there were victims on the other side too, and some of those supplies were badly needed at the ABiH hospital on the city's eastern side. In spite of the chaos and misery brought on by the war, a written agreement between the warring sides had called for the safe delivery of medicine to East Mostar. To accomplish the mission, a one-hour cease-fire was put into effect so that the Spanish Battalion (SPABAT) of the UN peacekeepers could safely provide the humanitarian escort.

During the early evening hours the SPABAT convoy slowly began traveling eastward on Herzegovina Brigada and over the Tito Bridge. A number of armored personnel carriers (APCs) and an ambulance were in the middle of the convoy. One last APC provided security from the rear. Lieutenant Aguilar was in command.

The scene was tense. The Spanish officers were on the lookout for snipers—and for good reason. SPABAT had been attacked by the HVO in the past, even when providing assistance to local Bosnian-Croats.

The convoy soon came under fire. Round after round struck the APCs as they attempted to cross the bridge. The peacekeepers were being hammered.

"Take cover! Take cover!" Aguilar yelled to his men.

In the pandemonium, the lieutenant placed the safety of his men above his own. As Aguilar was warning them, he exposed himself to gunfire and was mortally wounded. The lieutenant fell, his blood spattering the interior of the APC. The driver immediately sped away, taking up a more secure position behind a building nearby. SPABAT soldiers fired back at the snipers with heavy machine guns. Soon, sirens blared as a Bosnian ambulance rushed the fallen legionnaire to the ABiH hospital. A doctor tended to Lieutenant Aguilar, but it was too late.

Evidence remained at the scene, however. Investigators ascertained that the fatal shot had been fired from the HVO side of the battle line. The field of fire was limited; the shot must have come from the Bank Building, which the HVO controlled. Based on Aguilar's position in the APC, the pathological examination, and an analysis of his flak jacket, the investigation showed the trajectory of the bullet, which had traveled downward from an elevated position.

The peacekeeper's killing had prompted several investigations, including a UN Civilian Police inquiry and a joint SPABAT, HVO, and ABiH inquiry. Years after Lieutenant Aguilar's death, my job was to pull all the information together to cover the elements of international law so that the case could be prosecuted successfully.

As before, my first mission on this case took me back to Mostar. I anticipated that the defense would claim that the legionnaire was killed by a stray bullet owing to a mistake of fact, or that his death was simply collateral damage. I needed to demonstrate that his killing was part of a pattern of criminal activity. In fact, a score of HVO actions against SPABAT had been registered. The most significant had occurred over about two weeks in early June 1993. Similar episodes from the Muslim side of the conflict had not been reported.

My investigation actually began with the events of May 10, 1993, almost one month to the day before Lieutenant Aguilar's murder. It was the day after the HVO's initial attack on the Bosniaks in West Mostar, and the same day that police officer Nenad Harmandžić was first abducted and taken to the Heliodrom.

Amid the death and carnage, there had been a loud cry for help. The request for assistance had come from the ICRC. The international aid agency had received a shipment of blood and medicine that was desperately needed in East Mostar. As part of their mission to support humanitarian efforts in the region, SPABAT picked up the supply of blood and medicine in Međugorje, the town where the Virgin Mary is said to have first appeared in 1981.

At this moment in 1993, when it seemed as though the world had abandoned the helpless people of Mostar, assistance from mortal beings was needed—fast. The Tactical Group las Canarias, an element of the famed Spanish Legion that formed the SPABAT, was on the scene near Mostar. SPABAT had been tasked with providing the security escort on May 10 for a blood transport from the HVO military hospital in West Mostar to the hospital on the Muslim side, where civilians and soldiers from both sides were being treated. Again, an agreement between the HVO and the ABiH would allow the medical escort through, in spite of the hostilities. In exchange for letting the escort pass, the HVO requested the return of a Catholic priest who was being held on the Muslim side of Mostar.

Authorization was given for two APCs to cross over into ABiH territory. The HVO Intelligence Command was present to ensure that SPABAT was allowed to proceed as agreed. The next day the mission was under way.

The officer in charge of one of the APCs was 1st Lt. Arturo Muñoz Castellanos of the Second Tercio, or regiment, which is known as the "Duke of Alba." At the entrance to the city, Muñoz's APC was stopped at the HVO checkpoint. Next, he and his men passed along the confrontation line on Mostar's Bulevar and picked up an ABiH officer, Col. Esad Humo, commander of the Forty-First Motorized Mostar Brigade. In investigating this case, I traveled this route back and forth several times. I needed to conjure the time when the murders took place.

I went to the location of the hospital where the medicine and blood was delivered. My investigation revealed that once they had arrived at the hospital, SPABAT officers assessed the casualties and visited a nearby building where HVO prisoners were being held. One of the ABiH IV Corps commanders presented SPABAT with a list of the HVO prisoners to be provided to representatives of the ICRC and the UN Human Rights Council (UNHRC).

With UN peacekeepers at the hospital, Bosnian military doctors seized the opportunity to request that SPABAT transfer a civilian woman who badly needed blood to the Mostar General Hospital, which was under HVO control. The HVO agreed to the transfer.

As arranged, SPABAT officers proceeded to retrieve the Catholic priest—but the streets and alleyways were crooked and narrow, and the APC couldn't make its way directly to the house in which he was being detained. Muñoz took the APC as far as he could. Then a small team, traveling on foot, went to get the priest.

Once the clergyman was secured, the team, hearing gunfire and mortar rounds exploding, began to run back to the APC. But in the meantime, Muñoz had become concerned about their well-being. He left the APC in search of his colleagues and the Catholic priest, while the remaining APC crew stayed with their vehicle.

Without warning, mortars were fired from atop Mount Hum, the highest point in Mostar. Hum was a critical military objective during the war. Whoever controlled Mount Hum controlled the city, and at this point it was firmly in the hands of the HVO. Before the rest of the team, together with the priest, arrived at the APC, a mortar launched from this vantage point struck Muñoz directly.

It was clear that the mortars were fired intentionally at the humanitarian convoy. To this day, I don't know whether the perpetrator employed predicted-fire, using ballistic computations, or observer-adjusted fire, using spotters and forward observers. He could have undertaken a root-sum-square analysis to determine the designated mean point of impact and other factors, such as precision error, taking into account standard deviation, sensitivity, wind, and component error. But none of it matters. A cease-fire agreement was in place, and the UN peacekeepers had been lured into an ambush.

Attacks on the Bosniaks and civilian structures were prohibited under a number of different international laws. I was beginning to suspect that once a crime against humanity was under way, many of the applications of the laws of war would no longer apply. I would come back to this legal hypothesis several more times during and after my time at The Hague.

Based on the rulings of the ICTY, we knew that the Bosnian-Muslims in West Mostar were protected under the laws and customs of war, even though the perpetrators, the HVO, were of the same nationality. The illegal acts the HVO committed included unlawful forcible expulsions to the east, which were carried out by coercion, trickery, and often a combination of the two. But first, many innocent civilians were murdered; either they were shot to death or their throats were cut. Women were brutally raped, sometimes by multiple perpetrators, before they were murdered or forcibly expelled with the rest.

As the Bosniaks fled to the east, many were shot at and killed. Those civilians who somehow made it to the "Muslim side" were still under fire. The deadly attacks by the HVO persisted. Crying children and frantic elderly women came under fierce attack as they tried to make their way to safety. But there was nowhere to run. Like their neighbors in Sarajevo, the people of East Mostar were under siege, and the HVO savored their terror.

The scene at the hospital that received the blood transports wasn't much better. I examined the premises, interviewed witnesses, and viewed videos and photos of the area. The hospital building was riddled with bullet holes, and in many places the roof was falling in. According to witnesses and news accounts, screams of agony had echoed inside the unsterile rooms. There was no oxygen, running water, or electricity. Doctors treated children who had been injured, including one who had been shot in the head. Under fire, physicians worked heroically to save lives.

In this context of persecution based on ethnic and religious differences, Lieutenant Muñoz was intentionally struck by a mortar round while on an international humanitarian mission to save lives.

Down below Mount Hum, Muñoz never heard the *whoosh* as the mortar was fired. A SPABAT officer and one from the ABiH spotted his motionless body at the epicenter of the kill radius. The Bosniak officer yelled, "It's your soldier!"

His fellow legionnaires dragged Muñoz, who was still conscious, from where he'd fallen. Time is of the essence in situations like this, and rescuers must resist the tendency to be overly delicate. Soldiers and police officers have learned that the quicker a victim is transported for expert medical care, the greater his chance for survival. The SPABAT officers loaded Muñoz into their ambulance APC and sped back to the Muslim hospital they had just left.

The operator of the SPABAT combat radio keyed the mike, and a flash message crackled across the airwaves: A legionnaire was down. His fellow legionnaires never left his side. But at an HVO checkpoint, the SPABAT soldiers transporting the injured peacekeeper were brought to a screeching halt. The HVO soldiers on the scene refused to allow the seriously injured Muñoz and his fellow legionnaires to pass. A heated argument ensued, guns were drawn, and the SPABAT officers eventually made their way through.

Incredibly, the SPABAT escort team was stopped once again, at another HVO checkpoint. This time, some twenty armed HVO soldiers stuck machine guns in the faces of the Spanish legionnaires. The HVO soldiers' actions were inhumane and illegal. The SPABAT soldiers, who also brandished their weapons, found themselves in a hopeless situation. If they forced their way past the checkpoint, they could all be killed, particularly since several RPGs were aimed their way. But unless they hurried, Lieutenant Muñoz would surely die.

Furiously, frantically, they tried to make their way through the second checkpoint. The HVO soldiers were aiding and abetting a crime against humanity through their efforts to obstruct the passage of the wounded peacekeeper. Finally, the legionnaires were allowed to proceed.

The ambulance APC and its armored escort raced to a hospital, where a Spanish military physician and a medic from the ICRC provided medical aid. Lieutenant Muñoz then was transported to a SPABAT detachment, with the APCs taking heavy fire along the way. Back in East Mostar, the other members of the humanitarian convoy—the soldiers who were still with the priest and the injured woman—also remained under fire.

Eventually, a Medivac unit transported Muñoz to Madrid, where on May 13, 1993, he succumbed to his wounds. In a videotaped interview that was later played during a trial at the ICTY, a Spanish peacekeeper, identified only as "Blue Helmets 4," commented on his fallen comrade,

> Whether the memory of Lieutenant Muñoz can influence us somehow when it comes to accomplish the mission—I think in reality that it doesn't, that we fulfill the mission the same as always. We take the same precautions, only when we are in the middle of some incident, when the bombing or the firing is going on, unconsciously always appears the image of the dead people. Only when somebody dies then one takes even more precautions, hopefully, which makes us accomplish it. My friend Arturo wanted to be a Legionnaire. He was a Legionnaire; he lived a life of a Legionnaire. And thank God, [he] died as a Legionnaire.[1]

Lieutenant Muñoz was buried in Avila, Spain. I traveled there some thirteen years after his death, four years after my work with the tribunal was done. As I looked at his well-tended gravesite, I imagined the sad day when, at a special memorial Mass, Lieutenant Muñoz's fellow legionnaires had recited the "Espirtitus de Disciplina, Legionario y la Bandera de la Legion" (The Spirits of Discipline, Legionnaire, and the Flag of the Legion) while onlookers wept. Even more moving was the legionnaires' song, "El Novio de la Muerte," or the Groom of Death, whose poignant words penetrated the souls of all who were present as this hero was laid to rest.

Back in Mostar on a forensic mission in 1999, I worked with the Spanish legionnaires, who by then formed part of SFOR. Some of the Spanish SFOR officers had been in Bosnia years earlier, as part of the SPABAT. In fact, one of the captains, a lieutenant at the time of the murders, had been good friends with both Lieutenants Aguilar and Muñoz. Coincidentally, his wife was having dinner with one of the widows the very night we sat in the French base finalizing plans for the next day's mission. The captain became my friend too, and I told him that I would do what I could to prevent the deaths of these two brave soldiers from going unknown to the world.

The evening before my mission team and I departed Mostar for the Hague, we had a papaya dinner on the Spanish base. Not to be outdone by the Spaniards, after that the Carabinieri took us to the Italian camp for some espresso, which they called "real coffee." As I was leaving the next morning, I turned to my left and saw the two French gendarmes who had been my personal escorts on the mission. One of the policemen removed his silver badge and presented it to me. The two stood at attention and saluted. I saluted them back and, using the little French I knew, said, "Merci beaucoup, mes amis."

As an investigator, I needed to take certain steps after I left Mostar to ensure that those responsible for what happened to Lieutenant Aguilar and Lieutenant Muñoz would be brought to justice. I undertook a mission to UN headquarters in New York City, where I sought information and evidence on UN peacekeepers who had been murdered. There had been many, but most of the deaths were not particularly relevant to our investigation. However, I did find evidence deep inside UN files that assisted in this case.

My work on the legionnaires case was interrupted by events in Kosovo and two full years leading the investigation of crimes committed against Croats and other non-Serbs throughout Croatia. But before I left the tribunal to return home to the United States, I met with the senior trial attorney (STA), who was preparing the indictment related to the overall persecution and crimes that had occurred in and around Mostar. This was a leadership case much larger than Tuta and Štela's. It would include all the crimes that had occurred in the region.

I provided the STA with the dossiers I'd prepared on the deaths of the two Spanish legionnaires. I was confident that what had occurred was criminal—in my view, both crimes clearly were murder. I asked the STA to read the files thoroughly with the view to including these crimes in the larger indictment of the military and political leaders of the criminal enterprise. He made no promises, except to say that he would review the evidence. The decision was his, and I fully respected that, but a lot of work had gone into those dossiers. It was time for me to go home, yet I didn't want these two fine men and their families to be dismissed without the justice that was due.

The deaths of these two men have never left my mind. At the University of Notre Dame, I dedicated my doctoral dissertation to them.

6

Kosovo

I SAW HORROR SEIZE THE YOUNG MAN'S FACE AS THE MUZZLE OF MY gun flashed twice and the report echoed inside my car. The first round went through the car door and struck his hand as he leaned against the doorjamb. His eyes were wide open as the bullet—and his right thumb— hit the wall of the "stop-and-rob" convenience store behind him.

The bandit's other hand was inside the driver-side window, holding a lock-blade knife to my throat. As I leaned away, the second round from my .38 Smith & Wesson Chief Special tore into his heart. My own heart was pounding. The serial armed robber I'd been looking for had found me.

On a hot summer night in July 1999, I awoke in a sweat to the sound of explosions and the smell of smoke. For a moment I was caught between past and present, reliving the fatal shooting from my days as a twenty-five-year-old plainclothes policeman and realizing that right this minute smoke was filling my apartment. It didn't take me long to become oriented to my surroundings and to get the hell out of there. I was in Kosovo, and the house next door had just been firebombed.

My investigations in Bosnia had been interrupted by the events occurring in Kosovo. Serb military and paramilitary forces had entered the autonomous province and were pursuing a campaign of ethnic cleansing and terror, murdering innocent women and children, the elderly, and the infirm. Many of the Serb police officers with the MUP in Kosovo joined the criminal enterprise and participated in a pattern of ongoing criminal activity. Among them were special police units (PJP) and special antiterrorist units (SAJ). Also involved in the criminal activities in Kosovo were members of the special operations unit of the Serbian State Security (DB), called the Red Berets or JSO. Milorad "Legija" Ulemek, a.k.a. Milorad Luković, operating then under the code name "Brazil," was their commander. The Federal Republic of Yugoslavia (FRY), where Slobodan Milošević was president, claimed these police and security forces were doing nothing more than defending their homeland from groups of violent terrorists and racketeers.

I didn't know it then, but it would not be long before killers and assassins such as Legija, who took the nom de guerre Legionnaire after he served with the French Foreign Legion, would play critical roles in my investigations of previous crimes that had taken place in Croatia.

In some respects it all began on June 28, 1389—St. Vitus Day—at Kosovo Polje (Kosovo Field). There the Serbs lost a major battle with the Turks, which opened the floodgates into Bosnia for the expansion of the Ottoman Empire. Thousands of Christians in Bosnia eventually fled north to the area that now comprises Slovenia and Croatia.

Centuries later, the battle reignited. With Tito long gone, ethnic tensions rose between Serbs and ethnic Albanians living in Kosovo. There was a call for Kosovo to become an independent republic of the SFRY, but many Serbs feared the republic could become a "Greater Albania." Serbs also alleged that they were being mistreated by the Albanians. In 1986 the Serbian Academy of Sciences and Arts published a report, the "SANU Memorandum," that outlined the physical, political, and cultural genocide that Serbs—the ethnic minority in Kosovo—allegedly were suffering at the hands of the Albanian majority.

These events and others brought Slobodan Milošević, then the president of the Socialist Party of Serbia, to Kosovo in 1987, when he made his infamous remark, "No one should dare beat you again," before a large group of angry Serbs. Many believe this speech prompted the secession of the republics in the SFRY and the outbreak of war and subsequent crimes in Slovenia, Croatia, Bosnia, and ultimately Kosovo. In early 1998 armed conflict broke out between Serb security forces and members of the Kosovo Liberation Army (KLA) in Kosovo. By that time, the KLA, whose members were largely Muslim, had already been listed as a terrorist organization by the U.S. State Department. Indeed, the SFRY had implemented "special measures" to suppress counterrevolutionary efforts in Kosovo against the SFRY.

With Serb forces "defending" Kosovo and the sovereignty of Serbia, allegations that Serb forces had murdered ethnic Albanians in Kosovo surfaced. The KLA was able to convince the United States and Britain that theirs was a just cause. Diplomatic efforts to resolve the situation failed, and NATO intervention on behalf of the Kosovar Albanians was anticipated.

The alliance never secured authority from the UN Security Council for the action. Instead, it relied on the inherent right of intervention on humanitarian grounds. Experts in international law disagree about whether NATO had the right to act unilaterally, but in the end, it did because it could. It was as simple as that.

Several weeks before my deployment to Kosovo, I was at my home in The Hague, switching between CNN and the BBC. President Bill Clinton and Prime Minister Tony Blair had given Slobodan Milošević an ultimatum: leave Kosovo or NATO will take appropriate action.

Milošević didn't flinch, and on March 22, 1999, NATO forces launched their first strike. The objective was to prevent the recurrence of murders and ethnic cleansing by removing Serb forces from the area and inserting international peacekeepers. Unfortunately, the NATO strikes seemed to turn up the heat on the Kosovar Albanians, who were being expelled by the thousands. In the end, hundreds of thousands of Kosovar Albanians are believed to have been forced unlawfully from their homes.

Many other innocent Kosovar Albanians were brutally murdered. Daily newscasts with NATO spokesman Jamie Shea, U.S. State Department spokesman James Rubin, and CNN reporter Christiane Amanpour gave the world an upfront view of the situation. The attacks by Serb forces on ethnic Albanians in Kosovo were widespread. Two distinct images emerged—the convoys of frightened women, children, and old people being deported from Kosovo to Albania and Macedonia, and the CIA-, Pentagon-, and NATO-supplied photos of mass graves.

Together these painted a picture of horrific crimes against the Kosovar Albanians. The Western powers joined forces with the international community. The UN war crimes tribunal was working on one hand and NATO on the other. Promises of criminal indictments were combined with military might—and both promises were fulfilled.

In time, Milošević began to realize that NATO wasn't going to give up its air strikes. A ground invasion also was anticipated, although this was an action President Clinton didn't want to take. Instead, members of special forces units from a number of countries entered Kosovo in the midst of the conflict. UN war crimes investigators were there too, already deep inside Kosovo gathering actionable intelligence on major criminal activity and the perpetrators. UN prosecutors were working night and day to put together an indictment that would include charges of war crimes and crimes against humanity against Slobodan Milošević and members of his inner circle.

On June 12, 1999, Milošević agreed to certain conditions and allowed the NATO-led Kosovo Force (KFOR) to enter Kosovo. I joined one of the first teams that was redeployed in country to investigate murders and other atrocities that had taken place. I will never forget the stench of death that permeated the air. Homes were still on fire, and I could hear shooting everywhere I went.

We were processing one of the largest crime scenes in history. I saw evidence of the murders firsthand. I also saw the effects of the NATO strikes. The MUP station near my base had been hit dead on. So had the Hotel Yugoslavia in Pristina, where Arkan, the infamous Serb criminal and warlord, and his Tigers had been based. The Chinese embassy also had been hit, and three journalists had been killed. The United States said that a CIA-supplied map that NATO forces had used had included an error, but other intelligence indicates that agents of the Chinese Ministry of State Security (MSS) may have actually been assisting the Serbs, including Arkan, with SIGINT, since Serb communications had been struck and disabled by NATO. Many people believed the strike on the Chinese embassy was both intentional and precise.

I had not been assigned to the Kosovo case officially, but the chief of investigations was pulling investigators off other teams to provide immediate assistance with this enormous task. All hands were on deck. Help was also coming in from many national law enforcement agencies in Spain, Germany, Canada, the United States, and many other nations. Agencies such as the Royal Canadian Mounted Police and the Federal Bureau of Investigation (FBI) helped collect evidence from many of the scenes to assist international war crimes investigators with the massive undertaking.

My area of responsibility was the municipality of Prizren. I was assigned to a Dutch military camp that was squarely in the middle of the German army sector. Prizren municipality is in southern Kosovo, bordering Macedonia to the east and Albania to the west. Our investigations revealed that in late March 1999 many of the villages in this municipality were attacked by FRY and Serb forces, including paramilitaries. Bold, vicious, and deadly, the modus operandi was the usually the same: Tanks and other military vehicles surrounded the villages; then the villages were shelled. Civilians were killed in the initial attacks.

Then ground forces entered the little towns, murdered surviving residents, and set their homes on fire. Those who were able to escape fled to other villages, where they often were attacked again. Some villagers were shot in the back as they fled. Others were machine-gunned as their families huddled together and trembled in fear. Often, men wearing ski masks robbed families and raped women before shooting them, setting their homes on fire, or exterminating them by other means. Children witnessed the horror before they were murdered too.

The warning order (WARNORD) laid out the situation and my mission: to coordinate the exhumations of human remains conducted by the British forensic team to ensure that relevant evidence corresponding with the allegations in the indictment was secured. To do this, I first went to villages in Prizren. Through my interpreter, I spoke with residents to learn about missing persons and their possible whereabouts. I was frequently accompanied by a British police officer who served as a sort of wingman. Sometimes I worked alone.

An entire family had hidden in the woods behind one house I visited. I could see where they had been discovered by the killers and murdered. A doll lay near the place where a young girl had been peppered with machine-gun fire. My immediate job was to find the bodies. Finding the killers would come later.

In an effort to locate missing persons we believed had been murdered, I flew a number of air missions with the German army, which was operating militarily outside of Germany for the first time since World War II. Speaking through the headset in mixed German and English, I communicated with the helicopter pilot and the copilot. From the air, we searched for anomalies in the ground. The freshly turned earth of shallow graves was easy to spot. Once we found the graves, I marked their locations in the air with the global positioning system (GPS). At night I wrote up situation reports (SITREPs) and communicated my findings up the chain of command by satellite communications (SATCOM). Mobile phone communications were completely down.

The next day's missions were on the ground, where we searched for the suspected mass graves. We traveled by UN vehicle, often accompanied by a German army explosive ordnance disposal (EOD) team. I'd learned to read maps and use a compass years ago as a young airman and later acquired other relevant skills at the U.S. Air Force Special Operations School at Hurlburt Field, Florida.

I also had knowledge of land mines, but it didn't take an expert to recognize the danger of the shiny metallic objects in the fields. On one mission, I saw three young Kosovar boys throwing rocks at one such object in a playground. "Hey!" I yelled at the top of my lungs to get their attention. It worked, and soon the German EOD team was on the scene. The mine was live—and absolutely deadly.

During exhumations we also had to be on the lookout for booby-trapped gravesites. Some of the killers were thrilled with the prospect of killing or injuring an exhumation team member. These criminal acts were entirely premeditated—and it got worse.

Those of us who worked in Kosovo, or other "killing fields," will never forget the experience. Not many people, including police and soldiers, have seen so much fresh human death by violence. Like most cops, I thought I had seen it all. From an empathic perspective, I thought I had felt the pain of families whose children and other loved ones had been killed, but I cannot begin to accurately describe the emotions of the families I met. Their cries echoed throughout the valleys of Kosovo as the bodies of their loved ones, or what was left of them, were recovered, examined, and ultimately returned to them for burial.

Everyone, including the exhumation team, was overwhelmed with grief. The indefatigable British forensic team recovered body after body from the ground—young and old—with competence and compassion. The team members included a forensic anthropologist, an army X-ray specialist, a crime-scene photographer, and an evidence control officer. The head of the exhumation team was a senior police officer with the London Metropolitan Police.

The forensic team brought much of its own equipment, but the team members still needed certain supplies. I took on the responsibility of searching for some of those items, but obtaining them in the middle of a war zone was no easy task. First, the team needed a refrigeration unit in which exhumed bodies could be stored until autopsies could be performed. It took significant effort, but within days we had a UN refrigerator unit about the size of an eighteen-wheeled tractor trailer flown to the location of what had once been a schoolhouse. It was now a makeshift morgue.

The team also needed a protective apron to use when taking X-rays. None of the area's military units had one. I concluded that the most likely place to secure an apron would be a hospital outside of war-torn Kosovo. I selected Skopje, Macedonia, as the target, but the mission proved difficult. En route, we encountered our first obstacle at the Kosovo-Macedonia border. We waited for hours, but the Macedonian police would not let anyone cross. Finally, a U.S. Army officer in a Humvee approached me as I waited in the convoy of vehicles at a standstill near the border.

"Sir, can you move your vehicle up a bit?" he asked.

"Sure, what's up?"

"I'm not waiting any longer. I am just going to go through. You can follow me if you like."

As we passed through the Macedonian police checkpoint, I displayed my UN laissez-passer. The officer attending the post motioned me to go through. I wondered at that moment what might be waiting for us as we went through, but the border crossing was otherwise uneventful.

In Macedonia, things appeared calm. But that didn't last. Soon I saw a Macedonian police officer striking a teenage boy in the face. My interpreter told me the boy was Albanian. I yelled to the officer to stop. He turned and looked at me. I didn't know if he was going to try to arrest me or turn back to the boy, but he just walked away looking at the ground and shaking his head.

Next we stopped at the local hospital. We walked into the X-ray unit, and I asked to speak to the person in charge. After what seemed like twenty minutes, a man arrived, and I asked about the X-ray apron. He just stared at me. Eventually, after making more than a half dozen telephone calls, I procured what we needed. I had to sign a number of documents, sometimes more than once on the same page. This was the Communist style—the more signatures and stamps, the more proper the arrangement. It was official, all right: I had the X-ray apron, and they had the documents.

The earlier holdup at the border had delayed our return to base. Daylight was quickly fading as we crossed back into Kosovo, and Prizren was still several hours away. The situation became even more problematic as we drove on the R-115 Highway through the Šar Mountains, traveling northwest from Skopje toward Prizren. About halfway into our ascent, we ran into a severe thunderstorm. I was driving. I'd taken the wheel for good after once allowing the British police officer who was now riding shotgun to drive. He'd kept driving on the left side of the road—the wrong side. That may be OK in the UK, but it was not a smart thing to do with tanks and other heavy vehicles coming at us head on.

It was pitch black as we climbed the mountain, and the vehicle's headlights reflected off the thick fog. Blinded, I turned off the lights. I could see the road only when flashes of lightning dissipated, momentarily illuminating the fog. There was no room for error. If I veered to the left, I surely faced a head-on collision. Veer right, and I'd drive off the side of the mountain. I was creeping ahead in darkness and fog so thick that I couldn't see the road at all.

"Do you believe in God?" I asked my interpreter, a Kosovar Albanian who spoke Albanian, Serbian, and English.

"Yes," he nodded.

"You'd better start praying."

I thought we were done for when, all of a sudden, I saw two lights fighting to penetrate the fog only a few meters ahead of me. They looked like eyes, and they gave just enough light to guide us without blinding me. I followed the eerie beams of light until the storm broke as I crested the mountain and began my descent. When we dropped below the storm clouds, I could see that the "eyes" were nothing more than ordinary taillights on a tractor driven by an elderly farmer. As I passed him on the road, I blew the horn in acknowledgement. When I looked in the rearview mirror, he was gone.

There were three parallel worlds in Kosovo. First, there was the Kosovo that the world saw: a place where ethnic Kosovar Albanians were victims of forced deportations and murder. I saw evidence of this treatment firsthand. But the victims weren't just Kosovar Albanians. In the second real world, there were Serb victims too—many of them. Indeed, the house that had been firebombed as I slept next door was a Serbian home. I learned that most of the gunshots I was hearing every day were attacks on Serbs. Most were civilians who, like their Albanian counterparts, had done nothing wrong.

Unrecognized at the time was a third world in which al Qaeda had a significant presence. I was in Kosovo a little more than two years before the 9/11 attacks. In my own parallel world—as a reserve special agent working counterintelligence and national security investigations with U.S. Air Force Special Investigations—I, like many of my colleagues, knew little about "the base" and nothing at all about Osama bin Laden's planning, which was already under way.

Al Qaeda members were in the Balkans helping the KLA. Bin Laden himself is said to have supplied one of his top operatives to assist in their training. In fact, Milošević tried to raise this issue during his trial in an effort to prove that he was fighting terrorists, but as was often the case, the judge shut him down and prevented him from raising potentially relevant issues before the court.

The KLA members I encountered during my missions appeared to be either ragtag fighters or mobbed-up gangsters. We exchanged glances before we spoke, and these men were easy to size up. Nevertheless, those I talked with provided excellent information concerning the location of missing or buried Kosovar Albanian victims. On the surface, the KLA operated openly as freedom fighters, but the group had a darker side. Perhaps Milošević had more than a minor point to argue. Certainly the Western intelligence community knew what the KLA was really into. As in Afghanistan during its conflict with the Soviets, the CIA had a hand in helping the KLA too.

This wasn't just a war zone; it was also the underworld. I was smack in the middle of major auto theft, heroin smuggling, and human trafficking for purposes of prostitution. Narcotics trafficking throughout the Balkans funded many of the KLA's operations. In fact, many KLA members were directly linked to syndicated crime in Albania. They also were involved in arms smuggling and had connections to the Italian mafia.

On top of all that, the KLA ran deadly extortion rackets. It is important to remember that while I was in Kosovo there were virtually no border controls between Kosovo and Albania, which made smuggling, trafficking, and other forms of transnational crime relatively risk-free endeavors. This was a lawless state, and the only trained criminal investigators—war crimes investigators from the UN—were focused on crimes against humanity, such as murder, rape, and torture. Consequently, the KLA was free to run whatever rackets it wanted with impunity.

My work over the past two years, and everything I had done during my twenty-year career in state and federal law enforcement, paled in comparison to the journey ahead. In October 2000 I was promoted and appointed to lead the overall investigation into the murders, rapes, tortures, and persecution alleged to have been perpetrated throughout the entire Republic of Croatia by Slobodan Milošević, as the president of Serbia, and fifteen major coperpetrators at the head of a murderous international criminal enterprise. During one of Europe's darkest hours, I was entering a bright moment in my career.

7

Team Four

Every special calling in life, if it is to be followed with success, re-quires peculiar qualifications of understanding and soul.

—Carl von Clausewitz, *On War*

IT WAS A DARK DAY FOR THE SOUL IN SEPTEMBER 1991 WHEN MEM-bers of the JNA began a frontal attack on the small Croatian village of Škabrnja. Flashes of light and the sound of explosions filled the air as the armed, violent attackers began shelling the village. Residents who tried to extinguish the resulting fires fell one by one, shot by Serb riflemen. Scores of JNA combatants and other Serb forces raked the area with machine-gun fire and strafed the fleeing victims from the air.

The mostly civilian defenders were outmaneuvered and outgunned at every step. JNA ground forces overran the village, showing no mercy. A woman lay face down on a dirt road, crushed to death by a slow-moving tank. The surviving villagers hid in their cellars, trembling in fear. Their cover didn't last long.

Serb special forces soldiers in dark uniforms and black berets soon arrived by helicopter. The dusty, makeshift landing zone became their staging ground. House by house, these trained killers worked their way through the village, dragging screaming residents—including women and children—from their hiding places. Scores of villagers were killed in the attack; many were viciously murdered as they pleaded for their lives. Those who were not killed were used as human shields.

Inhabited since the eleventh century, Škabrnja had been home to nearly two thousand residents. When the assault was over, the soldiers razed the village.

Nine years after the attack on Škabrnja, I was at the FBI Academy at Quantico, Virginia, attending an international homicide investigators' conference when I learned that I had been promoted to lead the investigation of a number of high-level war crimes perpetrators, including police, military, and political leaders. I was now the team leader—the UN first officer in charge of the investigation. The men I was to investigate were behind the murders, rapes, torture, and persecution that had been committed throughout Croatia, including the crimes committed in Škabrnja. For me, this is when Slobodan Milošević entered the story. As the powerful former president of Serbia and, at the time, the equally heavy-handed president of the FRY, he was at the center of an unprecedented, international criminal conspiracy. It would prove to be the case of a lifetime for everyone involved.

When I returned to The Hague from the United States, my first order of business was to meet with the investigative team that I would work with to bring Milošević to justice. I needed to gain an intimate knowledge of the mass murders and other atrocities they had been investigating. It was an extraordinary undertaking, but these were no ordinary investigators. The members of Team Four had come to The Hague from all over the world. Collectively, they were experts in investigating homicides, organized crime, conspiracies, sexual assaults, financial crimes, and mass murders. Among them were lawyers, crime analysts, military intelligence analysts, political research officers, investigative assistants, and interpreters.

Working with dedication, integrity, and perseverance, this team would bring the case to a successful conclusion. And these determined international civil servants would take von Clausewitz's understanding of the soul one step further: They would look inside the spirits of the dead and expose the hearts of the killers.

In my office at The Hague, war crimes investigators briefed me on the specific crimes in Croatia they had been examining.

CRIMES IN THE SERBIAN AUTONOMOUS DISTRICT OF THE KRAJINA

Brent Pfundheller was a retired police sergeant who had conducted criminal investigations with the Washington State Patrol. He also had served as commander of the Serious Crimes Unit, part of an international police force, at the UN mission in Kosovo. Tall and kind, Pfundheller understood people as well as he did criminal investigations.

His partner was just as impressive. Bill Hardin was a retired supervisory special agent with the U.S. Drug Enforcement Administration and a former police officer in Oakland, California. Both men had experience with complex drug conspiracy cases—expertise that proved invaluable during their investigation of Serb crimes in Croatia.

Together we discussed the region, the perpetrator groups, and their crimes, referring often to a large military map pinned to my office wall. Files of witness statements, military orders, and videos pulled from the tribunal's Evidence Unit informed our conversation.

Pfundheller and Hardin were working the war-ravaged area of the Serbian Autonomous District of the Krajina (SAO Krajina), which lay within the borders of Croatia. Even then the area was difficult to work, but not too tough for the two veteran police detectives.

The SAO Krajina was formed on December 21, 1990, as an artificial state created by Serbs and for Serbs. By its own statute, the region proclaimed territorial autonomy and independent rule from Croatia. Many Croatian-Serbs, as well as officials in Serbia, believed that if Croatia could declare its independence from Yugoslavia, then the Croatian-Serbs could separate themselves from Croatia. And that's exactly what happened.

The SAO Krajina included territory in Croatia where relatively large populations of Croatian-Serbs lived. Parts of its borders followed a line connecting the Croatian towns of Ogulin, Karlobag, Karlovac, and Virovitica. In fact, much of the border followed the same path as the historical "Military Frontier" that my great-great-grandfather, Šime Sanković, once patrolled as a member of the Landesgendarmerie-Kommandos (Austro-Hungarian gendarmerie) on the lookout for Turks and highway robbers.

This new threat had nothing to do with the Ottoman Empire. It was a complex criminal enterprise headed by Milošević. The objective: to annex approximately one-third of Croatia as part of a "Greater Serbia." Serb forces had standing orders from their superiors to accomplish the mission by deporting and transferring non-Serbs from the self-proclaimed Serb-dominated territory and destroying whatever was in their tracks.

The amputation of Croatia would prove to be not only painful but also protracted and bloody. To accomplish Milošević's goals, armed men were needed, mostly on the ground. The JNA played a pivotal role. This army dated back to its predecessor armed forces and to the liberation of Yugoslavia from fascist control. On November 22, 1951, the Yugoslav Army (JA) officially became the Yugoslav People's Army with soldiers, NCOs, and commissioned officers coming from each of the Yugoslav republics. The JNA was created to protect the Yugoslav state and all its citizens. But in Croatia at this time, under Milošević's watchful eye, the JNA was taking the side of the Serbs.

Working in conjunction with the JNA were members of local territorial defense (TO) units. Under a total-war military doctrine, each Yugoslav republic had its own territorial defense much like a home guard or reserve unit in other countries. When the SAO Krajina was formed, so was its own TO. The unit was made up mostly of Croatian-Serbs.

To wrest the Krajina from Croatian control, agents, operatives, and other armed men from Serbia's State Security Service (DB) were sent into Croatia. Additionally, a new, armed police force was created in the region. It was called the Krajina Milicija, which is translated as "the militia of the Krajina," but in common parlance, the group was known as Martić's Police, named for the force's first commander, Milan Martić. I didn't know it when I first discussed the case with Pfundheller and Hardin, but one day I would come face to face with this abject killer, the man behind so many brutal slayings.

In the meantime, I needed to get a handle on the region and the Serb forces in general. I couldn't lead the investigation from the rear. My in-depth discussions with Pfundheller and Hardin moved next to the principal villages they had been working, including Škabrnja and Nadin. Not long after they had hit the streets, the two war crimes investigators had cultivated an important witness who provided key details about the horrific attack on Škabrnja and its civilian inhabitants. It was evidence that helped us begin to link the JNA to war crimes committed in Croatia.

Col. Ratko Mladić was the man in charge of the JNA's Ninth Corps, which was responsible for many of the criminal attacks in the area. According to Pfundheller and Hardin's witness, when a subordinate officer had run out of ammunition, Mladić had ordered him to continue his advance on Škabrnja, lest he be executed by Mladić himself. This brutality came as no surprise. In May 1992 Mladić commanded the Bosnian-Serb Army (VRS), and in July 1995 he was indicted by the tribunal and subsequently placed on trial for his alleged participation in the genocide committed at Srebrenica. More than seventy-five hundred Muslims, including many boys, were exterminated at Srebrenica. It will undoubtedly go down as one of the worst mass murders on European soil since World War II.

Our detailed analysis turned to what happened after the Škabrnja attack. The next day Serb forces advanced on Nadin, where they began another bloody killing spree. A young woman—a teenager—who had somehow survived the Nadin attack gave war crimes investigators detailed evidence. I listened intently.

The attackers came to her home, where members of her family and friends had been hiding. It was like a drug raid back in the States: occupants of the house jumped out of windows as police burst through the door. But the people inside the house in Nadin weren't bad guys fleeing justice, and the armed men coming through the door weren't enforcing the law. They were there on a deadly mission.

Ten elderly men and women and one girl were unable to escape from the house. Our teenage witness, by then protected by Team Four investigators, described how they were lined up against a bedroom wall. Then the killers opened fire.

I could see the emotion in Pfundheller's eyes as he continued the witness's story: "All in the room were killed, except our witness, who had been the first in the room and had been shielded by the bodies of the others. She lay there until nightfall, and then escaped to the woods."

I can't imagine the terror she experienced lying all alone among the lifeless bodies, feeling them grow colder with each passing hour. Eventually, the young witness slipped away into the night. Little did she know that even more pain and misery would be inflicted on similar small towns and villages throughout the region.

I researched the victims of Škabrnja and Nadin one by one and examined the evidence in depth. The body count was high. All told, at least forty-five inhabitants of the two towns had been cruelly murdered during the attacks. One victim was as old as ninety-two. Most fell dead from gunshot blasts. One victim was found strangled, and another's left ear had been hacked off.

Another eyewitness from Škabrnja explained that his father, a seventy-three-year-old stroke victim who needed a wheelchair for mobility, couldn't escape the violence. His mother, loyal to the end, stayed by her husband's side. The witness never again saw his parents alive. He later learned that his father had been shot in the back of the head; he fell from his wheelchair face down on the floor. His mother was found with a bullet hole in the back of her head and another in her chest. To verify this information, Pfundheller and Hardin provided autopsy reports obtained during their field investigations. I read each of them, and the corroborating evidence was there. The witness's father had indeed been shot in the right ear and cheek. His mother had multiple gunshot blasts to the head and chest.

To facilitate Milošević's objectives, other crimes were committed by fifth columnists in the region. By artifice and treachery, JNA intelligence operatives carried out special black-flag operations. Saboteurs destroyed churches and synagogues, and agent provocateurs staged murder scenes. These efforts were not intended to throw off criminal investigators, as is usually the case. Instead, they were meant to make the Serb minorities believe that Croatian terrorists—so-called Ustaše forces—had rekindled their World War II–era ethnic hatred for the Serbs. In reality, Serb forces and intelligence agents were carrying out murders of their own people.

It is no wonder that many ethnic Serbs in Croatia were panicking. These perfidious acts laid the groundwork for the persecution of Croats and attacks on their homes, churches, villages, and helpless families.

At one home in Marinovići, a hamlet of Bruška, death came knocking at the door.

"Who's there?" a teenage girl asked.

"Krajina Milicija!"

Our witness, barely fifteen at the time, took the words as a joke—until she heard a burst of fire from an automatic weapon. The girl bolted out of the house with a mad killer in pursuit. She ran toward the woods, but before she reached shelter, bullets struck her arm and her hip. She fell to the ground hard, in pain and panting. Her face void of all color, somehow her mother pulled her to safety. Now the tormented teen was working with investigators under the code name "Jump Rope."

"I felt my body flash with heat, and I fell down," Jump Rope told us. "I realized I had been shot. I was having a hard time standing up, and I realized there was something wrong with my arm."

The attack had occurred just four days before Christmas in 1991, and the bloodshed in the town was far from over. Martić's Police slaughtered at least ten more unsuspecting civilians in Marinovići that night, investigators learned. Nine of the victims were members of the Marinović clan, the family for whom the lovely hamlet had been named generations ago.

The village of Bruška was next. Surrounded by a number of Serb-dominated villages, it was a Croatian enclave located deep in the forested mountains of Zadar County and had a population of less than two hundred.

Again, Martić's Police attacked many innocent civilians. Those who weren't killed were taken to Serb-controlled prisons, where they were psychologically and physically tortured. Martić's Police ran one prison, the JNA another. On October 15, 1991, Mladić himself was seen inspecting one of the facilities. He was escorted by the man who came to be known as Captain Dragan, a member of the deadly Red Berets.

Shortly after the attack on Bruška, a Serb judge visited the village. As in most jurisdictions, the law in the region required the investigation of suspicious deaths. But when the judge arrived, members of Martić's Police tried to persuade her to say that Croatian terrorists had committed the killings. The judge, a prudent and righteous woman, refused even to acknowledge the request. Years later Pfundheller and Hardin tracked down the courageous Serb judge and obtained a witness statement from her. Again I was reminded that criminals had committed these crimes, not the Croatian-Serbs as a whole.

When I took over as leader of Team Four, Pfundheller and Hardin were in the early stages of their investigations. They were also tired of running into bureaucratic roadblocks and politics—and they were ready to resign. I quickly realized that these experienced investigators knew what they were doing. They just needed some leadership to help them contribute fully to the ultimate objective. In any organization, internal issues sometimes become obstacles. We sorted things out relatively quickly, and the crew agreed to stay on.

Then I told the team members what they had been longing to hear: "From this point forward, this will be a multidisciplinary investigation. But it will be a police-driven investigation with only one person in charge."

The investigators worked what we called the "crime base," that is, the murders, rapes, tortures, and other crimes perpetrated at the scene. Obviously, there was no way to investigate every single crime that had been committed in Croatia. That would have taken years. Instead, we chose crime sites for investigation based on a number of elements, including geographic location, demographics, and "solvability" factors such as the presence of forensic evidence and available witnesses. We also employed intelligence-led investigative strategies. In other words, we needed to have a good idea of which perpetrator groups were involved in the crimes before we spent too much time on the scene. Otherwise days or even weeks could be lost on redundant or unnecessary investigations.

Our team of war crimes investigators worked in a precarious environment. Depending on the specific area of operation, they faced threats from land mines, booby traps, organized crime, and foreign intelligence and secret police agencies. Black-bag jobs were a frequent concern, meaning we knew foreign intelligence operatives surreptitiously entered the flats, hotel rooms, and other structures occupied by or associated with our investigators. Our investigative activities, witness identities, and evidence were top priorities of a number of governments. Consequently, running counterintelligence and countersurveillance tactics was of paramount importance, and we used confidential sources and methods to protect witnesses, documents, communications, and ourselves.

With both the investigative missions and the omnipresent security concerns in mind, the enormity and complexity of the task cannot be overstated. Eventually, war crimes investigators would have to work their way from the crime base and the street-level killers to the commanders of police and military units and from there to senior political leaders. At every step, we needed to keep the end in mind.

By early 2002 Team Four was hot on the trail of the killers, torturers, and terrorists who had wreaked havoc in Croatia. Critical evidence came from diverse sources: members of nongovernmental organizations (NGOs), military alliances such as NATO, intergovernmental organizations such as the Organization for Security and Co-operation in Europe (OSCE), local police and courts, intelligence agencies, journalists, and survivors. We also had confidential sources—often people involved in the crimes—who provided us with an inside look at the killers, their leaders, and their motivations.

While war crimes investigators did their work, I spent considerable time negotiating with diplomats, intelligence operatives, and law enforcement chiefs. I even made my way to the head offices of ministers of interior, ministers of justice, prime ministers, and presidents. My objective was to smooth the way for Team Four to obtain evidence, witnesses, and information that would be crucial in our investigations. It wasn't at all unusual for me to meet key officials in third-party countries in order to receive confidential information and evidence that was useful to our work.

Even when the information came from Western intelligence agencies, we endeavored to verify and corroborate each relevant detail. We read suspects their rights. We detailed the chain of custody on every piece of evidence. This was a modern and methodical criminal investigation following the rules of evidence before a truly international court.

The evidence included detailed forensic analysis and reconstruction of complex financial records, so I brought onto the team an expert in forensic accounting. Morten Torkildsen of Norway analyzed financial structures and followed the money all the way from Serbia to Austria, Bulgaria, Cyprus, Greece, and Switzerland. With his expertise, we determined that Milošević and members of his inner circle had used at least eight front companies in Cyprus and Greece alone to fund the supply of illegal arms and otherwise avoid international sanctions being imposed on Serbia. Working from his office and on missions throughout the region, Torkildsen uncovered deposits of large amounts of cash and other surreptitious and suspicious financial transactions, which Milošević classified as "state secrets."

I approved scores of operational mission orders to process crime scenes, take aerial photographs from helicopters, and obtain reams of documentary evidence, including autopsy reports and intercepted military transmissions that were spoken or written in a variety of languages. On top of that, investigators and analysts sometimes had to interpret communications that had been encrypted or otherwise coded. We had access to spy satellite and aerial surveillance imagery that provided evidence linking perpetrators to killings, and we obtained forensic evidence, including DNA results, that helped put the cases together. Most important, we relied on brave survivors, men and women who assisted war crimes investigators by filling the gaps in ways only an eyewitness can.

One of those eyewitnesses was a sixteen-year-old schoolboy we codenamed "Skater." One night in November 1991 Skater and his family were inside their home in Vukovići, a hamlet not far from Knin near the border with Bosnia. The boy was sitting at a table when he glimpsed something strange outside the window.

"It happened so fast that I couldn't tell who it was," he told us. "I was curious, so I told everyone what I saw and that I was going to check and see who was out there. These were the last words I spoke to my family members."

The deadly silhouette quickly came alive. When Skater opened the door, he found JNA and TO soldiers pointing machine guns at his face. The gunmen ordered everyone out of the house. Skater's father, grandfather, and two aunts came out with their hands high in the air, begging for mercy. They were killed straight off. But for whatever reason, one of the murderers favored Skater and protected him from being executed.

The killers then went into the house, looking for a bedridden man who was nearly eighty years old. The elderly man let out a bloodcurdling scream as one of the gunmen clutched his hand and cut his wedding ring from his finger. After the intruder withdrew from the house, another gunman swung around, broke a window with his rifle butt, and fired multiple rounds through the broken window into the old man, who lay helplessly in his bed with blood spurting from his hand. To complete their murderous operation, one of the men lobbed a hand grenade into the house. The killers left the dead behind and set the hamlet ablaze.

Days and nights went by, and Pfundheller, Hardin, and I were still at it. I learned how civilians had been abducted, tortured, hanged, and murdered by Martić's Police and JNA soldiers. I also learned how these two groups had worked in concert toward the commission of their crimes. Witnesses, documents, and confidential informers provided us with evidence that TO forces, equipped and commanded by the JNA, were directly involved in criminal activities in and around Saborsko, an area well known for its virgin forests and crystal-clear streams and lakes. The beauty of the countryside was tainted with death.

In October 1991 TO soldiers entered Lipovačka Dreznica, a hamlet near Saborsko, and massacred seven Croats in their homes. War crimes investigators located a mournful witness who described how a local Serb commander instructed him to help bury some of the bodies. Homes in Lipovačka Dreznica were in flames. The witness found one man, shot in the stomach multiple times, lying on the kitchen floor of his house. The bodies of his wife and son were lying in front of their home. Our witness went to a second home with the gunmen. There they found a man and his wife, along with two others—Marija Cindrić, also known as Marija Brozinčević, and her elderly mother, Katja Cindrić. They all had been killed by machine-gun fire and were subsequently buried in a mass grave.

One family of about twenty members hid in the basement of a house owned by a relative. They overheard Serb forces talking outside and came to believe the house was about to be torched. Not knowing what awaited them outdoors, one brave woman decided to risk facing the Serbs rather than being burned alive. She left the house waving a white flag of surrender. Immediately she came face-to-face with heavily armed JNA soldiers. The frightened woman assured the gunmen that only civilians were inside the house. Then she began pleading for their lives. The entire family was removed from the house at gunpoint. Just in case someone was still hiding inside, one of the attackers tossed a grenade into the basement. The gunmen robbed the male victims of whatever cash and other valuables they carried. Then the killers fired automatic machine guns, cutting down the unarmed men. The terrified women cried and continued to beg for mercy. For some reason, the gunmen allowed the rest of them to leave the village. But as they fled the area, another group of Serb forces opened fire on them, killing one woman and wounding another.

As I continued to examine the evidence, the case of an elderly woman caught my attention. Based on all the facts provided to us, we knew she had been incapacitated, trapped in her bed as her house burned to the ground. Small fragments of bone and teeth were the only human remains found in her bedroom, which had been reduced to ashes. According to a forensic anthropologist, these remains were consistent with those of an elderly female.

To help us better understand what actually took place at Saborsko, we cultivated an inside source, code-named "Achilles," who provided us with critical details. Achilles outlined the events surrounding the murders and described the members of the joint criminal enterprise who had committed crimes in the area. He provided a vivid picture of how Martić's Police and other Serb forces played an integral part in the carnage. He was in a good position to provide accurate information. Achilles was one of the Serb fighters who had participated in the attack.

In the end, there were at least twenty-five more murder victims. Some had been shot. Others had been killed by blunt force trauma or burned to death. Homes were burned to the ground, and the town's two Catholic churches were bombed. Saborsko had been destroyed.

———— ««◉»» ————

On a rainy Sunday morning in October 1991, an armed man in uniform accosted a resident of Hrvatska Dubica who had been standing in front of his house. A truck bearing the words Milicija SAO Krajina was parked nearby.

Many of the village resident's days were numbered. The man we code-named "Apple-1" was marked as Number 53 on a list of people to be exterminated, but he didn't know it yet.

"Is this your house?" the militiaman asked.

"Yes."

"Well, get ready, because we're going off to the fire brigade building for a meeting there."

In recent days Apple-1 had heard gunfire in the village, and he knew his family was in imminent peril. Under cover of night he had sent his wife to safety, but he had returned to protect his home. Now Apple-1 climbed into the back of the truck, where four women were already seated on a rough wooden bench. As the militiaman drove to the firehouse, he made a number of stops. Each time he forced other neighbors and their loved ones to climb into the truck. "Old men and women" and "two pensioners" were among them. By the time the truck pulled up to the firehouse, twenty-three victims were riding in back.

A short time later a bus pulled into the firehouse with more residents on board. JNA soldiers guarded the fire station and the men and women who had been taken there. Many of the victims must have suspected they had been driven to their deaths.

By Apple-1's count, fifty-three captives were ushered into the firehouse. Most were Croats. All except a boy with a cast on his leg were older than sixty, and about half of them were women. Their names were called in order, corresponding to a previously numbered list. Apple-1 was last on the list—Number 53.

The men and women were held against their will all day. There was never a meeting. By the time it grew dark, Apple-1 was restless—and he knew what was coming. He approached one of the guards, who seemed to have a sad look on his face.

"Listen here. I'm cold," Apple-1 said. "If you don't let me go home, I'm going to go home of my own free will, and you can shoot after me."

"Please don't leave while I'm on duty!" the guard pleaded, and he began to cry.

About that time a car drew up and parked near the fire station. A man in a rain cloak exited the vehicle and gave a sign to the guard. Apple-1 was summoned to the car and told to get in. He and the man in the rain cloak exchanged glances, and Apple-1 recognized him. The villager entered the vehicle and was driven away to freedom. The last words spoken by the mysterious man warned Apple-1 not to expose his rescuer should he be recaptured. Ultimately, nine other residents of Dubica also were released.

The forty-three victims left behind simply vanished. For years villagers suspected they were buried somewhere in an unmarked mass grave. Their suspicions proved to be true. Team Four later learned that on the Monday morning after Apple-1's release, the forty-three elderly prisoners were herded onto a bus, transported to a site along the river near Baćin, and executed by machine-gun fire. Drunk with power, the killers released a deadly taste of gunpowder into the air, as the victims' screams echoed along the river. In fact, Bosniaks on the other side of the river, which served as a border between Croatia and Bosnia, heard the awful sounds of death.

For five years the only traces of the victims were the memories held by their loved ones. Then Apple-1 attended an exhumation of a mass grave at Baćin, not far from his village of Dubica. At least thirty-two victims buried there were identified as having been at the firehouse. Two were Serbs, ostensibly branded as collaborators. The rest were Croats—people for whom no transgressions were necessary in order to become enemies of the new state.

The evidence showed that Apple-1 was on the death list because he had objected to the treatment of Croats and other non-Serb minorities. He had refused to hold public office, and the Serb forces were distrustful of him. Apple-1 was a Serb.

Two highly experienced investigators made up the lead investigative crew working the streets and backwoods roads of Dubica, Baćin, and other towns in this area of the Krajina. Rajie Murugan, Azim Arshad, and I spent several days together poring over maps, photos, and witness statements from another part of the Krajina—Hrvatska Dubica and the villages of Cerovljani and Baćin.

Murugan, a police captain from South Africa, understood persecution better than most. During apartheid, he had had to ride in the back of the police car. Yet his demeanor, words, and actions reflected no animosity toward anyone. He was a true gentleman, but he also was streetwise and tough as nails. His experience working a number of mass murders and political assassinations for South Africa's Truth and Reconciliation Commission made him the perfect investigator for the job.

Arshad, a senior police superintendent from Pakistan, had a master's degree in political science and knew more about the U.S. Constitution than I did. I personally brought him on board, and the combined intelligence and integrity of these two men was phenomenal.

In June 1991, Murugan and Arshad told me, local Croats observed JNA soldiers unloading weapons that had been brought in by helicopter in a forest. The scene was Hrvatska Dubica, the village where Apple-1 lived. It sits on the border with Bosnia where the sister community on the other side of the river is known as Bosanska Dubica. Angry residents contemplated firing their hunting rifles at them, but they knew it would only make the situation worse. Ultimately, weapons and ammo from the helicopters were loaded onto trucks and transported by caisson to Serb enclaves just outside of Dubica. Members of Martić's Police and JNA soldiers were there in the thick of things.

Soon Hrvatska Dubica was shelled from all sides, including from the nearby communities of Hrvatska Kostajnica and Bosanska Dubica. Most of the population fled, including Croat police and Croatian National Guard (ZNG) members. Those were the people who could escape. About sixty inhabitants, mostly infirm elderly and women, remained behind. Their only consolation was going down with the homes in which their families had lived for generations.

Serb forces surrounded Dubica and began searching houses. They abducted several Croats and other non-Serbs. Some were used as human shields and forced to walk ahead of the Serb forces as they searched for Croatian defensive positions. This action by itself was a war crime.

Some of the abducted men, including one who became a cooperating witness, later were taken to an old schoolhouse being used by Serb forces. Several victims were locked inside a bathroom where they were showered with insults, beatings, and torture. Some were pummeled into unconsciousness.

The next morning one frightened witness and a companion saw the bodies of two abductees in the back of a truck. "We were ordered to lie on top of the bodies," he said. "We were both too weak to climb the trailer. The Serbs put us there."

Once he was inside the truck, the witness could see that both the men's throats had been slit from ear to ear. He could feel their bodies moving. The next thing the witness knew, he was at the River Una, where the Serb forces threw the mangled, near-dead bodies over the bridge. Death plunged into the river not far from the site of the notorious Ustaše Jasenovac extermination camp from World War II. The Ustaše were brutal. They had killed and tortured thousands of Jews, Orthodox Serbs, Gypsies, and—less well-known—Croats, most of whom were Communists. Even the Italian forces shuddered at these horrific acts of inhumanity.

As was often the case, local Serbs were joined by strangers from other parts of the former Yugoslavia. Our investigation showed that through these exterior alliances, Serbs turned up from Bosnia, and other compatriots arrived from Serbia proper. They did whatever they could to stir up the fears of the local Croatian-Serbs. Soon their propaganda turned to death.

The bodies of many victims from Dubica and Baćin were never recovered, which had raised concerns that we wouldn't be able to prosecute these murders successfully. I worked with war crimes investigators to build a case based on the strategic use of strong circumstantial evidence that would lead a trial chamber of the tribunal to conclude that the missing victims were murdered by Serb forces. The approach was similar to the homicide case involving Nenad Harmandžić, which I'd investigated in Mostar, but much bigger.

Other crimes were committed in the area. In September 1991 about fifty Serb paramilitary soldiers, mostly wearing civilian clothes, moved in on the nearby village of Cerovljani, killing Croats and torching their homes. The local Catholic church was intentionally struck by a rocket. Residents tried to steer clear of trouble, but within a couple of weeks Serb forces had abducted the remaining Croats in the village and executed them. They were buried in a mass grave near Baćin. The bodies of three victims were never recovered.

When Serb forces took Baćin itself, all remaining Croats were seized. Twenty-two people, most of them elderly, were murdered near Baćin, along with the victims from Cerovljani.

Throughout the region, Catholic churches were destroyed. Houses were looted and then reduced to rubble. The nearby village of Predore was razed.

CRIMES IN THE SAO WESTERN SLAVONIA

As I walked the streets of Voćin, I reviewed the evidence and read witness statements taken after I'd sent in a new team of investigators, including a police officer from the Norwegian Police Service. I learned how Serb TO forces had taken over the Voćin police station in August 1991, and how JNA soldiers had followed them into the village. Croatian residents were assembled and told that a new Serb government was in power. The total subjugation of the Croatian population of Voćin was in progress, and a pattern of systematic persecution was under way.

The town of Voćin is nestled in an enchanting valley not far from Papuk Mountain in Western Slavonia. Perhaps the most exciting thing that happens in this community of less than two thousand is the annual pilgrimage to a centuries-old Catholic church in tribute to the Virgin Mary. But Voćin's serene atmosphere changed on August 12, 1991, when local Serbs declared Western Slavonia's autonomy from Croatia, just as they had done farther west in the SAO Krajina. The SAO Western Slavonia was born—and all hell broke loose.

Like storm troopers, Serb forces burst into the homes of Croats and searched them, seizing hunting rifles and other personal weapons. Civilians were vilified, abducted, and taken to detention facilities. The whereabouts of some victims were never ascertained. My experience told me these were not random acts of violence. Categorical criminal calculation was in play.

Team Four's geographic, demographic, and perpetrator-group analyses were coming together. I knew that the investigators' work was precise, and this had helped to identify an area of Croatia that would provide critical evidence of the criminal plan and key political players in the overall conspiracy. This is what led us to Voćin.

Our investigation revealed that in October 1991 paramilitary soldiers entered Voćin in buses bearing Belgrade number plates. After initiating a sustained pattern of persecution against the local Croats, the Serb forces withdrew on December 13, 1991. They had orders to take no prisoners.

What transpired next constituted both a mass murder and a crime against humanity. Cutthroat killers went door-to-door murdering thirty-two people in Voćin and the surrounding villages. Several tons of explosives were detonated, destroying Our Lady of Voćin Church. The savage conduct of the killers was difficult to understand, but I knew some of them were sadists. Many of the victims had been beaten with chains, tortured, and burned to death. One woman was brutally murdered by several ax blows to the head. In another case, a Croatian couple had their heads cut off and placed in fertilizer bags. The offenders' pleasure in mutilating the bodies was manifested through their deeds.

Fortunately for us, some of the malefactors left critical evidence at the scene—their military leave records. These records, together with witness statements, inside sources, and a profusion of circumstantial evidence, later would be used to allege, from an investigative and prosecutorial standpoint, that some of the perpetrators were members of a volunteer paramilitary force known as Šešelj's Men.

To corroborate this information, I undertook a secret mission into the region to meet with a potential witness. I believed she had key information about crimes committed in the area, including details that could help us link the criminal enterprise to Serbia. This reluctant witness had good reason to fear for her life. My job was to gain her trust and cooperation.

I could offer her no assurance of any kind. I could only remind her that working with us was the right thing to do. Winning her over was no easy task, but we did it—and this well-placed source had information that was even better than what our intelligence had suggested. She gave us words spoken to her directly by the highest-level leader in the joint criminal enterprise: Slobodan Milošević.

CRIMES IN SLAVONIA, BARANJA, AND WESTERN SREM

Stretching east all the way to the Serbian border with Croatia was another Serb autonomous region, the SAO Slavonia, Baranja, and Western Srem (SBWS). The area's proximity to Serbia proper meant certain misery for Croats and other non-Serb minorities living there. Vladimir Dzuro, a former police captain from the eastern bloc, helped me get up to speed in this region. Dzuro was the primary UN war crimes investigator of Serb crimes committed in Vukovar and other areas of the SAO SBWS. He knew the area, the victims, and the perpetrators well.

The SAO SBWS was declared autonomous in late June 1991. Within its borders lay cities, towns, and villages of extreme interest to war crimes investigators—places such as Vukovar, Erdut, Ilok, and Dalj. Here too was Lovas, a village a little more than three kilometers from the Serb border. The tragic events that occurred in Lovas stay with me even today.

The local Croats and other ethnic minorities didn't offer any opposition when armed Serb TO forces and a ruthless paramilitary force known as Dušan Silni (Dušan the Mighty or Dušan the Great), named for the fourteenth-century king of Serbia and emperor of the Serbs and Greeks, entered what had been a sleepy village during the early morning hours of November 10, 1991. A protected witness code-named "Oscar" told Team Four how he and his wife and small children hid in their cellar when the shooting started. Then a terrifying voice called out to them: "Come out now, or we'll throw a grenade in!"

Although he knew that grave misfortune had befallen them, Oscar had no choice but to bring his family out. They were required to put on white armbands identifying themselves as Croats. Like the homes of other local Croats, their house was marked with a white sheet. This set the stage for the looting and burning of Croats' homes by Serb forces, including paramilitaries such as Dušan Silni and the Beli Orlovi (White Eagles). Both heavily armed groups were well known for their callous disregard for the lives of civilians, including women and children. In Lovas, they did not touch a single Serb home.

Eventually Serb forces seized Oscar and a number of other Croats. Oscar was placed among a group of victims who were used as human shields during a search for alleged Ustaše. Fifty of the seventy captives were organized into two columns and led to the outskirts of the village. Not far from Lovas, the prisoners began a forced march. At gunpoint, the men were compelled to join hands and become human mine ploughs. As I stood at the scene of the crime several years later, I could practically hear the shouts of "Wire!" and the subsequent explosion and gunfire. As I continued to read witness statements at the scene, I scanned the field and felt the wild beating of the panicked prisoners' hearts. The decimation was about to begin.

In all, twenty-one unarmed men were killed on that field, either blown up by mines or shot by soldiers. Others were maimed or crippled. Those who could walk were forced to pick up unexploded mines and carry them from the field.

Back in Lovas, the twenty men left behind became *desaparecidos*. They simply vanished from the face of the earth. They weren't the only ones.

———✦———

Blood spattered the ground, and screams filled the night air. In the distance, the sound of heavy machinery hinted at the horror still to come. The burial site was nearly ready.

The last known victim to escape later became a protected witness. He provided crucial evidence about what became known as the "convoy to darkness." Under cover of night, a truck driven by a Serb soldier took away a group of about fifteen victims. After only about ten to fifteen minutes, the truck returned empty. This scene was repeated several times until it was our witness's turn to be ordered at gunpoint into the back of the truck.

Once he and the other victims were inside the truck, a large tarp was thrown over them. But even before the truck was in motion, the witness's mind was formulating a plan. With the basic human instinct for self-preservation kicking in, our witness bailed out of the truck at a decisive moment and made a daring escape. The more than 250 victims left behind were shot to death; most of them were buried in a mass grave at a pig farm near Ovčara. These were the victims of Vukovar Hospital.

The events that led up to the single bloodiest mass murder in Croatia began when Serb forces besieged the city of Vukovar for three terrifying months, beginning in August 1991. The Yugoslav Air Force even strafed civilians. Hundreds were killed, and most of the city was destroyed.

Vukovar Hospital itself became a target of the illegal campaign as early as August 15, 1991. Some of the bombs made direct hits on the hospital, which held hundreds of patients. Fires broke out, electrical wires sparked, and water pipes burst. Food, water, and other provisions were scarce, just as they were in the Mostar hospital I had investigated earlier. The medical staff members in Vukovar risked their own lives trying to save their patients. It was utter chaos.

Hospital staff sent urgent pleas for help to the international community. Desperate, they groveled before senior members of the JNA in theater. Even though the hospital staff was also tending to JNA soldiers, no respite was in sight.

Only at the eleventh hour, with the bombed-out city ready to fall, was an agreement reached with the JNA. The hospital would be evacuated under the observation of NGOs, including the ICRC. The evacuation would be carried out at precisely 8 a.m. on November 18, 1991.

What happened next gave an all new meaning to perfidy. The time came for the evacuation, but not a single representative of an international organization appeared. Fearful that something was amiss—and placing herself in immense peril—one physician made her way to a nearby town, where she immediately made contact with a senior JNA officer, Col. Mile Mrkšić. Without emotion, he assured the doctor that the evacuation would proceed as planned.

When the physician returned to the hospital the next day, she couldn't believe her eyes. JNA soldiers were removing people without international observers present. She objected strenuously, but Maj. Veselin Šljivančanin, the JNA officer in charge at the hospital, simply carried on. To make matters worse, the doctor was seized and held there against her will overnight.

The next day, November 20, 1991, the doctor was abducted and taken to a JNA barracks, where she was conveniently unable to witness anything going on at the hospital. She eventually was informed that the patients and others had been evacuated. In reality, they were being transported in a caravan of death.

The JNA loaded approximately 264 patients, hospital employees, and others, including some of Vukovar's former defenders, into six olive-green military buses and drove them across a bridge to a drop-off point at a JNA barracks. The hard work of war crimes investigators paid off when they recovered video footage of the buses crossing the bridge over the River Vuka. The video captured Šljivančanin's ominous image in the foreground, looking straight into the camera.

From Vukovar, the buses headed toward Negoslavci and then made a left turn onto an asphalt road that ran between cultivated fields. A right turn brought the buses to the hangar at the pig farm. The abductees were at Ovčara, in the custody of members of the TO and JNA military policemen. Before long, the JNA withdrew, leaving the helpless victims in the sole clutches of the TO, which already had a history of beating, abusing, and murdering innocent Croats and prisoners of war. Soon the bulldozer would do its work.

The author in Sarajevo preparing to embark on an investigative mission.

Remains of the Sovići schoolhouse where innocent, unarmed civilians, including women, children, and elderly, were herded following an attack by the HVO and members of the KB.

Remains of homes after an attack by the HVO and members of the KB on Doljani.

The confrontation line on Mostar's Bulevar.

The author flying an aerial mission in a French SFOR helicopter over Mostar in Bosnia.

The author (left) *briefing a Spanish legionnaire* (center) *and an Italian carabiniere* (right) *before the execution of a mission in Bosnia.*

Briefing before the execution of a mission in Bosnia. Left to right: *French gendarme, author, Italian carabiniere, Spanish marine, Italian carabiniere, Spanish legionnaire, and Dutch police officer.*

Author (center) *briefing members of the Irish Garda, Italian Carabinieri, French Gendarmerie, and Dutch police prior to the execution of a search warrant mission in Bosnia.*

Inside a structure on the ABiH side of the confrontation line in Mostar looking toward the HVO side, with the Health Center and the fountain in the background. This was the scene of the wooden rifles incident described in chapter 3.

At an Irish pub in Sarajevo after a mission. Left to right: *author, member of the Royal Canadian Mounted Police, and member of the Swedish Police Service.*

The author preparing for the next day's mission from inside a French billet at the Multinational Division NATO compound in Bosnia.

The scene in Kosovo as the author arrived on a mission following the NATO campaign against Serbia.

The scene in Kosovo as the author flies aerial missions with German KFOR in search of mass graves.

Graves of Kosovar civilians who were alleged to have been murdered by Serb forces, discovered by the author and team members.

Makeshift morgue in Kosovo where the British forensic team examined exhumed remains.

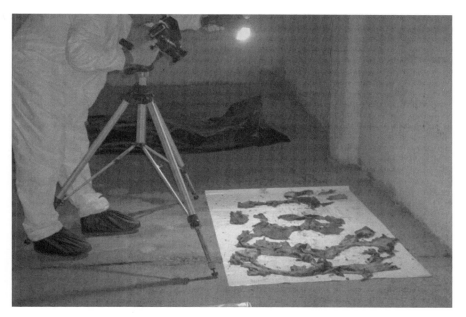

Scotland Yard police photographer processing evidence recovered from a murder crime scene in Kosovo.

The author's great-grandparents, Josip and Paulina Cenčić, at their wedding in Lokve, Croatia.

The local tambura band in Lokve in front of the Zagreb Inn, 1928. Top (left to right): *Šimun Čop (Tomakov), Petar Magdić, Alojz Žagar (Rokičev);* bottom (left to right): *Marijan Grgurić (Korenov), Milan Briški (Skubetov), Franjo Malnar (Boretov) (child's name is unknown).* Courtesy of Mirjana Pleše

The author in front of a World War II Nazi bunker in Lokve, 2007.

The snow-covered village of Lokve during wintertime. Courtesy of Mirjana Pleše

Crosses of Rejection, Repentance, and Redemption in Lokve, 2007.

The author (left) *and Mirjana Pleše examining the Lokve schoolhouse logbook, c. 1880 (photo taken in 2007).*

Outside the village of Lokve in the Gorski Kotar region of Croatia, 2007. Left to right: Jonathan Cencich (son), author, cousin Boris Cenčić, cousin Edo Cenčić.

Son Sebastian Cencich (left) *and daughter Catalina Cencich at the gravesites of the author's great-grandparents, Josip and Paulina Cencich, at Detroit's Mt. Olivet Cemetery.*

During the course of the evening, the soldiers loaded groups of about ten or twenty victims into a truck, which left the farm building and returned empty a short while later. The truck traveled south from the Ovčara farm building on the road leading to Grabovo. About one and one-tenth kilometers southeast of the building, the truck turned left and then traveled northeast on a dirt-filled road that ran between a cultivated field on the left and a wooded ravine on the right. At the head of the ravine, about nine hundred meters from the Ovčara-Grabovo road, the soldiers removed the captives from the truck.

Within hours, the victims were crushed. The deadly sounds of terror disappeared, and the pitch-black farmland became an unholy burial ground. The massacre was complete.

Five years later the remains of two hundred victims, mostly men, were exhumed from a mass grave. Approximately fifty victims remain unaccounted for. I distinctly remember standing at the site of the mass grave, which had been made into a permanent memorial. It bore sharp witness to man's inhumanity to man. I have seen death many times, even at my own hands. And by the grace of God, I've escaped my own demise too many times to have been simply lucky. At the memorial site, a heavy sadness fell over me. What happened at Ovčara caused me to look deeper into my own soul and to seek answers to questions lingering within.

Is such evil bound to be?

My moment of silence was interrupted by the sobbing of two elderly women who stood nearby. It was time for me to move on with the investigation.

Once military operations in and around Vukovar had ended, the JNA deported thousands of Croats and other non-Serbs into Serbia. But that wasn't good enough. Goran Hadžić, the president of SAO SBWS, allegedly made a request to detain those non-Serbs who were suspected of participating in the fight. Consequently, the JNA transported many Vukovar residents to the detention facilities in Dalj. There, selected detainees were interrogated, beaten, and tortured. Thirty-four were murdered.

I was by no means the first to examine these crime scenes. By the time I came to The Hague in the fall of 1998, the OTP had already taken a mid-level perpetrator of the Vukovar Hospital massacre to trial, and it had indicted three others. But the victims' family members received little justice. Although the investigators and prosecutors were definitely on top of their job, the trial unexpectedly was brought to a halt.

Slavko Dokmanović, a Serb who had been president of Vukovar municipality, was indicted and arrested. By all accounts the prosecution team—including Grant Niemann, the STA, and Clint Williamson, the team legal adviser who later became U.S. ambassador at large for war crimes—laid out the evidence before the court, piece by piece. But Dokmanović hanged himself in the UN detention wing of Scheveningen Prison before a verdict was reached in his trial.

Dokmanović hadn't acted alone. I quickly learned that three JNA officers were dead center on Team Four's radar: Mrkšić, Šljivančanin, and Miroslav Radić. The "Vukovar Three" were fugitives from justice, and international warrants had been issued for their arrest. War crimes investigators worked the streets of many countries in an effort to locate these alleged killers. We worked with Interpol, foreign intelligence services, and national law enforcement agencies from around the world in an effort to identify their precise whereabouts and place other war crimes suspects, yet to be indicted, under surveillance.

Assisting Team Four was a dedicated fugitive squad from the Investigations Division of the OTP. The Fugitive Investigative Support Team (FIST) was staffed with experienced operatives from American, British, and French intelligence services, including Britain's MI5 and the ultra-secret U.S. Intelligence Support Activity (ISA).

───※◈※───

Meanwhile, there were more crimes to investigate. Some were committed by ruthless men who often wore black tactical uniforms and carried Yugoslav- and Russian-made automatic weapons and radio headsets. Bold and razor-sharp, their very appearance inspired terror.

These were Arkan's Tigers, death squads notorious for their extraordinary violence. When necessary, they hid their faces behind black ski masks, but most of the time they didn't bother. They simply murdered any witnesses, including everyday people such as Juliana Pap.

Juliana was a fifty-year-old ethnic Hungarian woman living in Erdut, a village and municipality in eastern Croatia, where both the Danube and

Sava Rivers flow. Erdut sits right on the border with Serbia, and it was not a safe place for ethnic non-Serbs.

In mid-November 1991 Juliana went to the TO training center in Erdut looking for her husband, Franjo, and her son Mihajlo. She knew where to go. Mihajlo and Franjo had been abducted several days earlier and fettered in chains. But for some unknown reason, her son had been released. He had run home and told his mother what had happened to him and his father. But before long the terrorists returned and seized Mihajlo again, sending him back to the training center.

The multipurpose facility was used for detentions, interrogations, and murder. It had been established originally by Radovan Stojičić, a.k.a. "Badža," a police general from Serbia who had headed the SAJ. A highly trained killer, Stojičić reported both to Milošević and to the head of the DB. Although the SAJ called itself an antiterrorist unit, its members were the terrorists, not the other way around.

Juliana didn't know it was already too late to find her family alive. When her son was taken back to the training center, he and eleven other ethnic minorities, mostly Hungarians, had been taken to a nearby Catholic cemetery and executed. Her husband was among them.

Anguished and desperate, the iron-willed Juliana tried to suppress her fear as she went looking for her loved ones. She found herself face-to-face with both the head of Arkan's military police and the head of Serbian National Security (SNB). I can only surmise the content of their conversation.

"I'm here for my husband and son."

"They're not here."

"Yes, they are! Please release them! They've done nothing wrong."

We don't know the exact words of her plea, but we do know that she paid for her persistence with her life. From the very moment she pleaded for the release of her family members, she didn't have a prayer. Juliana, another of her sons, and Mihajlo's fiancée were promptly executed.

On June 3, 1992, the head of Arkan's military police once again ordered SNB forces to murder an ethnic Hungarian who was asking about her missing relatives. A simple-hearted woman, Marija Senasi, fifty-four years old, was related to the Pap family. Like Juliana, she never gave up looking for her loved ones.

Under Arkan's orders, gun-wielding SNB forces abducted Marija as she pedaled her bicycle down the road between Erdut and Dalj Planina.

Like Juliana, she'd been asking questions around town—and like Juliana, she paid with her life. Marija was taken to a house that was used as an interrogation center and subsequently murdered.

The despot leading the Tigers was Željko "Arkan" Ražnatović, a man with unbridled power and a murky past. His men were vicious executioners enraptured by suffering and death. Often they killed for sheer pleasure; some sanctimoniously made the sign of the cross after taking an innocent life. The fearless Arkan savored the terror, too.

Even before Juliana Pap and her family members were murdered, Serb forces had been busy in the area. During September 1991 members of the TO and the area militia "arrested" a number of local Croats and took them to a police facility in Dalj, a community just north of Vukovar. Arkan was right behind them. On September 21, 1991, he and about twenty of his bloodthirsty men went to the holding tank. Arkan removed eleven prisoners and summarily executed them.

His thirst for blood unsatisfied, Arkan and his men returned to the same detention center the following month. They removed men from the cell block and fatally shot twenty-eight unarmed captives. Their bodies later were dumped into the Danube River.

Arkan's Tigers and their accomplices were just warming up. In early November, killers from the TO led by Arkan and the militia rounded up more ethnic Hungarian and Croat civilians in Erdut, Dalj Planina, and Erdut Planina. They took their captives to the training center in Erdut and executed twelve of them the following day. A few days later seven non-Serb civilians in the village of Klisa were similarly abducted. Two of the victims who had Serb relatives were released, but the remaining five civilians were not so lucky. They were taken to the TO training center in Erdut to be interrogated. All five were brutally treated, then killed, and finally buried in a mass grave in the village of Ćelija. About a month later, on December 10, 1991, members of Arkan's Tigers and local militiamen whisked away five non-Serb villagers from their homes in Erdut. They also were taken to the TO training center in Erdut and subsequently murdered.

The holiday spirit meant nothing to these killers. Even on Christmas Day, celebrated by Orthodox Serbs and Catholic Croats on December 25 (which corresponds with January 7 on the Gregorian calendar), Arkan's Tigers, members of the TO, and local militiamen went after seven ethnic Hungarian and Croat civilians in Erdut. The victims' pleas for mercy went unanswered. They were conveyed to the TO training center in Erdut, and on the day after Christmas their blood spilled into the snow.

The New Year brought little respite. Within two months Arkan and his band of killers were back at it again. Their modus operandi was the same. They abducted four non-Serb civilians in Erdut and interrogated them in the TO training center. A bloody execution soon followed.

By now the names "Arkan" and "Tigers" caused civilians to tremble in fear. Even hardened criminals blindly obeyed Arkan's every word, lest they suffer the same fate as the Croats and ethnic minorities who fell victim to his terror. Make no mistake: Arkan wasn't operating alone. Although he had direct connections to Milošević, he took orders and pay from the head of the DB—and the DB had its own band of ruthless killers.

In nearby Grabovac, members of the deadly special operations component of the secret police struck hard and fast. This unit of the Red Berets was staged out of Tito's castle in SAO SBWS. On May 4, 1992, a special operations team came to Grabovac and abducted a number of civilians. The kidnappers sped away with the victims in a van, their destination unknown.

Eventually we learned that the kidnap victims, three men and two women ranging in age from forty-one to fifty-eight, were taken to Tikveš Park, near the border with Serbia. There they were executed and buried in a primary mass grave. A secondary dumping site, in an effort to better hide the bodies, would come later.

Investigators knew Grabovac was a hunting ground under the control of the Red Berets at the time of the murders. But the hunters had turned from wild game to innocent civilians.

Throughout the region, many victims' remains were never recovered. Those that were found and returned to surviving family members can be credited, in large part, to the tireless efforts of Col. Ivan Grujić and Dr. Davor Strinović. The mostly expressionless Grujić worked hard as the head of the Croatian Office of Missing and Detained Persons. I respected him immensely, mostly because he worked just as hard to find Serb victims as he did Croats and other non-Serbs. Grujić and his team literally left no stone unturned. Strinović was the deputy head of the Institute for Forensic Medicine at the University of Zagreb. He and his staff of expert medical pathologists worked to identify victims and determine the cause and manner of death. This helped war crimes investigators prepare cases for the prosecutors who would present them in court. More important, the victims' families would have some closure to the tragedy they endured.

UN war crimes investigators from Team Four also were working aggressively. They had the compassion to interact with survivors and relatives. They also had the guts and the sophisticated know-how to work the dark, tough streets and backwoods roads of the region, as well as the inside sources and war criminals who walked them.

This was all evident on October 28, 1998, when members of Team Four solved the mystery surrounding the whereabouts of the abducted civilians from in and around Erdut. War crimes investigators recovered the remains of twenty-three victims, bearing evidence of gunshot wounds, in an abandoned well in Daljski Atar.

It was an excellent operation. The investigative team worked hard and took their missions seriously. Hours upon hours of old-fashioned police work finally paid off. Investigators, together with Croatian authorities and medico-legal experts, were able to determine the victims using the dates they had gone missing. The first kidnapping victim lay at the bottom of the narrow well. The twenty-two others were piled on top of one another in the precise chronological order of their abductions.

The work continued. In September 2000 investigators found Juliana Pap, her son Franjo Pap, and her other son's fiancée, Natalija Rakin, in a well in Borovo Selo, near Dalj. The remains of Marija Senasi were found too, in another long-abandoned water well not far from the confluence of the Sava and the Danube, at Dalj Mountain near Erdut.

CRIMES IN THE DUBROVNIK REGION

Mount Srđ was the high ground. Standing on the summit, where hundreds of spent casings from 7.62 mm rounds still littered the ground, I could see the beautiful Adriatic Sea and the Old Town, a walled area of the city of Dubrovnik protected by the UN Educational, Scientific, and Cultural Organization (UNESCO).

A salvo of serious criminal proportions had been launched from Mount Srđ against Dubrovnik and its inhabitants. Beginning October 1, 1991, JNA ground forces and TO soldiers from Montenegro had come in from the hinterlands and covered the city from three sides. On the fourth side was the Yugoslav Navy, with JNA warships lying in wait on the Adriatic, somewhere between the devil and the deep. Serb forces gripped Dubrovnik by the throat. The local defenders stood fast, but to no avail. Theirs was an untenable situation. Light arms and the soft-skinned vehicles of the civil defense and local police were no match for the mighty JNA.

The investigative crew of Murugan and Arshad was on this job too. Joining them were a retired sergeant from the Royal Canadian Mounted Police and a former detective sergeant from Australia. Together they did an outstanding job of investigating the barrage of fire that rained down on this beautiful city and its inhabitants.

This component of the investigation was beginning to wind down when I took over as leader of Team Four. But the investigators' briefings and the evidence I reviewed supported the theory that the siege of Dubrovnik was part of an overall criminal enterprise masterminded from Serbia.

Although the majority of the region consisted of Croats, advocates of a Greater Serbia pushed for a so-called Dubrovnik Republic that would be detached from Croatia and connected with Serb-aligned Montenegro.

The seven-month siege in 1991 and 1992 crippled Dubrovnik and upended the lives of its inhabitants. Power and water were cut off, and the inhabitants suffered profusely. On October 1, 1991, the situation grew worse: Serb forces shelled the Dubrovnik region from sea, land, and air. The JNA and TO forces from Montenegro overtook scores of villages as they advanced on the city.

In many of the overtaken villages, Serb forces looted homes. Some hijacked trucks and other vehicles to transport their illegal war booty to Bosnia and Montenegro. Many of the local Croat villagers were rounded up by Serb forces and unlawfully sent to prison camps in Serbia, Bosnia, and Montenegro. Most of the "prisoners" were civilians, some as old as ninety. But it made no difference whether the detainees were civilian or military. They were beaten and tortured; some were sodomized.

Those civilians who somehow eluded Serb forces fled toward Old Town. They took refuge in large hotels that had been mostly vacated by tourists. Protected by UNESCO, they believed they would be safe from attack. They were dead wrong.

The Serb forces that shelled, looted, and burned civilian homes on their way to the city did not give a second thought to what was about to happen in Dubrovnik. They intentionally fired on the Old Town, committing a war crime that, from the very beginning, also constituted a crime against humanity. Strictly speaking, the offensive had been a part of a widespread or systematic attack directed against a civilian population within the context of state policy.

The heaviest shelling occurred on November 8–13 and December 6, 1991. Thousands of shells fell on Old Town buildings, some directly striking the hotels where the fleeing villagers had sought refuge. At least forty-one people were killed. The attack was not justified by any lawful military objective. These were intentional assaults directed at civilians and civilian objects.

Since our prosecutors took a conservative approach, Team Four investigators sought to demonstrate that these killings were not the result of collateral damage. In order to prove willful murder or unlawful killing, we had to go well beyond the evidence necessary for an ordinary homicide investigation. Like nearly all the other homicides Team Four investigated, what happened in Dubrovnik constituted a mass murder in and of itself. Yet we needed to learn about the shooters and the orders given to them; their past conduct and that of their superior officers; the accuracy of the ordnance and its trajectory; the occupations of the victims; and the presence of combatants or other legitimate military objectives nearby. We were told this was all necessary to prove beyond a reasonable doubt that each of the forty-one victims was a civilian noncombatant, and this would take us one step closer to murder charges.

I did what our legal advisers said was necessary and instructed the investigators to pursue the evidence that we did. But it didn't sit well with me. I had difficulty accepting the notion that collateral damage had any application whatsoever to a crime against humanity. In my view, traditional concepts of the law of war, such as belligerent reprisals, the rule of distinction, and the rule of proportionality, weren't relevant in this case. This was a criminal operation that, once under way, eliminated traditional law-of-war factors from consideration.

But this wasn't the time to debate the philosophical issues surrounding the laws and customs of war versus criminal enterprises. I had a job to do.

CRIMES THROUGHOUT THE REPUBLIC OF CROATIA

The team had to put together the entire Croatia investigation—from Dubrovnik to Vukovar and from Zagreb to the Krajina—in order to present the master case for an indictment against Milošević and his senior coperpetrators. Throughout the country, the process started with the crimes on the ground and ended with the police, military, and political leaders at the top.

As far as the crime base was concerned, there is no precise accounting of the murders, tortures, assassinations, and destruction that occurred in Croatia during the ten-month period from August 1991 until June 1992. But it is estimated that almost five thousand civilians, many of them children, elderly, or infirm, were the victims of criminal homicide. Among them were 335 victims who were younger than eighteen and at least 1,526 older than sixty.

The dead included oft-forgotten minority groups such as Hungarians and Muslims. Byzantine Ruthenians from Eastern Slavonia, including the brave men and women from Petrovci who risked their lives to bring food and water to the helpless patients at Vukovar Hospital, were murdered too. In the end, the indictment listed 688 murder victims by name.

But these murder statistics don't take into consideration the more than six thousand Croats who died while defending their families, homes, and homeland against thousands of armed participants in the criminal enterprise who descended on them and their communities. In my view, since the offensive was criminal in nature from the outset, these defenders became homicide victims too. A criminal enterprise is different from the commencement of war or armed conflict. It casts an entirely different light on the traditional legal notions of *jus ad bellum* and *jus in bello*, which relate to the legality of going to war, and once under way, the laws governing the conduct of combatants, respectively.

In addition, thousands more were unlawfully imprisoned and subjected to inhumane treatment. Both civilians and prisoners of war were unlawfully beaten, tortured, and raped. Great masses of people, at least 170,000 Croats and other non-Serb minorities, were forcibly transferred from their homes. Approximately fifty thousand more civilians, including women, children, and elderly people, fled the region in fear for their lives.

Moreover, much of Croatia was ravaged and pillaged. The willful and deliberate destruction of homes, places of worship, hospitals, and cultural monuments was widespread and systematic.

Team Four's overall investigation in Croatia revealed that the principal perpetrator groups responsible for these atrocities were members of the regular and reserve JNA forces; KOG, the federal military counterintelligence unit of the JNA Security Administration (UB); the TO; Martić's Police; the DB and its special operations component, known at different times as the JSO, JATD, or Red Berets; Četniks or Šešelj's Men; Arkan's Tigers; the White Eagles and members of Dušan Silni; and the SNB. They were killers indeed. Many were even decorated for their criminal ambitions and successes.

Soon it would be Team Four's job to link the murders, rapes, tortures, and other crimes against humanity to the perpetrator groups horizontally, as part of the joint criminal enterprise. Then we would connect their leaders vertically in two ways, through criminal enterprise associations and their various modes of participation. As a precautionary strategy, we would also demonstrate individual criminal responsibility through traditional police and military chains of command.

Our undertaking would link violent crimes at an unprecedented level. It would piece together the joint criminal enterprise and penetrate the once-impregnable inner circle of top-level military and political leaders, headed by the president of a country.

8

The Conspirators

THEY CAME FROM THE SECRET POLICE AND FROM THE HIGHEST ranks of the JNA. They included members of the Presidency of the SFRY and individual presidents of several constituent republics. One was perhaps the most feared and deadly killer in all of Europe.

Sometimes they met behind the closed doors of a president's office. On other occasions their violent ambitions took them to smoky dens frequented by gangsters and prostitutes. They employed both old-fashioned coded messages and encrypted electronic communications systems to further their deadly conspiracy.

These were members of Slobodan Milošević's inner circle, the alleged participants in a joint criminal enterprise that was spawned in Serbia and reached throughout the Balkans and beyond. They held the innocent citizens of Yugoslavia at their mercy—and they dispensed cruelty instead.

These conspirators were tapped into organized crime, and they often controlled the mob. Political assassins were at their disposal. They were never quite sure who was working for whom, but they had connections with members of foreign intelligence services, including the U.S. CIA; the Soviet Union's KGB; and Shin Bet, the Israeli State Security Agency.

They had one objective: to seize about one-third of Croatia and form a Greater Serbia.

History is replete with territorial ambitions and human rights violations in Eastern Europe. In 1990 the conspirators' ambitions were focused on the Republic of Croatia, an area largely inhabited by peaceable civilians.

Most of its residents were Croats or Croatian-Serbs, but they shared their neighborhoods with other ethnic and religious groups—Muslims, Ruthenians, and Hungarians among them. Members of all these groups would fall victim to the conspirators' perfidy.

To carry out the objective of the joint criminal enterprise, Milošević's inner circle set a number of strategies in motion. Croatian generals in the JNA were abruptly relieved of their commands. Weapons were taken away from Croatian citizens, and Croats were removed from government posts in their local communities.

In some ways, the Croats who were only forced from their homes were the lucky ones. Too many others fell victim to extermination, murder, rape, torture, and unlawful confinement. Their homes and churches were destroyed. In some cases, entire villages were razed, leaving no trace of the peaceful inhabitants who had lived there in an atmosphere of brotherhood and unity.

To carry out these unlawful operations, the conspirators needed forces on the ground. And in one way or another, they controlled them all: the JNA, the DB, TO, special volunteer paramilitary units, and the police—both regular uniformed officers and special operations units. Their reach was so pervasive that many otherwise amiable Croatian-Serbs came to believe they must persecute their own Croatian neighbors, lest they themselves be killed.

The propaganda machine became an essential component of the criminal enterprise. Through black-flag special operations and effective use of the media, the conspirators convinced many Croatian-Serbs that the atrocities committed against their people during World War II were occurring once again. Serbian TV networks broadcast images of brutally murdered Serbs—although, in reality, many of the bloody corpses were either dead Croats or Serb victims who had been murdered by Serb forces.

To make the operational aspects of the conspiracy possible, the inner circle gained control of all organs of the federal government, including the Presidency, and gave itself the ability to pass laws whenever it chose. The conspirators controlled the banks, and other revenue came streaming in from both legal and illegal sources. With these funds, the conspirators purchased weapons and ammunition, paid informants and assassins, and saw that regular and irregular forces were properly trained and equipped.

This circle encompassed the men ultimately responsible for the heinous crimes that occurred throughout Croatia—crimes that shocked the conscience of humanity: The destruction of Vukovar, including the abduction and murder of 264 unarmed hospital patients and others; the siege and attack on Dubrovnik; the execution of innocent civilians from Erdut, whose bodies were dumped into wells; and the ruthless murder of helpless women, children, and elderly men, some of them wheelchair-bound or bedridden, in Croatian villages such as Baćin, Voćin, and Škabrnja.

Through our investigations, we identified the units—and sometimes the triggermen—directly responsible for perpetrating these crimes. Through diligent police work, we often tracked down the individual commanders on the ground. But orders to commit such widespread and systematic atrocities didn't normally originate with captains, majors, or even colonels. The orders came from much higher. The planning involved general officers and political leaders, including ministers and other cabinet-level officials. And a criminal conspiracy this big could not have come to fruition without the president's knowledge.

In this case, his treacherous machinations were at the heart of the conspiracy. Once the plot was hatched, the redoubtable Slobodan Milošević was never more than a heartbeat away from the evisceration of Croatia.

SLOBODAN MILOŠEVIĆ

Slobodan Milošević was born in Serbia during World War II. In 1959, when he was just eighteen, he joined the League of Communists of Yugoslavia.[1] Milošević attended the Faculty of Law at the University of Belgrade, where he first met and became friends with Ivan Stambolić, the future president of Serbia. In 1984 Milošević became chairman of the City Committee of the League of Communists of Belgrade, and two years later he was elected chairman of the Presidium of the Central Committee of the League of Communists of Serbia.

On July 16, 1990, the League of Communists of Serbia and the Socialist Alliance of Working People of Serbia united, forming a new party named the Socialist Party of Serbia (SPS). Milošević was elected the party's president, a post he held until 2006.

He was already a political leader, having been elected president of the Socialist Republic of Serbia in May 1989. When a new constitution was adopted on September 28, 1990, the Socialist Republic of Serbia became the Republic of Serbia. Three months later, in December 1990, Milošević was elected to the newly established office of president of the republic.

Team Four's investigations into the crimes that occurred in Croatia began to come into focus around this time. By 1990 certain political and conspiratorial events leading up to the atrocities already had begun.

By August 1991 the murders and other crimes in Saborsko and Poljanak were in progress. September brought more horrific events, this time in Dalj. By October murders, exterminations, and other crimes were widespread, reaching the many villages, towns, and hamlets, including Hrvatska Kostajnica, Lipovanić, Dubica, Cerovljani, Baćin, and Lovas. During this time Dubrovnik came under attack by land, sea, and air. As winter began in the Balkans, Vukovići, Škabrnja, Nadin, and Vukovar became targets of violence, along with Erdut, Borovo, and Dalj Planina. Just days before Christmas, the murders in Voćin, Bruška, and the hamlet of Marinovići were carried out. By the spring of 1992 members of the special operations component of the DB also had murdered several people at Grabovac.

Milošević was president of Serbia when these crimes against humanity and many others were carried out. Our investigation later revealed that he directed or otherwise participated in a number of overt acts that helped to further the objectives of the joint criminal enterprise. From Belgrade, Milošević pulled the strings of the political leaders in the SAO Krajina, the SAO SBWS, the SAO Western Slavonia, and the Republic of Serbian Krajina (RSK). Even as president of Serbia, he was able to take effective control of the JNA. He directed the creation of Serb armed forces outside the federal government, and he sent them to Croatia to participate in the forcible removal of Croats and other non-Serb minorities. Milošević financed the special operations unit of the DB. He provided financial, matériel, and logistical support for regular and irregular forces that committed war crimes. And to ensure that Serbian television networks broadcast what he needed to further his objectives, he controlled the Serbian state-run media. Milošević allowed nothing to stand in the way of his rise to the top or his omnipotence once he got there. Not even his good friend and mentor Stambolić was safe.

On August 25, 2000, precisely between my involvement in Tuta's arrest for war crimes committed in Bosnia and in the interrogation of Andabak in Croatia, Stambolić went missing, with no clues left behind. It was a political assassination, we now know. Stambolić's remains were later recovered from a lime pit in Fruška Gora, a mountainous region of northern Serbia. The ruthless Milošević had ordered the hit.

Milošević also used his influence with other state organs to carry out his plan. The constitution of the SFRY contained provisions for a collective Presidency. Members of the Presidency rotated service as the actual president of the Presidency, a role that functioned much like a chairman. During Tito's reign, choosing the top man was simple: the former Partisan leader was president of the republic. In 1991, Milošević began the process of exercising influence and control over certain members of the Presidency who, as participants in the conspiracy, would contribute to the destruction of Yugoslavia. His orders were not to be countermanded by anyone, regardless of their official position of power—and that included the federal Presidency.

MEMBERS OF THE PRESIDENCY OF THE SFRY

Borisav Jović was born on October 19, 1928, in the village of Nikšić, near Batočina, Serbia. He was at various times a member, vice president, and president of the SFRY Presidency from May 15, 1989, until April 1992. He also was president of the SPS from May 1991 to October 1992, and he held other key positions in the SPS until November 1995.

Jović took over leadership of the Presidency in 1990. When it came time for him to vote or make other official decisions, he was known to excuse himself from the meeting so he could contact Milošević for instructions. During one session of the Presidency, a motion was made to declare a state of emergency that would have allowed the JNA to operate independently—that is, without direction from members of the collective Presidency or from the president of the Presidency, who served as the supreme commander of the JNA. The measure was not approved, so members of the Presidency who were aligned with the Serbs resigned and formed the Rump Presidency, which consisted of the four Serb-aligned members of the Presidency.

Once the measure failed, Milošević appeared on television and announced that Yugoslavia had ceased to function as it had in the past. He then directed the creation of his own Serbian armed forces and refused to recognize the legitimacy of the collective Presidency.

At one point, Jović took over for the minister of defense and began directing the JNA himself. In many respects, his actions represented a bloodless coup d'état against the Yugoslav state.

But before long, the machinations of the politicians would turn to treachery as blood poured into the streets, the rivers, and the hinterlands of Yugoslavia.

Branko Kostić was born in 1939 in Rvaši, Montenegro. He served as vice president and then as acting president of the SFRY Presidency from December 1991 to June 1992. Kostić represented Montenegro, and in his role as presiding officer, he is alleged to have rendered illegal decisions, including some that affected the JNA. He and Borisav Jović served as collective commander in chief of the JNA. They were able to do this as members of the Rump Presidency. This position gave them effective control over the JNA and other Serb forces that committed crimes against humanity throughout Croatia. All this was done on Milošević's orders.

After meeting with the minister of the interior during a mission in Montenegro in March 2002, I went to Kostić's home in the rolling hills outside Podgorica. It was a sunny, warm day. Kostić's front door was partially open, and I could hear voices inside. I knocked on the door and announced my presence. The voices went silent, and no one came to the door. Eventually I left my business card with a handwritten note telling Kostić to call me. I never received a reply. Within a few days, however, my name showed up in a Montenegrin newspaper story claiming I had made contact with Kostić in an attempt to enter into a secret deal with him. Only history will tell whether he made the right decision by not contacting me.

POLITICAL PARTY LEADERS

Vojislav Šešelj was born on October 11, 1954, in Sarajevo. He holds bachelor's and master's degrees, as well as a doctorate in law, from the University of Sarajevo. A former Communist, in 1984 he was convicted of counterrevolutionary activities and sentenced to eight years' imprisonment. His sentence was commuted, however, and in 1989—on the anniversary of the "Battle of Kosovo"—he was appointed a *Vojvoda*, or Četnik duke.

In 1990 Šešelj became the leader of the Serbian Freedom Movement. In the same year he founded the Serbian National Renewal Party, which was later renamed the Serbian Četnik Movement (SČP). The SFRY soon declared the SČP illegal, though, and Šešelj subsequently was appointed president of the new SRS.

In June 1991 Šešelj was elected a member of the Assembly of the Republic of Serbia. His political platform called for the unity of Serbia and war against Croats, Muslims, and Albanians throughout the territory of Yugoslavia. He used the historic Karlobag-Ogulin-Karlovac-Virovitica Croatian line as the western border of a new Greater Serbia.

To accomplish the objectives of the joint criminal enterprise, the ardent Šešelj is said to have engaged in a number of illegal activities. These included recruiting, financing, and forming special volunteer units that were used to commit war crimes throughout Croatia; instigating the perpetration of criminal activities by way of inflammatory hate speeches in the media; calling for the expulsion of Croat civilians in areas of Serbia; and planning the takeover of a number of towns and villages in Croatia.

In November 1991 Šešelj is alleged to have been at Vukovar. During one of his speeches there, he reportedly exclaimed, "This entire area will soon be cleared of Ustaša!" Only days later 264 patients and other occupants of Vukovar Hospital were seized and transported to a pig farm at Ovčara, where they were executed and buried in a mass grave.

SENIOR OFFICERS OF THE JNA

Gen. Veljko Kadijević was born on November 21, 1925, in Glavina Donja, Croatia, the son of a Serb father and a Croat mother. He became the federal secretary for national defense on May 15, 1988, and held that position until January 6, 1992. In this capacity he commanded the JNA, the TO, and the volunteer units acting in coordination with and under the supervision of the JNA.

Officially, Kadijević was a subordinate of Stjepan Mesić, a Croat, who was president of the Presidency at the time. Under the constitution of the

SFRY, Mesić was also the supreme commander of the JNA. Nevertheless, Kadijević refused to meet with Mesić.

Having been put on notice about the war crimes in Croatia and Milošević's illegal plan, Kadijević also refused to follow Mesić's orders. That is not surprising. After all, Kadijević publicly referred to the Croats as fascists. He has since said that he was interested in protecting the Serbs in Croatia from neo-Nazis, but as a member of the SFRY, he made no mention of protecting Croats and other non-Serbs from violence. In fact, the JNA was directly involved in many of the deplorable deeds committed throughout the region.

Col. Gen. Blagoje Adžić was born on September 2, 1932, in the village of Pridvorica, Bosnia, in what is now the Republika Srpska near the Montenegrin border. He served as chief of staff of the JNA from October 1989 until May 8, 1992, and as acting federal secretary for national defense from January 1992 until May 8, 1992. Together with others, he commanded, directed, or otherwise exercised effective control over the JNA and the TO units and volunteer units acting in coordination with and under the supervision of the JNA.

Maj. Gen. Aleksandar Vasiljević was born in 1938 and began his career in the UB in 1961. In 1982 Vasiljević became the head of the UB detachment at Sarajevo. From 1986 to 1988 he served as chief of counterintelligence for the Federal Secretariat for People's Defense (SSNO). In 1990 he became deputy head of the UB, and on June 16, 1991, he was appointed the overall commander of the UB. He held that position until May 8, 1992, when he was prematurely pensioned off. Two months later he was arrested by the state as the result of an unauthorized interview he had given to a journalist, but in the end he was acquitted of all charges.

Vasiljević is noted for interrogating Janez Janša, who was arrested for his dissident writings against the JNA in 1988. Janša later became the Slovenian minister of defense, a position he held during Slovenia's Ten-Day War of Independence, and ultimately prime minister of Slovenia.

As a war crimes investigator, I was most focused on Vasiljević's role in the UB and KOG during the Croatian War of Independence. During this time KOG participated in activities designed to stir up hate, fear, and violence, which furthered the overall objectives of the joint criminal enterprise. KOG did far more than disseminate misinformation. Members undertook clandestine missions that produced widespread fear and panic, which spread rapidly with the support of the propaganda machine. KOG operatives engaged in a number of black-flag operations, including bombings, murders, and other violent crimes. The UB also directed and supported the local Croatian-Serb political leaders and the local Serb police and military forces, including the TO staff and volunteers from Serbia.

Gen. Tomislav Simović acted in response to Milošević's statement that he no longer intended to recognize the collective Presidency. Milošević appointed Simović to create an entirely new armed force in Serbia. It still isn't widely known that Serbia established its own Ministry of Defense with the aim of replacing the JNA. The JNA was never actually supplanted, largely because of Milošević's ability to ultimately bring the federal forces under his control.

Simović nevertheless functioned as minister of defense for the Republic of Serbia, and from July 31, 1991, until at least December 19, 1991, the Serbian Ministry of Defense formed, deployed, and provided substantial assistance or support to Serb volunteer units and other Serb forces involved in the perpetration of crimes throughout Croatia.

SENIOR OFFICERS OF THE DB

Jovica Stanišić was born on July 30, 1950, in Rakovo, in the autonomous province of Vojvodina in the Republic of Serbia. In 1975 he began his career in the DB, part of the MUP of the Republic of Serbia. He rose through the ranks to become the deputy head of the DB in 1991, served as the de facto head of the agency, and was formally appointed as chief of the DB on December 31, 1991. He held this position until October 1998.

By May 1991 illegal secret police units had been formed under the auspices of the DB. These units committed crimes throughout Croatia; at various times they were referred to as the Red Berets, the JATD, and the JSO. Acting alone or in conjunction with other Serb forces, members of these special operations units engaged in a pattern of persecution that included murder, forcible transfer, and deportation. Stanišić, in his capacity as chief of the service, is alleged to have directed the regiment and provided arms, training, and logistical support to these men, who committed war crimes throughout Croatia.

Franko "Frenki" Simatović was born on April 1, 1950, in Belgrade, Serbia. He began working for the DB in 1978 and held numerous roles until 2001.

He initially worked on counterintelligence operations. Sometime later he was transferred to the new Intelligence Administration, or Second Administration, where he commanded the DB's special operations component.

In April 1991 Simatović helped to establish a training center at Golubić, near Knin, for the special operations units. Additional training centers were established and financed by the DB. Volunteers, conscripts, and many others who were involved in the war crimes committed in Croatia were also trained there.

PRESIDENTS OF REPUBLICS (INCLUDING THOSE THAT WERE SELF-PROCLAIMED)

Milan Babić was a Croatian-Serb born on February 26, 1956, in Kukar, which lies within the municipality of Sinj, Croatia. A dentist by profession, he became a member of the League of Communists of Croatia, and later a prominent figure in the Serbian Democratic Party (SDS). In 1992 he assumed the role of SDS president, a position he held until 1995.

On April 30, 1991, Babić was elected president of the Executive Council of the SAO Krajina, which was renamed the RSK on December 19, 1991. The RSK's first president, Babić held that position until February 15, 1992. In April 1994 he became the minister of foreign affairs for the RSK, and in July 1995 he was elected prime minister. He held that position for only one month; then he and other RSK officials fled after Operation Storm, a Croatian offensive to regain territory.

While he held these powerful government posts, Babić formulated policies to advance the objectives of the joint criminal enterprise. He was involved in creating and funding the local TO. Accordingly, he was the lawful commander of the TO forces, and he was the one who appointed Milan Martić as deputy TO commander. Babić later appointed Martić to a number of other political positions. In his official roles, Babić supervised the police and military forces, including Martić's Police.

He also provided financial, logistical, and political support to Martić's Police, the TO, the JNA, and other Serb forces that were involved in the joint criminal enterprise to remove Croats from the region. Babić made ethnically inflammatory speeches that created or contributed to the Croatian-Serbs' fear of their Croat neighbors. He requested assistance from the JNA to further the criminal enterprise's objectives and provided aid for their unlawful activities. He also helped to acquire arms for Croatian-Serbs to further the objectives of the joint criminal enterprise.

Milan Martić was a Croatian-Serb born on November 18, 1954, near Knin. A graduate of Croatia's police academy, he worked his way up the ranks to senior inspector. Martić established, commanded, directed, and otherwise exercised effective control over members of his police force, Martić's Police. He later became secretary of the Secretariat of Internal Affairs of the SAO Krajina, a post he held from January 4, 1991, to May 29, 1991; he was minister of defense of the SAO Krajina from May 29, 1991, until June 27, 1991, and minister of internal affairs for the SAO Krajina from June 27, 1991, until January 1994. On January 25, 1994, he was elected president of the RSK.

Martić's Police were responsible for some of the most outrageous acts of inhumanity committed throughout Croatia, and Martić was as brutal as his men. Even before Team Four began investigating crimes committed in Croatia by Serb forces, Martić had given the order to fire rockets armed with cluster bombs on Zagreb's city center. As one might expect, innocent civilians were killed and injured in the attack.

Goran Hadžić, a Croatian-Serb, was born on September 7, 1958, in Vinkovci, Croatia. He worked as a warehouseman at a plant in the municipality of Vukovar. A member of the League of Communists since his youth, he later joined the SDS and became chairman of the local Vukovar party in June 1990. Hadžić held a number of other elected and appointed positions, and in June 1991 he was appointed president of the self-proclaimed government of the SAO SBWS. On February 26, 1992, he was elected president of the RSK, a position he held until December 1993.

In these high-level positions, Hadžić formulated policies that facilitated the joint criminal enterprise. He was instrumental in creating the governmental bodies that oversaw the police and other Serb forces that were responsible for committing violent illegal acts to further the enterprise. He is alleged to have personally given orders to members of the SNB who committed a number of war crimes, whether as the sole perpetrator group or in conjunction with Arkan's Tigers. Hadžić is also alleged to have been involved in creating, financing, and directing the TO in SBWS, the Serbian Volunteer Guard, and the SČP.

Throughout the territory for which he was responsible, crimes were widespread and systematic. These included the destruction of Croatian communities; forced deportations of thousands of citizens; murder, torture, and extermination; and the unlawful confinement of civilians. Areas that were affected by these crimes include Ćelije, Daljski Atar, Dalj, Dalj Planina, Sarvaš, Ernestinovo, Laslovo, Erdut, Aljmaš, Lovas, Šarengrad, Tovarnik, and Bapska. And there was Vukovar, where violent criminals devoid of even the slightest hint of humanity perpetrated the single largest massacre in Croatia during the war.

Momir Bulatović was born on September 21, 1956, in Belgrade, Serbia. He served as president of the Republic of Montenegro from 1990 to 1998, and during this time he advocated for a close alliance with Serbia and alignment with Milošević's policies.

The Dubrovnik region of Croatia had historical ties to Montenegro, and President Bulatović mobilized and provided substantial assistance to Montenegrin troops, including TO, police, and volunteer units, that were deployed to the Republic of Croatia. There they formed part of the JNA and participated in criminal activities in and around Dubrovnik.

LEADERS OF PARAMILITARY GROUPS

Radovan Stojičić, also known as "Badža" (Brutus), was born in 1951. A general officer in the MUP of Serbia, he had previously commanded a special police unit in Kosovo. On Milošević's orders, he was deployed to Croatia in the summer of 1991 and established the Serb TO units of the SBWS, which fell under the command of Goran Hadžić.

Stojičić and members of the TO were responsible for perpetrating a number of war crimes and crimes against humanity in Croatia. These atrocities include the execution of thirty-nine detainees who were removed from their cells in the police building at Dalj. Their bodies were either buried in a mass grave or dumped into the Danube. This was just one of the horrific crimes committed under Stojičić's command. Many others were perpetrated in cooperation with Arkan's Tigers and with Arkan himself.

Željko "Arkan" Ražnatović was born on April 17, 1952, in Slovenia. As a young man, he left Yugoslavia to find his own version of capitalism. Violent crime became his trade. We know he committed armed robberies and murders throughout Western Europe. He worked as a government assassin, targeting enemies of the state. In turn, the Yugoslav Security Service was often instrumental in getting him out of trouble with the police. He operated a mobbed-up casino, he was involved in hijackings, and he smuggled and sold drugs, weapons, and other contraband on the black market. These were all useful skills for the soon-to-be warlord.

In 1990 Arkan established and commanded the Serbian Volunteer Guard, an elite volunteer unit commonly known as Arkanovci, or Arkan's Tigers, which at different times operated under the command of the TO of the SAO SBWS or the DB. These bloodthirsty soldiers followed Arkan's orders with blind obedience. Their exploits caused the masses to tremble in fear for their lives.

Arkan also maintained a significant military base in Erdut. It served as the training center for other TO units, and from here members of his unit took part in bloodcurdling crimes.

Unlike those who strictly ordered violent attacks, Arkan took pleasure in personally participating in murders and other despicable crimes, including the executions of the thirty-nine detainees removed from the Dalj police station. Arkan was also responsible for the abductions and slaughter of ethnic Hungarians and Croat civilians in Erdut, Dalj Planina, and Erdut Planina. The bodies of his victims either were buried in gruesome mass graves or were thrown into abandoned wells.

By many accounts, Arkan knew too much about Milošević's activities—and Milošević was acutely aware of the danger inherent in this situation. Some even say that Milošević believed Arkan had been approached by war crimes investigators and asked to serve as a secret witness against him. The day would come when Milošević's concerns about Arkan would be allayed once and for all. A deadly hammer would fall.

In the meantime, our job was to investigate the men alleged to have been members of the joint criminal enterprise headed by Milošević. To obtain the evidence needed to prosecute them, war crimes investigators had to venture deep into the shadows of the Balkans and other dark corners of Europe.

9

Inside the Shadows

IN THE DARK CORNERS OF THE SERBIAN CITY OF NOVI SAD, AND DEEP inside the shadows of Milošević's inner circle, was the MP Royal. A mob-owned casino run out of the Hotel Putnik, it looked from the outside like nothing more than a large, Cold War–era building in a dodgy area of a city along the Danube. Inside, however, the MP Royal was a mix of glamorous nightlife, hookers, and gangsters. By no means a place for the fainthearted, the casino was owned by a professional assassin who worked for both the Yugoslav federal state security service (SDB) and the DB. The place also was known as the Royal Casino. It provided a seductive fast life for the underworld, as well as a pipeline to Interpol's Red Notices, international requests for arrest and extradition.

Operating under the cover of a "fashion agency," high-priced call girls at the MP Royal turned tricks for politicians. The secret police used prostitutes, narcotics, and other vices to gain control over whomever they wanted.

Although strong words often pierced the thick smoke inside the casino, their muffled echoes were hard to discern. One by one, the men who spoke softly in this shadowy place would change the face of Yugoslavia, victim by victim.

As a hit man, the casino owner killed a human rights activist in Brussels at the behest of the DB. In fact, this was the first assassination ordered by the Serbian secret police that was not sanctioned officially by the federal security service. At the top of the casino owner's secret portfolio were the political liquidations of Albanians throughout Europe.

The MP Royal was a key rendezvous point for the Bačka Palanka Lobby. On the surface, the lobby was an unlikely group of men—members of the police, the secret police, the propaganda machine of the political apparatus, and organized crime. Operationally, members of this circle of conspirators and professional killers worked in concert with one another to implement the calamitous orders of Slobodan Milošević. In doing so, they wove a deadly web of connections between politicians and the underworld.

Within this highly selective circle was Jovica Stanišić, chief of the secret police and, by many now-published accounts, an asset for the U.S. CIA. The lobby also included his deputy, Franko "Frenki" Simatović, who headed the merciless special operations component of the DB. Mihalj Kertes, the head of the Federal Customs Administration, allegedly figured prominently in the inner circle. So did Goran Hadžić, who somehow went from being a simple warehouse manager to president of the SAO SBWS and later the RSK.

These were key conspirators who were responsible for extortion rackets, kidnappings, political assassinations, war crimes, and the overall bloody catastrophe in Yugoslavia. They were members of an ongoing criminal enterprise that reached far beyond the rugged scenery and wild frontiers of the Balkans.

The MP Royal's guest list also included none other than the man who would come to be called the "Butcher of the Balkans"—Slobodan Milošević himself.

A DB operative we code-named "Blackjack" was there too. His job was to keep an eye on the money and to control the sticky-fingered cashiers so they wouldn't steal from the casino. But unbeknown to the conspirators, including Milošević, Blackjack would one day risk death by providing us with the information only a well-placed insider would have.

Vice, organized crime, and spies: This was my world. It reminded me of my undercover days working shot houses, topless bars, and organized gambling enterprises on the gritty streets of South Richmond, Virginia, where some of the operations had links to the Bruno/Scarfo mob in the South Philadelphia/Newark area and to the Lucchese crime family in New York City. For dealing with espionage, secret intelligence, and treason, I drew on my past experiences working national security and counterintelligence investigations for the U.S. government. But what went on at the

MP Royal was much darker and had far greater impact on the region and throughout the world.

I will never forget receiving a message on my mobile phone telling me to move to a special room in our headquarters at The Hague to speak with one of my investigators. He was on a mission, working the dangerous streets of Belgrade and Novi Sad in a well-planned effort to track down mobbed-up gangsters and war criminals and turn them into inside sources. After "going secure" on an encrypted communications system, the experienced investigator gave me the news: He had scored, big time.

"Boss, we have Blackjack."

Roger that.

Blackjack's first introductions to the shadowy world of espionage were through the DB and with men who ran cloak-and-dagger departments that covered both internal and external extremism for the Republic of Serbia. They penetrated all walks of life.

Blackjack met with his handlers secretly at the MP Royal and at an exclusive club known as Legat, situated just behind the Libyan embassy. They even met at the DB office in Novi Sad.

Blackjack learned technical methods—bugging and countermeasures. He learned how to elicit critical information. And we learned from him.

Through Blackjack, we were able to demonstrate that Milošević referred to the Serb-occupied territories of Croatia as "our territory," and members of the lobby planned to do everything they could to cleanse the area of "Ustaše." The territory was to be "conjoined with the Republic of Serbia." And it was to be a fait accompli prior to the forthcoming London Conference, during which the UN and the heads of many states would meet in an attempt to find a solution to the ongoing violence in Yugoslavia.

The head of the local DB told Blackjack that members of the lobby wanted as many Croats as possible out of the area of Vojvodina, which bordered Croatia; these people would be replaced with hard-line Serbs. Blackjack also learned about how Serb forces eventually would carry out this part of the criminal enterprise. Secret agents were instructed to "intimidate the richest and well-to-do" but not to employ "violence and liquidations" against Croats and other minorities in the Serb province; violence could cause problems with the international community. Exterminations in Croatia proper, in contrast, could always be shifted away from Serb forces in one way or another, including anarchy. In fact, this happened many times throughout the region at the hands of fifth columnists that could make the murders appear to have been perpetrated by Croats on Croats, or simply general lawlessness in certain areas.

Funds to carry out the extreme operations were not a problem. "Not to worry, there always has to be money for the needs of the Service [DB] and for such things," Milošević told his underlings.

Team Four began putting more pieces of the conspiracy together. According to Blackjack, Serb forces and other members of the criminal enterprise employed multiple strategies and tactical operations. In a move reminiscent of La Cosa Nostra's activities in Harlem, New York, during the 1960s, Stanišić was recruiting dangerous street thugs to import heroin into Croatia. His aim was to get as many young Croats as possible hooked on narcotics, so they would become demoralized. In fact, Stanišić's thugs practically gave the heroin away, and in great quantities at that.

Members of the criminal enterprise viewed the heroin operation as a necessary subversive activity. But, not surprisingly, sometimes their drug dealers were caught in the crossfire. One such DB-hired gangster who distributed smack on the streets of Zagreb was killed in a gunfight involving Serb and Albanian gangsters who also were working the dangerous streets of Croatia's capital.

There were mixed messages about this "special warfare." On one hand, according to Blackjack, the DB wanted to keep their heroin distribution activities, especially in Zagreb, secret. In fact, when Stanišić heard that one of the mobsters had been talking about the heroin operation, he said, "Fuck him, I hope he is not saying that." But that was more than likely just a cautionary comment because in another breath he attempted to justify what they were doing when he said, "Well, the Siptars [Albanians] in Belgrade are doing the same to us."

More important to war crimes investigators was evidence of connections between key players in the joint criminal enterprise. We learned that Hadžić was in direct contact with Simatović, and Simatović was connected to professional killers. Arkan met often with Kertes, and Stanišić was directly linked with Milošević himself.

We also identified links to the unrest in Montenegro, where Momir Bulatović was president. Bulatović had sent his territorial defense troops to fight alongside the JNA in the Dubrovnik region of Croatia, where innocent civilians were killed, homes were looted, and entire villages were destroyed.

Evidence pointing to the criminal intent to remove Croats and other non-Serb minorities from their homes and villages for the purpose of forming a Greater Serbia was also found through Milan Panić, the federal minister for internal affairs. Milošević believed that Panić would be a puppet who would do whatever he was told. But on the contrary, Panić actually fired Kertes as his deputy over the ethnic cleansing that was taking place in Croatia. Panić himself was subsequently terminated after the London Conference, and from then on, Milošević and his men considered Panić a traitor to their cause.

Through the enigmatic words spoken within the Royal Casino, investigators also corroborated connections between several of the perpetrator groups responsible for the murders and other crimes in Croatia. I was not at all surprised to hear that in a barracks near Belgrade, Šešelj's Men received arms and training from the "regime" before committing a series of murders and other crimes against humanity in Western Slavonia. This was a link to the ruthless killers who, operating in concert with members of the White Eagles, brutally murdered many inhabitants of Voćin who had done nothing more than attempt to protect their homes and their families. We also heard whispers about the paramilitary organization known as Dušan Silni, whose members were the sadistic torturers and killers responsible for the incomprehensible suffering at the Lovas minefield.

We cultivated more links and evidence in relation to Arkan, who was provided arms directly by Simatović. Arkan and his Tigers were responsible for the murders of at least eleven civilian detainees who were buried in a mass grave in Ćelija, twenty-eight more civilian prisoners who were executed and dumped into the Danube River, and other innocent Hungarian minorities who simply sought to learn the fate of their loved ones. Some victims were executed and thrown into a well, where their remains were discovered years later by war crimes investigators. And that was just the beginning of Arkan's reign of terror in Croatia and Bosnia.

The unfaltering words of members of the Bačka Palanka Lobby made it clear that these crimes were interrelated.

"The boss told me today to step up the actions in Slavonia, Baranja, and Western Srem, because I heard that the Croats would try to enter the Krajina by force," Stanišić told Simatović, according to Blackjack.

"Jovica, don't worry, everything is under control," Simatović assured his boss.

What immediately grabbed my attention was the fact that Milošević joined the group at a meeting in March 1993. This is when Milošević asked Stanišić about the situation in SAO SBWS, and Stanišić told Milošević that the area had been cleansed of Croats and the security situation was stable. Blackjack gave us the words directly from Milošević's mouth: "*Dobro*. So we have completed the main part of the job. Carry on like that but in a subtle way." Milošević went on to say, with what seemed to be a certain degree of pleasure, "Well, I'm really looking forward to how the Croats would ask for the Krajina with the majority of the population now Serbs."

He said to Kertes, "Bracika, you and Frenki just continue in this manner. You've done well so far. And as far as the material equipment is concerned, just ask Jovica for everything you need." Milošević then asked Kertes bluntly, "Is Arkan under control?"

"Yes, he is."

"*Dobro, dobro*. Don't let him gain control over you. We need people like this now, but no one should think that they are more powerful than the state."

Milošević would make sure that never happened.

There were other shadows to pierce. Blackjack provided details about the formation of the Red Berets, a handpicked special operations unit given unprecedented power and trust. Although a number of elite volunteer units and paramilitary bands of soldiers were operating in the region, the DB needed a unit under its own control. Creating one fell to Simatović. Like the KB in Bosnia, the secret Red Berets regiment was composed primarily of people who had been released from prison or who were seeking to avoid their prison terms through this special service. With Simatović in charge, the lethal special operations troopers began their bloody campaign in Croatia and later directed their killing rampage to Bosnia.

Indeed, crimes against Croats and Bosnian-Muslims were "heralded as some form of prestige," according to Blackjack, and many members of the Red Berets who frequented the MP Royal bragged about their crimes. One Red Beret discussed the massacre of Croatian policemen and the murders of nearly two dozen Croats at Borovo Selo; their bodies were thrown into the Danube.

The Red Berets were annihilative. Simatović acknowledged that when he responded to security concerns about the utter viciousness of a doped-up Red Beret member who had been running his mouth wildly: "Don't worry, I'll handle that," Simatović said. "But you need to understand that they're young fellows, and without them we wouldn't be able to achieve anything."

One of the components of the investigative plan was to dig deeper into the Red Berets. Investigators on Team Four and our colleagues on Team Five were able to penetrate deep into the criminal enterprise, cultivate witnesses, and procure evidence describing the actual creation of this deadly unit whose members terrorized, tortured, and murdered innocent civilians throughout Yugoslavia.

One key figure in the development of the Red Berets was Dragan Vasiljković, a.k.a. Daniel Sneddon, who operated under the nom de guerre "Captain Dragan." Born in Serbia and raised in Australia, Captain Dragan spent several years in the Australian military, where he acquired skills that he one day would use on the streets and in the hinterlands of Yugoslavia.

In 1990 Captain Dragan flew to Belgrade from the United States in a small, single-engine aircraft. He didn't intend on staying in Yugoslavia; his destination was actually Africa. But while in Serbia, Captain Dragan learned about the fighting going on between the Croats and the Croatian-Serbs, and he became concerned that ethnic Serbs would be victimized as they had been in World War II. He also believed the Croatian-Serbs were not prepared to defend themselves properly, so he decided to stay in the region and stand up for his fellow Serbs. This is Simatović's story anyway.

Simatović was one of the first men Captain Dragan met in Yugoslavia, and they have been close friends ever since. In April 1991 they traveled together to the Krajina, accompanied by a former British special forces officer. Captain Dragan next was taken to a training camp near Knin. The camp was populated with between eighty and a hundred men who had been armed with weapons ranging from hunting rifles to Kalashnikovs. Milan Martić was there too. He introduced Captain Dragan to the recruits as the instructor and told them to obey him—establishing another connection in the joint criminal enterprise.

This was when the Red Berets, the highly trained and violent special operations component of the DB, came into existence, and war crimes investigators learned that Milošević was involved in the creation and deployment of this new band of killers. We conducted extensive interrogations of Milan Babić at a Belgrade safe house, and the former president of the RSK made the connection. He told us he had informed Milošević that the Krajina government needed professional assistance with training police units. Babić admitted that he had written to Milošević in April 1991, asking that the DB supply people and technical support for that specific purpose. Martić, Simatović, and Captain Dragan all were involved in establishing the Red Beret training camp in response to Babić's request.

The lead investigator I assigned to Babić was the right man to drill into the inner workings of the DB. When I arrived at the safe house, I found that they had built a solid rapport. At first I exchanged glances with Babić. Then I looked deep into his eyes. Somehow I wanted to believe him when he said he had no idea the degree of terror that would fall upon his Croatian brothers and sisters as a result of his asking Milošević for help. But his logic on that point defied common sense.

From 1991 on, tortures, rapes, murders, and other forms of persecution and destruction were committed throughout the SAO Krajina and SAO SBWS. These vicious crimes were connected in multiple ways to the Red Berets and other special operations units of the DB that merged with or otherwise survived the unit originally stood up by Simatović under the orders of Stanišić and Milošević and trained by Captain Dragan.

These units included the JATD, an antiterrorism unit; the JSO, a special operations unit; and the Serbian Volunteer Guard (SDG), including Arkan's Tigers. Other Serb forces that were either trained by, subordinated to, or otherwise working together in concert with the special operations unit of the DB included the TO units of the various SAOs in Croatia and the members of the Serb National Security (SNB) force who operated in and around the SAO SBWS.

In April 1995 the Red Berets recruited a deadly operator. That man piqued our interest, and, consistent with our strategic and tactical investigations methods, war crimes investigators recruited him as an inside source. Code-named "K-2," he was able to provide us with firsthand knowledge of the secrecy that permeated the DB special operations unit. For example, we learned that instructors told Red Beret recruits that the unit dated back to Captain Dragan's work in Croatia in 1991. But they also were told never to disclose their work or otherwise acknowledge the unit's existence.

K-2, who was cultivated by Team Eleven, provided insight into his tradecraft, which included extermination and silent liquidations. He had learned how to wiretap when information was needed and how to break necks or kill with wire when silence was required. His secret portfolio of dirty tricks was plentiful. K-2 was able to provide evidence that placed Simatović in charge of the unit. He was also able to connect Captain Dragan, Martić, Simatović, and Arkan. And he had met, face-to-face, several notorious criminals who had been released from prison so that they could fight with the venomous Red Berets.

Another inside source, this one code-named "C-017," told investigators that he was assigned to a military base near Mostar that was shared by a number of special police and paramilitary units, including the Red Berets, Šešelj's Men, and the White Eagles. He said the base was under the operational command of the Red Berets, including some who were trained personally by Captain Dragan.

I was not at all surprised to learn that Serbian clandestine operatives had been keeping a special eye on Captain Dragan. After all, this was the world of double agents, and the Aussie was suspected of being an informant for the CIA. We know that his phone was tapped, and he was placed under around-the-clock surveillance. Unbeknownst even to the DB special operations soldiers fighting alongside Captain Dragan, an ultrasecret counterespionage unit of the DB known as the "American Group" or "AOS" was on the job.

We also learned that by the time the Red Berets became known as the JSO, a mobster-turned-special-operations-officer named Milorad "Legija" Ulemek, a.k.a. Milorad Luković, was commanding the unit. Before leaving the French Foreign Legion to join Arkan's Tigers after war broke out in Yugoslavia, Legija had fought in Libya, Lebanon, and French Guyana. He was well prepared to command—and to kill.

We had evidence of all this from a number of inside sources, as well as from survivors. We even had oral admissions and written statements given by some of our suspects. We also had gotten our hands on a videotape, recorded surreptitiously, that captured senior members of the joint criminal enterprise celebrating the many "combat" and "special warfare" victories of the Red Berets. The source of the videotape is sealed and protected under court order. I first viewed the tape at a secret location in Europe. It was, however, played openly in court, and it showed Slobodan Milošević himself inspecting the ranks. Stanišić was showing Milošević a map of the places where the Red Berets had fought, killed, and died. Simatović was bragging about the scope of the Red Berets' operations. And there was Captain Dragan, receiving a medal for his work launching the unit.

Years later, when he was shown the videotape, Captain Dragan was impressed with the work of the war crimes tribunal. "On this tape are absolutely all members of the Serb service. I believe that in the history of secret services, security services, this is a unique case, that you have all the members of a security service on one single tape," he said with a combination of utter disbelief and amazement. Captain Dragan had every reason to be astonished. War crimes investigators had gone to some of the darkest corners of the Earth to identify, locate, and cultivate evidence and witnesses of this nature.

I sat in my office in The Hague and opened the dossier on one of those witnesses whose official code name I won't reveal, lest it lead someone to his current whereabouts. The witness, whom I'll call Witness X, provided investigators with solid information on the conspiracy. His dossier provided a window into the underground world of espionage and sabotage. It contained photograph after photograph, plus information on wiretaps, blackmail, and extortion. Reading it, I learned about the clever methods used by Serb secret agents to exploit government officials by using prostitutes, narcotics, and bribes. And I read the innermost details of horrendous murders that were relevant to our investigation.

War crimes investigators had cultivated this witness to obtain just this sort of shrouded information, and he was in a good position to provide it. He had lived the mysterious and cunning life of a spy. Witness X said he was first approached by the KOS to work as one of its operatives. Other sources have informed us that he was most likely working with the Intelligence Administration of the General Staff of the JNA.

In any event, he was right there in the thick of operations from Sarajevo to London. On the lookout for internal subversives, Witness X had infiltrated student groups in Sarajevo in the late 1960s. He had trailed dissident Yugoslavs, undertaking foreign missions throughout the world. He had even spied on senior officials of the International Olympic Committee when the Winter Olympics were held in Sarajevo in 1984.

A charismatic and charming man who was following his father's chosen career path, Witness X spoke a number of languages fluently, including English and French. He had assignments all around the globe, but the intersection of his world and mine began with the Log Revolution of 1990. That singular event was portrayed as a spontaneous uprising by Croatian-Serbs, who put log barricades across roads in the Krajina to prevent Croatian forces from taking control of the area. In truth, there was nothing unplanned about it. The insurrection was all part of the larger scheme directed from Belgrade.

Witness X exposed the attack on the Croatian town of Cetingrad in October 1991. He had watched that night as explosions illuminated the dark sky and refugees began streaming across the Bosnian border. Civilians were killed; churches and homes were destroyed—all violations of the laws and customs of war.

Next, he told us about plans to assassinate prominent Croats in order to spread fear among the refugee population. In 1991 he was assigned to work with two JNA officers. Their targets were two brothers named Brajdić. The assassination was to take place on Christmas Eve, just before midnight Mass, at the King Restaurant in Velika Kladuša. The mission of the assassins was to approach the premises from three sides and kill everyone inside with bursts of fire from automatic weapons. But the massacre didn't happen. Witness X explained why:

> Four or five days prior to the attack, these two officers came to Velika Kladuša fully dressed in JNA uniform, and as I was sitting in one of the coffee bars with a number of prominent Muslims from the local area, they came to me. They were drunk and they were carrying on about me being a great Serb and everybody should respect me for it, and all this will be part of Serbia, and generally they made it very uncomfortable for me. So I refused to deal with them any further after that. I didn't take them to be serious at all.

I understood Witness X well. In my professional experience, spies and true operators are much more disciplined than that. This was the work of amateurs.

Witness X explained how so-called antiterrorist units in the JNA actually were created to perform *prljavi poslovi*, or "dirty jobs." About forty-five young men were members of one such special internal security unit of KOS. They had extensive criminal records, and they did what regular JNA officers refused to do. Their dirty jobs included intimidating people, creating disturbances, and killing Croats, Muslims, and even Serbs when necessary. Every JNA corps had one of these units.

Members of one of these antiterrorist units assassinated the mayor of Virginmost, for example. The victim was a Serb who believed in peaceful reconciliation with the Croats. Following the modus operandi typically employed by members of the criminal enterprise, the mayor's murder was staged as an attack by Croatian terrorists. In fact, it was a black-flag operation.

Witness X also told us that a member of another Serb dirty-job unit had admitted to him that he'd killed an elderly Croatian couple accused of using candlelight to send signals to Croat forces on the other side of the River Kupa. Eventually, he came to know that the elderly couple had been set up. They had harmed no one, and by no means were they sending signals to the enemy.

Another crime was staged to undermine peace efforts in Norway. A train was blown up, and several on board were killed. The Serbs blamed the Croats, but Witness X knew better. A subversive-tactics units must have been responsible. He said,

> Well, it more or less came to me; it was a simple deduction. The place where the antitank mine was placed, how far it is from possible penetration of the Croatian side, how possible for Croatian terrorists would be to get in, how quickly we have deployed our forces in the area to search the immediate area where the mine was planted. All those things didn't produce any result. Now, considering it was wintertime, we have come to considerable area, which had no footprints or anything in the snow, which would make it perfectly clear that nothing came from that side, so it had to be from within.

He also confirmed connections between KOS, local DB operatives, and Stanišić in Belgrade. The perpetrators had *crni fondovi,* or "black funds," from Serbia to pay for these operations and to purchase the necessary weapons and listening devices from the Ukrainians. Witness X detailed how he and other operatives acquired these funds from almost anywhere in the world:

It was rather a simple system and very workable. Within every embassy, no matter where it is—the Yugoslav Embassy, that is—there was always a little Yugoslav club adjacent to the embassy, which would have a security officer in there. You would go in there, introduce yourself, show the passport and then ask are there any messages for you. I remember, for example, the London one. There were a number of dead-letter boxes or "pigeonholes" with the letters of the alphabet. . . . If they had anything in there, they would give it to me. On the other hand, if I had to forward any information or a report, I would go there, place an envelope, seal it, and place it in this [hole], and somebody would obviously, you know, send it where it was supposed to go. My request for funds would go absolutely the same way. I would write down the request, explain why I need this amount of money, place in envelope, put in the pigeonhole, and maybe two days later come back and collect the money.

One operation that particularly struck me took place in 1994 and involved the exchange of a hundred Serb bodies for an equal number of Croatian dead. The problem was that the Serbs didn't have that many Croatian bodies at their disposal. Consequently, Witness X was sent on mission to find as many as he could. Time was running out.

Witness X first went to a deserted part of Vojnić, where Croatian prisoners dug up four bodies of their comrades. The bodies were badly decomposed. Even more worrying to him was the fact that their hands were fettered with wire, which provided evidence of death by execution rather than during the course of combat. Left with few alternatives, he removed the wire bindings and took the bodies anyway.

Ninety more bodies were found in a mass grave, but Witness X was still six short. Not a problem: Arkan's Tigers summarily killed five prisoners. But those bodies were too fresh. So to compensate and carry out the switch effectively, he had the bodies frozen in a refrigeration unit and then delivered to the other side by moonlight. The Croats never knew the difference.

Witness X furnished us with more direct links between Belgrade and Croatian-Serbs, establishing evidence of the relationships among members of the joint criminal enterprise and further demonstrating their motive and intent. For example, he divulged how on one occasion Stanišić traveled to Croatia to deliver a message from Milošević directly to Martić.

We also learned how Milošević controlled Hadžić. Although Hadžić held the title of president, he did exactly what Milošević told him to do. This was quite obvious during a meeting in Norway. Witness X was there, and so was the U.S. ambassador to Croatia, Peter Galbraith. At one point Galbraith entered the room where the Serb delegation was gathered and addressed Hadžić as "Mr. President." Witness X translated Galbraith's greeting. Hadžić, who was playing solitaire, showed his true cards. He responded, "Well, tell him I'm not a president, I'm a dispatcher." Everyone could see that Milošević was calling the shots.

Witness X also was detailed to obstruct UN peacekeeping efforts. With cunning ingenuity, he prevented international observers from visiting the places they wanted to see. Housekeepers and interpreters acted as spies at his behest. They took notes of what they overheard and stole any UN documents they could get their hands on. Once in Witness X's possession, the information was entered into raw intelligence reports and promptly transmitted to Belgrade for further analysis.

Witness X also touched UN workers and other international employees through bribes and other schemes. When those didn't work, he turned to liquor and women, which set the stage for extortion. Many Western governments would be shocked to learn just who was spied upon and blackmailed and what sort of vice they engaged in. That information won't be made public—at least not by me.

This was dirty work, and it was just what we needed. Witness X was the consummate purveyor of important information that war crimes investigators worked into relevant and admissible evidence. He provided us with firsthand information about ethnic cleansing and the links between Belgrade and the groups committing crimes on the ground. The evidence showed that the JNA and the DB were directing operations in Croatia.

Witness X connected Serb forces operating in Croatia to the JNA General Staff in Belgrade. He linked Krajina Interior Ministry officials and elite special operations units to the DB in Serbia. He described Milošević as "the boss" who directed the heads of all Yugoslav and Serb police, military, and paramilitary units that had committed atrocities throughout Croatia. And he demonstrated how Milošević called the shots, making political puppets of the men who were supposed to be running the Serb-controlled government in Croatia autonomously and negotiating peace agreements for the benefit of the Serbs and Croats in the region.

The connections were amazing. The links clearly showed the sophistication of the criminal enterprise. But for all its complexity and value, what hit me hardest, perhaps, was the direct evidence of the massacre at Vukovar Hospital that Witness X provided. Going right to the very core of our investigation, he pierced the veil of silence, right through the heart.

"Kill those shits!" With those exact words, Gen. Mile Mrkšić ordered Maj. Veselin Šljivančanin to murder unarmed patients in Vukovar Hospital, Witness X told us.

In December 1991 Witness X had been assigned to work with the JNA's Eighth Operational Group. It was headed by Mrkšić, the JNA officer who commanded and oversaw the near-total destruction of the eastern Croatian city of Vukovar. Mrkšić confided in Witness X that he had ordered Šljivančanin to seize and murder the unarmed Vukovar Hospital patients.

Years later, in May 2002, a strange feeling came over me as I supervised Mrkšić's arrest at Amsterdam's Schipol Airport. I pictured those helpless victims being executed and buried in a mass grave. I could almost hear the screams echo in the night as a bulldozer dripping with blood worked under the cover of darkness.

Many other shadowy figures emerged to help us with the investigation. They came not only from Eastern and Central Europe but from every corner of the earth. All were confidential witnesses. Some retain their protected identities to this day. Others eventually agreed to be identified publicly, understanding that they were—and still are—placing themselves at great risk. Only in those cases have I mentioned their names.

One such inside source was a member of the inner circle of Gen. Tomislav Simović, the minister of defense for Serbia. Code-named "Lady-O," war crimes investigators tracked her down through old-fashioned police work. After working out a number of issues with her attorney, I arranged to have her flown to The Hague for several days of intensive interviews.

We picked her up at Schipol Airport and took her to a temporary residence. At The Hague, Lady-O described to us being in the office of the president of Serbia and in the presence of "Comrade" Slobodan Milošević on multiple occasions. She was able to provide evidentiary links to Milošević's connections to and power over Kertes and Radmilo

Bogdanović, then the minister of internal affairs. She told us about the almost daily contact between Simović and Milošević. Many of these communications provided Milošević with information about the activities of Šešelj's forces. Others were reports from people such as JNA counterintelligence and security chief Maj. Gen. Aleksandar Vasiljević. There was no question that Milošević was never more than a heartbeat away from the action in the field.

Lady-O described how Milošević had ordered Simović to give full support, including military assistance, to Hadžić. On top of that, she helped to establish links among Milošević, Simović, and the Israeli State Security Service in connection with the acquisition of weapons to be used by Serb forces. Funds were acquired specifically for this purpose from the National Defense Fund and the Jugoskandik bank, all with Milošević's knowledge. Fortunately, our team's expert financial investigator was able to follow the money and corroborate much of the relevant information provided by this witness.

As with Witness X's information, everything Lady-O told us seemed to circle back to the atrocities at Vukovar. She told me that Milošević had ordered Simović to send air support to Arkan and other Serb forces engaged there. The next day Arkan showed up in Simović's office with a sniper rifle slung over his shoulder. On top of it sat a bloody "Ustaša" cap. Lady-O described the scene:

"What did you do with prisoners?" Simović asked Arkan.

"General, we have taken prisoner only two hens. As for the others, practically there were no prisoners."

"How is it possible that there are no prisoners in war?"

"General, we have no prisoners."

Arkan explained that during the encirclement of Vukovar he had killed a number of Ustaše. He had liquidated them. Lady-O was horrified, and Arkan said, "Madam, leave the room if you can't bear to listen to this."

"She's more—there's more of a man in her than you think," Simović quipped.

Based on my experiences with the witness, I'd say that Simović was right and then some. Lady-O is one tough woman, and I was not at all surprised to learn that she neither flinched nor budged from where she stood. Looking squarely at Arkan, she observed him making the gesture of the hand across the throat, indicating that the Croatian prisoners had been killed.

And Milošević was well aware of what had happened at Vukovar, Lady-O said.

Another inside witness was Mustafa Čandić, a former Yugoslav air force officer and assistant chief of the KOG. His protective measures were lifted in open session of the tribunal on December 6, 2002. I first met Čandić in Sarajevo, where I'd gone to assess his credibility and evidentiary value. In subsequent interviews he provided war crimes investigators with critical information about high-tech electronic measures used to fabricate conversations that induced people to "voluntarily" flee their homes. Čandić also corroborated Witness X's information about Serbs committing crimes in a way that made them appear to have been perpetrated by Croats.

Operation Labrador is a good example. At the time, Labrador was the secret code name for a "false flag" terrorist operation undertaken by KOG counterintelligence agents targeting Jewish cemeteries and synagogues in Croatia. The aim was to depict Croats as pro-fascist terrorists. Collaborators armed with weapons and explosives were in place in Zagreb to carry out the missions. But their presence was detected before they fully completed their seditious tasks, and the secret agents escaped to Belgrade.

Operation Labrador was followed by Operation Opera and then Proboj-1 and Proboj-2. These involved more black-flag missions that ran the gamut from sabotage to assassination. They were designed to raise fears among honest, law-abiding Serbs and make them believe that Croatian terrorists were murdering their people. Čandić's words kept me on the edge of my seat: "On several occasions . . . films with mutilated bodies were brought to the counterintelligence group to show us the footage that had been made and to show us what the Croats were doing to the Serbs in that part of Eastern Slavonia. And they were really terrible, dreadful pictures, dreadful footage. And some of those videotapes . . . played on Television Belgrade. And I recognized these images and the footage taken . . . [as being from] the area of Eastern Slavonia."

In reality, these weren't the bodies of Serbs murdered by Croatian terrorists. "To me as an officer this didn't seem to be quite logical. It wasn't logical that the Croats should carry out this massacre and slaughter in a particular area and to leave the area that they had won over. . . . I think what happened was quite the reverse; that the victims were Croats, in fact, and they were depicted as being Serb victims," Čandić explained.

To get to the heart of this, I subsequently sat down in a small room in a Belgrade safe house with none other than the chief of the JNA Security Administration himself, General Vasiljević. How ironic. Years earlier I would have been arrested for being this close to such a high-ranking member of the Socialist Party. And now, as a U.S. federal agent working for the UN, I was interviewing the former chief of counterintelligence for the entire JNA. It was definitely an awkward position for Vasiljević, who was neither accustomed to such a role reversal nor to the much softer, forensically based interview techniques I employed.

At one point Vasiljević asked me, "Why are you asking these questions? There is nothing criminal about those activities."

I was diplomatic, but firm: "General, I realize you are an experienced counterintelligence agent and interrogator, but today I'll ask the questions."

He acknowledged me with an affirmative yet professional nod of the head, and we continued. I got what I was after.

Adding another dimension, Lt. Gen. Imra Agotić, a Croat, corroborated much of the information provided by Čandić, a Muslim operative, and Witness X, the Serb spy. This was particularly important in relation to the operations of the UB and KOG, and it all tied together with the information Vasiljević unwittingly had given me. Ironically, many of these men, including Vasiljević, had worked together in the counterintelligence world of the JNA during the relatively peaceful days of brotherhood and unity under the SFRY.

I first met General Agotić at President Mesić's office. At the time he was the president's national security adviser. He had been an air force colonel working with KOG when the war broke out in Yugoslavia. He was able to describe the true inner workings of the stealth unit, including the operational aspects of the First and Second Administrations or Detachments. He did this in spite of attempts by the former head of JNA counterintelligence to mitigate his role and culpability in deadly clandestine activities in the name of the Yugoslav state and its people.

I will never forget how General Agotić, an intelligent gentleman with a master's degree in international relations, described his decision to leave Serbia and return to Croatia during the war. He understood that he might easily be shot in the back as he walked out of his Belgrade office.

Finally, Milan Babić contributed another vital piece of the puzzle. We had recordings of numerous intercepted conversations between key members of the joint criminal enterprise, but we needed to authenticate them. I suggested playing the tapes for Babić. We would demonstrate their authenticity the old-fashioned way, by having someone testify that he recognized the voices.

I flew to Belgrade to meet the investigators. Babić did a superb job. Of the many people I'd interviewed who had been involved in the perpetration of war crimes—Croats, Serbs, and Muslims—I sensed Babić's remorse more than any other.

Working among these spies, secret agents, and conspirators was not easy, but their contributions were priceless. These shadowy figures, and so many more, were key components in putting together an international criminal investigation that ultimately would sustain brutal legal challenges. They were instrumental in helping war crimes investigators and prosecutors tie the joint criminal enterprise together, all the way to Milošević.

10

Indictment of a President

I T WAS A TENSE THIRTY-SIX-HOUR ARMED STANDOFF. SLOBODAN Milošević was threatening to kill himself. Shots had been fired, and it wouldn't have surprised anyone if he had followed through on the threat. Years before, and at different times, both his parents had committed suicide. Now Milošević was brandishing a firearm with members of his family and armed bodyguards by his side.

In a predawn raid by Serbian authorities on April 1, 2001, special police and military units swept down on him at his heavily armed Belgrade villa and took him into custody. It was precisely 4:59 a.m. Even members of the JSO, who through the years had murdered untold numbers at Milošević's behest, were part of the team that took the once-powerful president down.

I knew it was coming. By this time Milošević was no longer the president of the FRY. He had been replaced in 2000 by Vojislav Koštunica in what has been referred to as the October 5 Overthrow. With Milošević out and Koštunica in power, the U.S. government gave the Yugoslav government a deadline to arrest Milošević or face significant economic sanctions that would be devastating to the Serbs. Koštunica attempted to have legislation passed that would "allow" the extradition of war criminals to The Hague, but such efforts were repeatedly shot down in the Yugoslav courts. Koštunica, who holds a PhD in law, refused to defy the Serb and FRY justice systems.

Milošević was taken into custody on federal charges of official corruption and abuse of power, mostly involving the embezzlement of public funds equivalent to millions of U.S. dollars. Ironically, Milošević's first written statement in defense of the corruption charges claimed that he'd used the money not for personal gain but to supply arms and funds to Serb forces fighting in Croatia and Bosnia. War crimes investigators and prosecutors were quick to secure a copy of that statement from Serb authorities, because it provided corroborating evidence of Milošević's active participation in the activities that resulted in major war crimes being committed throughout the territory of the former Yugoslavia.

In the meantime, the tribunal's efforts to have Milošević transferred to The Hague were in full swing, openly and through covert operations. We were working on investigative, legal, diplomatic, and intelligence-led operations to take Milošević into our custody so he could be put on trial for war crimes, crimes against humanity, and genocide. At this point the international charges were for crimes alleged to have been committed in Kosovo. Indictments for crimes in Croatia and Bosnia were yet to come.

Along with two other senior war crimes investigators—Bernie O'Donnell, an Australian federal agent who was in charge of the Bosnia investigation, and Kevin Curtis, a British police officer who took the lead on the Kosovo investigation—I was on rotational call to bring Milošević in.

People everywhere watched the event live as it was broadcast on all the major television networks. On June 29, 2001, almost three months after the Serbs had taken him into custody, Milošević lifted off from Belgrade. He was in a helicopter—and in the custody of UN war crimes investigators. Curtis, the British police officer who led the Kosovo team, was in command.

It was a delicate operation that was pulled off not with the assistance of President Koštunica but, to the public's surprise, under the top-secret orders of Zoran Đinđić, then prime minister of the Republic of Serbia. Many legal scholars have spent time discussing whether the transfer was legal from a Yugoslav constitutional perspective, but in the real world of international law enforcement, what mattered to many was that we had him in our custody.

Milošević was quickly shuttled to the U.S. air base at Tuzla, Bosnia. There he was promptly transferred to the Royal Netherlands Air Force, which flew him and UN war crimes investigators to the same Dutch naval air base I had come to several times before to secure international war criminals.

This single event has been hailed as one of the most significant developments in international law. For the first time in history, a head of state had been indicted and transferred to the jurisdiction of an international criminal tribunal. The event had occurred neither overnight nor by happenstance.

Investigations Teams Four, Five, and Eleven (Croatia, Bosnia, and Kosovo, respectively) had been working day and night linking crimes committed by triggermen, rapists, and torturers to their superior officers. From there, war crimes investigators followed complex mazes of secondary crimes that led to generals, corrupt politicians, money launderers, and assassins who kept the worst of the "corrupt" in line on Milošević's orders. One way or another, Milošević worked hard to keep enemies and allies straight—dead or alive—to ensure his impunity. All of that came to an end.

One turn in the complex navigation led to another. For example, our intelligence indicated that certain military and intelligence communities had intercepted wire communications in their possession. We wanted to get our hands on those intercepts. To make it happen, I made contact with a key governmental figure in Eastern Europe who flew to The Hague to personally discuss the situation and my request. He was working directly for the prime minister of his country, but even he had difficulty obtaining what we were after. Nevertheless, all doors had been opened, and to the extent possible, whatever the investigations team needed was placed at our disposal.

The military was not the primary obstacle; it rarely is. Soldiers are trained to follow orders. But no matter what country you are dealing with, the intelligence community is another story altogether. Its members are smart, secretive, and deadly. And they don't like following orders.

Nevertheless, it was only a matter of weeks before Team Four investigators were listening to audio intercepts and reading transcripts containing inculpatory statements. These materials proved crucial to our investigations. On another occasion I went deep inside a Western embassy to an encrypted communications center that connected us by audio and video to synchronous and simultaneous transmissions with intelligence, military, and diplomatic centers around the world. When we needed critical satellite imagery to pinpoint the locations of naval ships or mass graves, or to gain intelligence to assist in tracking international war criminals, we had unprecedented access to the advanced space technology required.

Quite naturally, I can't provide the specifics of the information or of its origin.

I even had operatives fly to The Hague with photographs and other documents that a clandestine service had obtained. The agency was proud of what it had in its possession. As criminal investigators, we had better sources, and we already had most of what the agency thought might be useful. But we didn't tell that to them.

Even deeper behind the scenes, something had occurred months before that promoted this sense of urgency and propelled our high-speed investigative missions and operations. I had participated in a meeting with chief prosecutor Carla Del Ponte. She had asked some pointed questions surrounding the indictment of Slobodan Milošević, or the lack thereof, for crimes alleged to have been committed in Croatia. I quickly told Del Ponte that before I took command of Team Four, there had been no dedicated investigative effort toward this outcome. Nevertheless, I had a plan:

"Madam Prosecutor, if you give me until the first of October, I will personally hand you the indictment."

"And if you don't?"

"I will resign."

"Deal." She nodded her head affirmatively, with what, for her, might have been a slight smile.

Graham Blewitt, the deputy prosecutor, turned and whispered to me in his Australian accent, "That's one ballsy move, John."

I don't know if that's how I'd characterize it, but Team Four's delicate investigative activities indeed were being undertaken against this backdrop. We had the crime base investigations just about locked down, and the time had come for me to approach the team with the news: I was suspending all investigative operations and missions except those that related directly to the indictment of the number one target, Slobodan Milošević.

With the deadline from Del Ponte looming, I called the team together.

"Each of you is the best and the brightest, sent here from all over the world," I told them. "Your work so far has been nothing short of amazing, but we have reached a point here at the tribunal that perhaps you thought would never come. All of our investigative efforts are to be strictly focused on the indictment of Slobodan Milošević. Yes, this team is going to do it; you are going to do it. I ask that you trust me that we can do this together.

"By the way," I added, "it has to be done by October 1."

Every member of the team looked astonished. One by one, I went around the room and told them they were here to do the job. We would do it together.

I was in charge and accountable for the overall investigation, but as the team leader, I needed to ensure that we had a true team. Based upon their expertise, investigative background, and operational history, I assigned each of the investigators one or more of the coperpetrators. In fact, each team member was given ownership of the investigative components.

A political research officer was assigned to support one or more of the investigators; these assignments were also based on background and experience. To add to this, criminal intelligence analysts and military intelligence officers were assigned to support the investigators and their investigative efforts.

Previously, all the research, military, and crime analysts had been publishing work products they felt were useful to the investigation. Investigators had to search through databases to find the information and ferret out the applicability or relevance to the case. This was the normal course of business. But it made absolutely no difference to me how the other teams were operating or how this team had operated in the past. We were forging a new path forward on this investigation, and we needed the organizational courage to reexamine the evidence. In the words of Hungarian scientist Albert Szent-Gyorgyi, the individual team members needed "to see what everyone else has seen and to think what nobody else has thought." That is exactly what Team Four and our colleagues on Team Five would do.

The next step was to get the entire team's input on the investigative plan. Ownership means teamwork, and teamwork means ownership. With that in mind, we worked together every step of the way to identify what had been done, what needed to be done, who would do it, and how it would be accomplished.

Thus, this investigative team of some of the brightest and most experienced investigators set off to accomplish the impossible. Whether it was examining and synthesizing evidence in house so that it made sense in a logical way or digging up new forensic evidence or cultivating inside sources, they were working to make the indictment a reality. The analysts also were on top of their game, providing critically relevant information in a timely fashion.

Team members analyzed thousands of documents and undertook scores of investigative missions throughout Europe. I established interrogation teams that would approach key inside sources in some of the toughest areas of Eastern and Central Europe. We spoke to national security advisers and entered the offices of presidents of countries. Evidence was transported across Europe in diplomatic pouches, witnesses were protected, and investigative strategies were discussed at locations ranging from safe houses in some of the most dangerous corners of Europe to encrypted communications centers deep inside the secure walls of military installations, consulates, and embassies.

Most of the targets had been under investigation already. There were some new faces, however. I prepared—and the prosecutor signed—the paperwork authorizing Team Four to investigate them and for me to direct the investigation. The investigation of these individuals was undertaken primarily in relation to Milošević. In time, these individuals would be named in the Milošević indictment. For some, indictments of their own would follow. That's how the job is done.

To build a strong case, I had to focus on the single most important issue of all: proving the individual criminal responsibility of Milošević. All investigative efforts ultimately go toward proving beyond a reasonable doubt that the accused is guilty or otherwise individually criminally responsible for the crimes charged. Tying the investigation to the prosecution is not as simple as it may seem. Indeed, there is nothing simple about either component.

While the first proceeding before the Trial Chamber of the ICTY involved a relatively low-level perpetrator, the jurisprudence that eventually would come out of the case of *Prosecutor v. Tadić* provided some interesting, albeit unexpected, leads for resolving the question of how to successfully prosecute Slobodan Milošević.

There were differences of opinion in the international community over how Milošević might be prosecuted successfully. After all these years, the issue finally was untangled by way of the common purpose doctrine (CPD), also known as the joint criminal enterprise. But how was this prosecution theory actually developed? Legal scholars all over the world have speculated and written about the use of CPD at the ICTY, but none of them have been accurate.

After numerous meetings I attended with Dermot Groome, a former Manhattan assistant district attorney and the legal adviser for Team Five, we proposed that the investigation and prosecution be built on the theory of the joint criminal enterprise. This was in 2001, more than ten years after the war had begun and seven years after the UN resolution that created the ICTY was passed. What we had in mind was a prosecution theory similar to that of the U.S. racketeer-influenced corrupt organization (RICO) approach based on the legislation drafted by Notre Dame law professor G. Robert Blakey.

Coincidentally, years after he drafted the RICO Act, Blakey agreed to be a member of my doctoral dissertation committee at Notre Dame. During one of our many conversations, he told me that events of World War II and the Nuremberg war crimes trials had had an impact on his drafting of the RICO laws. Now Blakey's work would have a similar impact on mine.

The genesis of the theory of the joint criminal enterprise at the tribunal goes back to a meeting about the prosecution theory for the Milošević investigation for crimes alleged to have been committed in Croatia, Bosnia, and Kosovo. The chief of investigations and the chief of prosecutions were present. Legal advisers from the Bosnia, Kosovo, and Croatia investigative teams were there. Also present were military intelligence officers, criminal intelligence analysts, political research officers, the previous acting team leader for the Bosnia Team and the new head of the investigations team for Bosnia, and me, the new head of the investigations team for Croatia.

The aim of the meeting was to discuss the prosecution theory and the theory of individual criminal responsibility for Slobodan Milošević. His case was pretty clear-cut for Kosovo: He was the president of the FRY, and he had de jure authority over the forces that were alleged to have committed war crimes there. But Bosnia and Croatia were much different. Milošević was the president of Serbia at the time the crimes were committed. He had no de jure authority over federal troops or agencies. An attorney in the meeting argued that Milošević, as the president of Serbia, could be held responsible for the activities of nonfederal Serb forces, but a political research officer quickly pointed out that it was the prime minister of Serbia, not the president, who had control over such forces.

Another attorney, who also had been at the tribunal for years, gave a typical legal answer: we would have to wait and see how certain things developed before making the determination on the prosecution theory. When he was pressed on certain issues, he couldn't give answers.

I walked out of the meeting scratching my head. It had been close to ten years and there was still no sound prosecution theory, and some of the lawyers were saying we needed to see how things developed. It didn't make any sense to me.

Just outside the meeting room I asked one of the lawyers about conspiracy laws and was told that the statute did not allow for the charge of conspiracy, except for the charge of genocide. Genocide might not be proven at all, but even if it were, you couldn't use conspiracy charges for crimes against humanity or for the violations of the laws or customs of war.

"What about alleging a conspiracy without placing the charge?" I asked.

"What? What are you talking about?" one of the legal officers responded.

"Look, the idea of the conspiracy allegation is to hold one person responsible for the acts of another who also participated in the conspiracy. The further advantages are the relaxed rules of evidence. For example, what one co-conspirator says, they all say; what one does, they all do. This holds true in many jurisdictions, even where a conspiracy is not precisely charged."

"No, it can't be done," said another attorney.

The next day Groome came to my office.

"John, how familiar are you with the common purpose doctrine?"

"Yes, of course, in principle I understand it. What about it?" I asked.

"John, it is like a conspiracy, and the Trial Chamber on the *Tadić* case has alluded to its utility. But no case has actually ever been built upon it."

The utility of the joint criminal enterprise was that it held coperpetrators responsible for foreseeable acts that occurred as the result of the pursuit of the underlying objective. Specifically, if the object of the joint criminal enterprise was to expel non-Serbs from their homes in different parts of Croatia, and people were killed in the process, members of the joint criminal enterprise could be held individually criminally responsible. What could be more foreseeable than deaths as innocent civilians attempted to defend their homes and families from terror and brutality?

Groome and I worked together on a memorandum putting the joint criminal enterprise forward as the principal prosecution theory. One of its problems, we knew, would be the divergence of opinions relative to conspiracy. Even though it was not pure conspiracy law, many would view what we were proposing as conspiracy in mask and wig.

Soon, Groome arranged to have many of the OTP legal advisers attend a meeting to discuss our proposal. Most of them were skeptical. It didn't matter what country they were from. The body language was strong. Many had their noses up in the air. Some smirked, some laughed, but really no one believed in the theory. At this stage, we were fighting with shadows. It was obvious there were many actors operating behind the scenes who were contaminating the air so that this theory would not go forth. How could these two Americans find the solution for one of the most pressing issues that had faced the OTP for years? Richard Overy put it well when he said, "Conspiracy theories [to support investigations and prosecutions] invite invention and provoke skepticism."[1] We were seeing this firsthand. The center of the problem was the fact that the terms "common purpose," "joint criminal enterprise," and "conspiracy" were nowhere to be found in the Statute of the ICTY, save for the latter term relative to the crime of genocide.

Interestingly enough, some fifty years earlier those who had proposed the conspiracy and common plan prosecutions at Nuremberg had also faced a strong reaction. According to Bradley F. Smith, "The Russians and the French seemed unable to grasp all the implications of the concept; when they finally did grasp it, they were shocked. The French viewed it entirely as a barbarous legal mechanism unworthy of modern law, while the Soviets seemed to have shaken their head in wonderment—a reaction, some cynics may believe, was prompted by envy."[2]

History was, indeed, repeating itself in more ways than one. Fortunately, the *Tadić* Appeals Chamber offered hope, and the investigative teams provided the solution.

In many respects, I had been lucky enough to walk into the perfect scenario: The new legal adviser assigned to my team was simply faced with too great a learning curve to provide any meaningful contribution at this stage of our case. Perhaps she would have been up to speed in time, but time was something we didn't have. Consequently, I was uniquely positioned not only to lead the investigation, but also to develop the prosecution theory that would guide the investigation. Had the circumstances been otherwise, the theory of the joint criminal enterprise may never have come to fruition—at least not for Croatia. In the meantime, however, the question was whether I could pull it off.

Straightaway the chief of investigations and the chief of prosecutions agreed with the joint criminal enterprise proposal Groome and I put forth. Not long afterward, Carla Del Ponte approved our plan wholeheartedly.[3]

For the next several months everything began to come together. The investigative plan was aligned with the theory of the joint criminal enterprise. Criminal investigative techniques, such as forensic science, informants, protected witnesses, financial tracing, and the execution of legal documents, were aimed at proving the common purpose and the activities of those within Milošević's inner circle.

As the evidence began to fill the holes that had been identified in the investigative plan, a new challenge emerged. Who was going to write the indictment? The previous legal adviser had prepared a "draft indictment" that contained some excellent historical background. It did not contain information from new crime scenes that since had been worked or new evidence relating to prominent figures in the investigation. More important, it was not written following the theory of the joint criminal enterprise.

Without a legal officer on the team who was experienced with the case and the theory of the joint criminal enterprise, I knew I either had to rely on lawyers from other teams or write the indictment myself. Choosing the latter, I began to put it together, paragraph by paragraph, following the evidence.

I knew that this new draft indictment needed to fully capture the essence of the joint criminal enterprise theory. I also knew it would be reviewed by skeptic after skeptic. Although Del Ponte had approved the theory, there were still knowledgeable senior attorneys who did not support this approach. In the end, this would prove to be good, because those attorneys actually made the investigation and subsequent indictment even stronger through their constructive comments.

I began by focusing on the word "commit" and what it meant and didn't mean. For example, in paragraph 5 of the indictment I wrote,

Slobodan MILOSEVIC is individually criminally responsible for the crimes referred to in Articles 2, 3, and 5 of the Statute of the Tribunal and described in this indictment, which he planned, instigated, ordered, *committed*, or in whose planning, preparation, or execution he otherwise aided and abetted. By using the word committed in this indictment the Prosecutor does not intend to suggest that the accused physically committed any of the crimes charged personally. Committing in this indictment refers to participation in a joint criminal enterprise as co-perpetrator.

To ensure there was no ambiguity as to the full scope of the meaning of the word "commit," a senior trial attorney who later reviewed this portion suggested that the second and third sentences in this paragraph be added. With this foundation laid, I was now prepared to describe the joint criminal enterprise.

Milošević had committed a crime, but not necessarily by physically killing or raping anyone. In some cases he had specifically ordered executions and assassinations, but most of the innocent murder victims died at the hands of forces that had sought to seize parts of Croatia and cleanse it of Croats and other non-Serbs. I wanted to state the objective of the joint criminal enterprise and at the same time tie it to crimes such as murder, willful killing, and torture that were specifically enumerated in the statute:

Slobodan MILOSEVIC participated in a joint criminal enterprise as set out in paragraphs 24 to 26. The purpose of this joint criminal enterprise was the forcible removal of the majority of the Croat and other non-Serb population from the approximately one-third of the territory of the Republic of Croatia that he planned to become part of a new Serb-dominated state through the commission of crimes in violation of Articles 2, 3, and 5 of the Statute of the Tribunal. These areas included those regions that were referred to by Serb authorities and are hereinafter referred to as the "Serbian Autonomous District/*Sprska autonomna oblast*/("SAO") Krajina," the "SAO Western Slavonia," and the "SAO Slavonia, Baranja and Western Srem" (collectively referred to by Serb authorities after 19 December 1991 as the "Republic of Serbian Krajina/*Republika Srpska krajina/*" ("RSK")), and "Dubrovnik Republic/*Dubrovacka republika/*."

Our investigative efforts had identified fifteen coperpetrators that we felt should be listed in the indictment. By this time two, including the notorious killer and paramilitary leader Željko Ražnatović, better known as Arkan, were dead.

Despite his death, Arkan remained named in the indictment. Although a smaller number of his crimes was committed in Croatia, as compared to Bosnia, the relationship between Milošević and Arkan nevertheless was exposed. And since a joint criminal enterprise was charged, the words and acts of Arkan and his subordinates, even in the context of what happened in Bosnia, would be admissible in the trial involving crimes alleged to have been committed in Croatia. This would give the victims some sense of justice.

> This joint criminal enterprise came into existence before 1 August 1991 and continued until at least June 1992. Individuals participating in this joint criminal enterprise included Slobodan MILOSEVIC, Borisav JOVIC, Branko KOSTIC, Veljko KADIJEVIC, Blagoje ADZIC, Milan BABIC, Milan MARTIC, Goran HADZIC, Jovica STANISIC, Franko SIMATOVIC, also known as "Frenki," Tomislav SIMOVIC, Vojislav SESELJ, Momir BULATOVIC, Aleksandar VASILJEVIC, Radovan STOJICIC, also known as "Badza," Zeljko RAZNATOVIC, also known as "Arkan," and other known and unknown participants.

I thought that the next step should be to demonstrate the connection between the specific crimes charged and the object of the joint criminal enterprise. It was also important to explain the relationship between the crimes that were foreseeable outcomes of the execution of the plan, which was to remove by force Croats and other non-Serbs from their homes and from within approximately one-third of Croatia: "The crimes enumerated in Counts 1 to 32 of this indictment were within the object of the joint criminal enterprise. Alternatively, the crimes enumerated in Counts 1 to 13 and 17 to 32 were the natural and foreseeable consequences of the execution of the object of the joint criminal enterprise and the accused was aware that such crimes were the possible outcome of the execution of the joint criminal enterprise."

"Counts 1 to 32" included persecution; extermination, murder, and willful killing; unlawful imprisonment, torture, and inhumane acts; deportation and forcible transfer; attacks on civilians and cruel treatment;

and wanton destruction and plunder of property. These were the crimes that occurred all across Croatia, in places like Voćin, Baćin, Dubrovnik, and Vukovar. They were crimes perpetrated by groups such as the JNA, Martić's Police, Arkan's Tigers, the White Eagles, Dušan Silni, Šešelj's Men, the JSO or Red Berets, TO, SNB, Serbian MUP, and other paramilitary and police units. They had one thing in common: They were all deadly.

Like a conspiracy charge, it was necessary to show concert of action. Indeed, such concert of action would form the basis, through circumstantial evidence, to demonstrate the existence of the plan. Consequently, I inserted the following language: "In order for the joint criminal enterprise to succeed in its objective, Slobodan MILOSEVIC worked in concert with or through several individuals in the joint criminal enterprise. Each participant or coperpetrator within the joint criminal enterprise played his own role or roles that significantly contributed to the overall objective of the enterprise. The roles of the participants or coperpetrators include, but are not limited to, the following . . . "

The roles of each of the coperpetrators were then laid out by showing the individual contributions of each of the members of the joint criminal enterprise and how they contributed to the common purpose. It was my intent to demonstrate that these individuals commanded, directed, or influenced other members of the joint criminal enterprise who actually committed the killings, tortures, or other crimes (when they did not do so individually themselves).

The link between these leaders or key members of the joint criminal enterprise and their subordinates, who typically committed the crimes, was demonstrated in the indictment. Volumes of evidence, including witness statements, suspect interviews, interrogations, and forensic evidence, went into establishing these links as referenced throughout the indictment.

Next, it was necessary to show what Milošević had done as an individual. The investigative results were reflected in the indictment, much as they would be in a racketeering investigation in the United States. I showed how Milošević exercised control or substantial influence over other members of the joint criminal enterprise, including members of the federal Presidency; how he assisted the new Serb-run governments in Croatia; and how he provided financial, matériel, and logistical support to paramilitaries, federal troops, and secret police who were involved in the perpetration of crimes that went toward the achievement of the common purpose.

By now the heinous crimes that had been committed on the ground were by no means secret, and the indictment reflected how they had been linked to members of the joint criminal enterprise. Working from the other direction, I now wanted to demonstrate how Team Four had linked Milošević not only to the joint criminal enterprise, which may very well have been sufficient, but also to the other members of the group. Thus, there was a series of unbroken links from Milošević to the victims of murder, rape, torture, and forced expulsions.

One more critical issue needed to be settled. The draft indictment was specifically written to contain the names and roles of the coperpetrators. This, I believed, enabled the inner workings of the joint criminal enterprise to be demonstrated effectively. I was also of the professional view that naming the coperpetrators would help to successfully elicit the cooperation of one or more of them relative to the prosecution of Slobodan Milošević himself.

As the October 1 deadline drew nearer, I experienced another fortunate step in my journey. The case was turned over to Hildegard Uertz-Retzlaff as the STA. Uertz-Retzlaff was an outstanding prosecutor and former judge from Germany. I wasn't sure I would like her at first, and perhaps I didn't, but she quickly grew on me. I came to appreciate the trust and confidence she had in me and my team's work.

As I worked up the draft indictment, I sent it to her for her review. I want to make one thing absolutely clear: Uertz-Retzlaff turned the draft indictment into a much better legal document. From my perspective, she didn't change any of my work substantively. By and large, the theory of the joint criminal enterprise and the manner in which it was laid out in the draft remained the same. But she made it flow better, and she added the persecutions count that I had not put into the indictment. And Uertz-Retzlaff did much more than that. She came to my office so I could explain the case to her. I had a map on the wall with many annotations. White points indicated the locations of villages and hamlets where the crimes included in the indictment had taken place. Uertz-Retzlaff quickly had a grip on this case and was moving it in the proper direction.

Once she finished going over the case with me, dossier by dossier, and improving the indictment, she submitted it to all of the attorneys in the OTP to review before we went to the indictment review.

Feedback was almost immediate. Senior legal officers said they "didn't think it could be done." They had "changed their minds" and were "convinced this was the way to go forward." Almost as quickly, other teams began to reframe their investigative and prosecution strategies along the lines of the joint criminal enterprise.

The October 1 deadline was closing in. I left work early one day in mid-September, shortly after 3 p.m. I made the thirty-minute drive to my home, a townhouse in a quiet, friendly residential area of The Hague, not far from the queen's residence. As I pulled into my driveway, I saw my wife standing in the foyer, and from the expression on her face, I knew something terrible had happened. I was right.

It was now about 9:30 a.m. EST on September 11, 2001. Like people everywhere, I couldn't believe what I was watching on the BBC news broadcast and CNN International. In addition to my shock and anger over the terrorist attack on the United States, another reality hit me. In just a little more than two weeks I was scheduled to lead the presentation of the case against Slobodan Milošević, for crimes in Croatia, before an indictment review panel. Yet as a U.S. federal agent, I was sure I would be called up for national service somewhere in the world.

I knew I would find a way to finish the international undertaking I had begun at The Hague. I contacted Office of Special Investigations (OSI) headquarters just outside Washington, D.C. I informed my superior officers that I needed time—and explained why. I was assured that they would work with me and delay the issuance of official orders.

By November, I would indeed receive classified orders for a counterintelligence deployment in direct support of the Global War on Terrorism. From a small communications center in the U.S. embassy in The Hague, I received verbal confirmation of my forthcoming orders via a cryptographic Secure-Telephone-Unit, which in the U.S. military and intelligence communities is known as a "STU" (pronounced stew). Other communications back to the United States went through what is known as SIPRNet or Secret Internet Protocol Router Network. Even the code number that uniquely identifies me as a special agent and as a member of the U.S. counterintelligence community was classified. But although my appointment with the UN technically precluded mobilization, I would never have been able to live with myself if I had declined the assignment. This meant I had approximately seven weeks to indict Milošević and prepare to serve my country.

On September 30, 2001, at The Hague, I led Team Four in presenting our case for the indictment of Slobodan Milošević. The presentation was made before a packed room of the world's leading international criminal lawyers. We had rehearsed this several times. Rather than the team legal officer presenting the entire case, as was the usual course of business, I decided to involve everyone. Investigators and analysts presented their chapters of the case in support of the indictment.

I opened:

> Today Team Four is prepared to present to you the evidence supporting an indictment against Slobodan Milošević, the former president of Serbia and former president of the Federal Republic of Yugoslavia, for crimes that were committed throughout Croatia. These crimes include those which were perpetrated in Vukovar, Dubrovnik, Western Slavonia, and throughout the Krajina. We intend to establish the individual criminal responsibility of Slobodan Milošević in a number of ways. First, as the leader of a joint criminal enterprise to forcibly remove Croats and other non-Serbs from their homes and villages for the purpose of attaching approximately one-third of Croatia to Serbia in order to form a "Greater Serbia." We assert his criminal liability for the killings and other crimes that occurred in the process as foreseeable consequences of the object of the joint criminal enterprise. We also have evidence to support alternative theories of criminal liability to include command responsibility for the acts of his subordinates.

One by one, each team member stepped up and provided video clips and other documentary evidence to support our investigation, including all charges and counts. Summaries were succinct and powerful. We set out to demonstrate the inner workings of the joint criminal enterprise and how it fit into the case from factual and legal perspectives.

In our possession, we had seized documents and intercepted oral communications. We had witness statements and survivors. We had forensic evidence to speak for the dead. We also had inside sources that included members of the criminal enterprise. We had pierced Milošević's inner circle.

The indictment review, which included intense questions posed to me and other team members, lasted about eight hours. Piece by piece we presented the case that everyone said could not be done. At the beginning there were some smirks, some whispers, and some comments like, "OK, let's see what you've got."

The STA and one of her key legal officers were there. It was amazing how much they helped out, although they had been assigned the case just a short time before. When it was all over, the indictment review committee voted unanimously for the indictment on all charges. This was the first case actually built upon the new prosecution theory.

With the recommendation of the STA and the indictment review committee, Del Ponte was prepared to sign the indictment. Before she did, however, another wrench was thrown into the case. A number of legal officers thought that the identities of Milošević's coperpetrators should not be included in the indictment unless they too were being indicted.

"Back in the United States, the Justice Department has rules against this," exclaimed one attorney.

What the hell is this? Is there no end to it all? I thought to myself.

"First, this is not the United States, and the Justice Department doesn't have anything to do with this case. Who cares about their rules?" I said. "Second, I am well aware of policies concerning the naming of unindicted co-conspirators so as to not damage their good names. That simply isn't the case here. The names of these alleged coperpetrators and the crimes they are alleged to have participated in have been in the open for years. Third, the joint criminal enterprise can't otherwise be properly described. Last, my experience has been that naming the coperpetrators will 'rattle the chains.' They will come running to us."

The names stayed in, Del Ponte signed the indictment, and just as I predicted, some of the coperpetrators eventually came to us.

But first, in order for the indictment to be a legal document with the full force and effect of law, it needed to be confirmed by a judge of the tribunal. This is not a simple procedure by any means. Judges at the tribunal require substantial documentation to support each and every allegation contained in an indictment. Their work is thorough, and in the Milošević case their scrutiny would be even more intense.

Consequently, carts of binders assembled by Team Four, together with a summary of our investigative efforts some twelve centimeters thick, were wheeled into the judge's chambers. I accompanied the STA to the office of Judge Almiro Rodrigues, a well-respected judge from Portugal, after he had spent several days reviewing the materials we provided. We spent about thirty minutes in the judge's chambers answering his questions. When we were done, I felt confident he would confirm the indictment, although he never commented on the confirmation one way or another.

I was correct. The argument for charging the joint criminal enterprise in connection with the former president of Serbia prevailed. On October 8, 2002, the indictment against Slobodan Milošević was confirmed for war crimes and crimes against humanity alleged to have taken place in Croatia as part of a joint criminal enterprise. Milošević had finally been indicted for crimes committed in Croatia. The chief of prosecutions would later describe the Croatia indictment as "the benchmark for all future indictments at the Tribunal and its successor tribunals."

His prediction was correct. The joint criminal enterprise eventually served as the underlying basis for almost every subsequent indictment at the ICTY or any other major international criminal indictment with jurisdiction on crimes ranging from terrorism to war crimes. For example, one of the coperpetrators named in the Milošević indictment had previously been subject to an investigation by another team. In fact, the entire investigation team had been created specifically for this man. Just prior to our formulation of the joint criminal enterprise theory, the investigation was closed without an indictment. With the new approach approved by the chief prosecutor, I approached the investigations team leader and asked for access to his files for use in our investigation.

"John, the file is closed due to insufficient evidence," he politely informed me.

"We are taking a different approach under a new theory and believe there is a way to demonstrate his culpability," I explained.

"That's impossible. His participation in the war was even examined by a highly respected and connected Western intelligence agency, and they said his role didn't rise to the level of a true military or paramilitary commander. There is simply nothing we can do."

"I understand, but we have a new prosecution theory. And besides, that agency doesn't do criminal investigations. They can't possibly say there is no case to be made."

He gave us special access to all relevant documents and databases. The coperpetrator has since been indicted for war crimes and crimes against humanity.

I returned to The Hague from my U.S. mission just before the first of the year. The case was no longer investigator driven. It was in the hands of the STA, who still needed help preparing the case for trial. By this time, Investigations Team Four was operating in support of the prosecution team. They were now locating witnesses, preparing discovery, authenticating documents, and making sure protected witnesses were prepared for their journey to The Hague and the aggressive cross-examination that would be put to them by none other than Milošević himself.

The chief prosecutor had added a new position to the prosecution team that oversaw the STAs responsible for Croatia, Bosnia, and Kosovo. Geoffrey Nice, QC, an Oxford-educated barrister, was the principal trial attorney in charge of all the Milošević cases. I had briefly met Nice in the past, but this was the first time I sat down with him to discuss the investigation. I explained how the case was put together and what went into the development of the prosecution theory of the joint criminal enterprise. He fully supported the approach and the investigation.

Nice led the prosecution of Milošević all the way to the end. He subsequently was knighted by Queen Elizabeth for his service to the UN.

For me, there was a sense of closure. This was the type of case that only a relatively small number of investigators in the world will ever be privileged to work. Even fewer will bear the responsibility for taking the lead on an investigation of crimes against all humanity and the indictment of a president.

11

Mala Jaska

*We must never forget that the record on which we judge these men
today is the record on which history will judge us tomorrow.*

—Robert H. Jackson, Chief U.S. Prosecutor, Nuremberg

THE C-47, HEADING EAST, ROARED OVER JOSIP CENČIĆ'S BELOVED
village of Lokve, occupied by the Nazis. My great-grandfather and
members of the Partisan resistance, including my relatives, had no
way of knowing that a clandestine mission to save hundreds of Americans
and Allies was just beginning. The event foreshadowed Lokve's liberation.

World War II was nearing its end when two undercover American
special agents embarked on a daring mission known as Operation Halyard. One was George Vujnovich, a Yugoslav-American who worked for
the Office of Strategic Services (OSS). His wife, Mirjana, worked at the
Yugoslav embassy in Washington, D.C. She secretly provided Vujnovich
with information about hundreds of Allied airmen, mostly Americans,
who had been shot down behind enemy lines.[1]

The airmen were still alive, but no one was coming to help them.
Despite the efforts of Gen. Draža Mihailović, the Serb Četnik leader, to
relay the information to officials in the West, no one would listen. But
Mihailović didn't give up. He kept sending coded messages to the Yugoslav embassy in Washington—messages that Mirjana eventually picked
up. She passed the intelligence on to her husband, who ultimately trained

many of the OSS and other military men who participated in the rescue. He was the OSS control agent for the overall operation.[2]

Also critical to the mission was George Musulin, another American secret agent working with the OSS. A mission leader, he twice parachuted into Yugoslavia behind enemy lines. Like Vujnovich, he spoke fluent Serbo-Croatian, a skill that enabled him to befriend and work with the local Serb villagers and armed Četniks, including Mihailović.[3]

Together these two men helped to put together one of the greatest rescue missions in history. Operation Halyard ultimately saved more than five hundred airmen, many of whom had been shot down in their B-24s while returning to Italy from bombing missions in Romania. The airmen, with the help of Četniks and Serb farmers—including women and children—built an airstrip by night, working with only their bare hands, rudimentary tools, and the aid of brute animals. The airstrip allowed C-47 cargo planes, like those flying over Lokve, to land surreptitiously under cover of night and ultimately fly the brave pilots and their crew members to safety.[4]

The successful rescue of these airmen would have been a wonderful ending to a great story but for the fact that Mihailović, an enemy of Communist Josip Broz Tito, was executed as a traitor and a war criminal by the new Yugoslav government after the war. I don't know the extent of Mihailović's collaboration with the Axis Powers as alleged, but I do know that he was a Royalist and staunch anticommunist. History is contradictory and controversial in this regard. According to the two American special agents, the men who participated in the rescue missions attested to Mihailović's deeds. They were brave men of unquestioned integrity who, after saving hundreds of lives, made it back home safely to tell the story of the secret mission that was covered up for a long time by the U.S. government.[5]

More than fifty years after Vujnovich and Musulin returned to the States, I too was preparing to return home from the same part of the world. One day I too would tell my story. The investigation and indictment against Slobodan Milošević was complete, and Team Four had helped prosecutors prepare the case for trial. The prosecution theory of the joint criminal enterprise had been set in motion. So had the investigations of several of Milošević's coperpetrators. The former president of Serbia had been brought to justice, and it wouldn't be long before some of his criminal associates—those who had not been assassinated—would be in the custody of UN war crimes investigators.

As I left The Hague, my colleagues presented me with a humidor, its interior inscribed with the succinct words of Justice Robert H. Jackson that served as a reminder of our legacy: "We must never forget that the record on which we judge these men today is the record on which history will judge us tomorrow." As I reflected on the memento, there was no doubt in my mind that one day history would judge our work based not only on the outcome of our investigative efforts, but also, perhaps more important, on how we arrived there and how the accused ultimately were treated in court.

It was difficult for my family and me to leave the Netherlands. We had spent four years in The Hague, and it had been the experience of a lifetime. I had engaged in meaningful work that, in the view of those who have worked serious crimes of this magnitude, was unmatched by anything else in the fields of criminal investigation and international security. I had made lifelong friends. My children had been educated at the British School in the Netherlands, and my wife's everyday experiences had included international art, languages, and culture. Now it was time to return home.

When my great-grandfather Josip came to the United States, he chose Detroit as his ultimate destination, but some of his cousins selected Pittsburgh as their American home. The hardworking, middle-class Steel City had caught my eye too. Years earlier I had worked on some interesting criminal cases in Pittsburgh, including an undercover operation that had led to the indictment and conviction of two men on corrupt organization charges. I really liked western Pennsylvania. Even better, I had a job waiting for me. After twenty-five years of police work and criminal investigations, I had been appointed as a professor at California University of Pennsylvania, a state university nestled in the Allegheny Mountains among working-class communities of coal miners and steel mill workers. My academic discipline was organized crime and international criminal justice.

Coincidentally, George Vujnovich grew up in Pittsburgh, on the city's South Side. His parents were Yugoslavs who, like so many others, had come to western Pennsylvania to work in the steel mills. At age nineteen, Vujnovich left Pittsburgh to attend a university in Serbia. That's where he met Mirjana. When the Nazis invaded her country, he smuggled her out of Yugoslavia and into the United States. Had it not been for that romance sparked in Belgrade, those five hundred airmen likely would have been summarily executed by the Nazis.[6]

George Musulin also came from western Pennsylvania, from the blue-collar city of Johnstown. He played football for the University of Pittsburgh, and before his secret missions with the OSS, he had played tackle for the Pittsburgh Pirates, a team that later became known as the Pittsburgh Steelers. Musulin was a huge man, so big that the OSS was concerned that his parachute wouldn't support him as he jumped deep behind enemy lines.[7]

I was proud to be settling in a region where these two Yugoslav-Americans who had made such an impact, not only on Pittsburgh but throughout the world, had lived. Pittsburgh is home to one of the largest Croat and Serb populations outside of the former Yugoslavia. In fact, Zagreb is the sister city of Pittsburgh, and the Tamburitzans of Duquesne University have, since 1937, been performing and preserving the music, songs, and dances of many Eastern European cultures.

Much of Pittsburgh's connection with Eastern Europe began at the end of the nineteenth century, when immigrants, including Josip's cousins, came to the city for a better life. Included in the mix were Russians, Ruthenians, Slovaks, Czechs, Poles, and Ukrainians. Many of the Croats settled in Mala Jaska, or "Little Jaska," an area on Pittsburgh's North Side that was once the City of Allegheny. Located at the junction of the Allegheny and Ohio Rivers, Mala Jaska took its name from Jastrebarsko in Zagreb County, Croatia. It was a community of immigrants who worked hard to take care of their families. Women swept the sidewalks as Croatian-speaking merchants sold chickens, vegetables, and sausages in the smoky enclave and children played ball on the busy street corners. Many residents of the community helped to build Pittsburgh and provide the rest of America with coal and steel, while others worked in plants, shops, or factories.[8]

Like their fellow immigrants, many were also taken advantage of by their employers. The Croats and members of other immigrant groups were working at some of the toughest jobs and earning the lowest wages. They had no insurance to protect their families or pay expenses if they became ill or died. If they missed work because of an injury on the job, they received no compensation. Consequently, in 1894 they formed the Croatian Union of the United States, later called the Croatian Fraternal Union (CFU). Headquartered in Allegheny City, the CFU was founded to help in many ways, including aiding orphans, widows, and the sick.[9]

These facts were easy to find in books, but I wanted to better understand Pittsburgh and the Balkan influence on the city. As I had done during my previous twenty years on the job, I set out to find my answers on the streets. I walked the sidewalks of what had once been Mala Jaska, exploring Troy Hill and other North Side neighborhoods in Pittsburgh.

I entered St. Nicholas Church on East Ohio Street. Built in 1901, it was the oldest Croatian church in the United States. Tucked into the hillside next to the main entrance was a grotto built during World War II. At candlelight vigils, parishioners knelt there and prayed to the Blessed Mother for their relatives in Croatia, thousands of miles away, who were being persecuted, tortured, and murdered by Hitler, Mussolini, and Pavelić. Their prayers were answered. Before long, Hitler and his puppet regimes were vanquished. But as those three murderous men departed the world stage, a darker side of Pittsburgh emerged.

The city's traditional organized crime family, La Cosa Nostra, flourished after World War II. Pittsburgh's gamblers, bootleggers, loan sharks, and other racketeers soon were joined by political assassins. From Yugoslavia, Tito sent secret agents—liquidators—around the world. They walked the dark alleys of Paris and Prague and prowled the gritty ethnic neighborhoods of American cities such as New York, Pittsburgh, Cleveland, Chicago, and Detroit. As a young boy, I didn't understand the complexity of the politics or the danger of the situation, but years later I found myself right in the middle of this complicated, conspiratorial web of terrorists, spies, secret police, and assassins.

Coincidentally, our international investigations years later focused on some of Tito's targets—killers in their own right who successfully evaded assassination. We also pursued their hunters: members of the state security or secret police operating under the SFRY (UDBA) and KOS agents who were hot on their trails. At various times some of these men fought together, took up arms against each other, and were jailed in UN prison cells across from one another.

Pittsburgh has changed since the collapse of Yugoslavia. The city's smoky skies are long gone. Its ethnic shops and markets are closed, and so is St. Nicholas Church on East Ohio Street—it was shuttered between the time I came to live in Pittsburgh and the writing of this book. Also gone are the bands of killers, terrorists, and secret agents who turned up the heat in the region's otherwise peaceful working-class communities.

In many ways, the current condition of Mala Jaska reminds me of Mostar's confrontation line, save for the number of bullet holes and spent shell casings. Instead of the roar of helicopters, there is the sound of traffic on a four-lane highway that is pushing for even more space. In the desolate area are many homes with broken glass where the boards that once covered the windowless buildings are gone.

As I had in Mostar, I sensed the ghosts of long-gone residents as I walked between some of the decrepit homes. But these phantoms bore no arms. Instead, they drank homemade *šljivovica* and ate their grandmothers' *sarma* and *pogatica*. They were the spirits of people like John Cencic, a former Allegheny County policeman, whose family undoubtedly came from Lokve and who was quite likely one of Josip's cousins.

As I walked through Pittsburgh's neighborhoods, I didn't hear Croatian being spoken on the porches of the once-colorful houses, although I know there are still many families in the area who continue to speak their mother tongue. They likely are the same people who have held on to what remains of the homes they grew up in—homes the state Transportation Department is trying to seize in order to expand the highways.

I came to Mala Jaska searching for clues to the past so that I could better understand the present. Leaving the Yugoslav war didn't close the book for me; it served only to open new chapters. Although the desolation of Mala Jaska covered some of the tracks to those clues, it did not preclude their discovery. Indeed, in some ways it made the journey all the more interesting. Every step I took seemed to be entwined with the past, illuminating connections between Pittsburgh and certain areas of the former Yugoslavia. One night I even walked down a dark, artistic alley in downtown Pittsburgh officially designated as "Tito Way."

I found the rolling hills of western Pennsylvania dotted with beautiful Serbian Orthodox churches—in Clairton, Aliquippa, McKeesport, Monroeville, and Pittsburgh itself. I walked into several of them and admired not only their iconic beauty, but also the ceremony of the Divine Liturgy.

In the boroughs of Whitehall and Baldwin, just outside Pittsburgh, I could hear the language of my ancestors and of the people with whom

I had just spent the last four years of my life. In these communities live entire families who fled the violence of the Balkans or were left homeless by the war. I saw many Bosnian refugees of various ethnicities standing in Prospect Park's Kockica, or "Little Square." These war refugees have become the new "South Slavs" of Pittsburgh. There is evidence of this in the *pivo, šlivovica,* and *ćevapi*—beer, slivovitz (plum brandy), and minced meat—in the area's markets and state liquor stores.

At the university I teach topics that include the investigation of international crimes. In my classrooms I recognize the students' surnames and sometimes their accents. I see Serbs, Croats, Bosniaks, and Kosovars sitting in class together. I wonder if they truly realize what has taken place in the lands of their ancestors and whether they recognize the connections between the Pittsburgh area and the former Yugoslavia.

I found clues to those connections, and the answers to some of my own questions, at St. Nicholas Cemetery, just north of the suburban borough of Millvale. Another Croatian church, also named for St. Nicholas, still stands there. This was the end of my journey. Or so I thought.

I arrived at the cemetery on a windy autumn day. I wanted to visit one of my distant relatives who had come to Pittsburgh and died young. I found his name: Stevo Cenčić. He died in 1929, at age fourteen. He'd slept through World War II and the war that killed so many in the 1990s. His parents had shared Josip's dream, and so did I.

The wind picked up, blowing fallen leaves off another grave marker. To my surprise, I recognized this surname too. Buried here was Marija Cindrić, who was born in 1876 and died in 1931. Sixty years later, on October 28, 1991, another Marija Cindrić and her elderly mother, Katja Cindrić, were executed by machine-gun fire in Croatia. Their bodies were exhumed from a mass grave in Lipovačka on June 12, 1996.

Resting beside Marija Cindrić in western Pennsylvania were several relatives whose gravestones bore the Anglicized spelling "Cindrich." As I looked around, I recognized even more names—the names of the victims of the murders I had investigated in Croatia. These were the names of my ancestors' friends, neighbors, and loved ones. They also are the surnames of friends I've made in Pittsburgh. I found the grave of Marko Covich, who died in Pittsburgh in 1937. Mijo Čović was murdered in Bačin, Croatia, in 1991 at the hands of Martić's Police. I saw a marker for Mate Vuković, who died here in 1937, and remembered Pero Vuković, who also was murdered in Bačin in 1991. Anna Bačić and her parents, Anton and Barbara, are buried side by side in St. Nicholas Cemetery. Mirjana Bačić, age seventy-two, was murdered in Voćin, Croatia, just before Christmas in 1991 along with more than thirty others. Martin Magdić was buried here in 1928. Six decades later Mile Magdić was abducted from Vukovar Hospital and executed with more than two hundred other unarmed noncombatants at a pig farm in Ovčara. The list went on. Again and again I found names shared by victims of the war in Yugoslavia and ancestors of my friends in Pittsburgh.

Before I visited the cemetery, I had believed that this was the end of Josip's journey, one that stretched from the thick forests of the Devil's Garden all the way to the New World. But it wasn't that simple.

During my early years of police work, I firmly embraced the "us vs. them" mentality. Like many of my colleagues, I saw a clear line of demarcation between the good guys and the bad guys. If you weren't one of us, you were one of them. It was as simple as that. Now I view life differently. My travels, and the people I've met, have changed my perspective.

In cities such as Sarajevo, Zagreb, and Belgrade, and in the hinterlands of Bosnia, Croatia, and Serbia, I could see myself as I spoke with victims of the Yugoslav war. Even stranger, I saw the same people—myself included—as I looked into the eyes of the killers I tracked down, arrested, and interrogated. I realized that mankind had indeed fallen victim at the hands of us all. With that realization, I understood the true essence of crimes against humanity. I learned quickly that my colleagues and I not only looked into the faces of death, but more important, exposed the many images of life.

This was our story. It is a war crimes investigator's story.

EPILOGUE

The Hague Crucible

O N MARCH 11, 2006, ON A QUIET SATURDAY MORNING, SLOBODAN Milošević was found dead. He was alone in his locked cell in Scheveningen, the same gloomy prison where my journey to The Hague had begun some eight years earlier.

Speculation began at once and included talk that Milošević had been murdered by poison. In fact, the tribunal's inquiry into his death revealed that nonprescribed medications at times had been found in Milošević's blood, most recently one month prior to his demise. Those drugs had been smuggled into the UN detention center and had the power to annihilate the desired effects of his prescribed heart medications.

Conspiracy theories of this sort have arisen around the world and throughout history—after the deaths of Rudolph Hess, Jack Ruby, and Pope John Paul I, for example. Why should the death of Slobodan Milošević have been any different? But the speculation was baseless, the coroner said. The official cause and manner of death: natural causes from a heart attack. Milošević was sixty-four.

Milošević's death occurred just a few weeks before he was prepared to rest his case. Milošević had been representing himself in his legal defense, although the tribunal also had appointed an amici curiae, a group of three attorneys who were "friends of the court," to be present and to assist the tribunal with ensuring a fair trial for the accused.

The legal proceedings on the charges against Milošević were both a test and a trial. It was a test of the prosecution theory of the joint criminal enterprise. Indeed, Milošević was the first president who stood in the dock before an international criminal tribunal for crimes against humanity alleged to have been committed while he was a sitting head of state.

As interesting as the court proceedings were, I have intentionally avoided discussing the trial throughout this book. This is, first and foremost, a war crimes investigator's story. Nevertheless, with Milošević's death coming before the end of the trial and without a final judgment from the court, I feel personally and professionally compelled to make a few observations.

Based on the investigation and the facts that it produced, I believe there was sufficient evidence to prove Milošević's guilt beyond a reasonable doubt. Surely this comes as no surprise. What lead investigator would suggest otherwise?

But some aspects of the proceedings against Milošević troubled me. From the comfort of my nineteenth-century farmhouse just outside of Pittsburgh, I watched as much of the live proceedings as I could over the Internet. And in the process of writing this book, I sat in my study and read transcript after transcript.

I first was taken aback by the number of times that prosecution witnesses barely testified, save for providing their names and confirming information and summaries of their statements, which were read directly into the record. To add to this, when witnesses needed to explain an issue or a question with more than a yes-or-no response, they often were told that details weren't important. Again, some of the witnesses simply were asked to confirm what was being read into the record. This was direct examination conducted in a way I'd never seen.

I realize that the process was streamlined because it was such a lengthy trial. And surely Milošević was stringing the proceedings along. But he was a defendant in a criminal trial, and many of the points he raised were, in my view, legitimate. By no means am I suggesting that Milošević wasn't criminally responsible for many of the acts for which he was charged, but in my opinion, reading statements and summaries into the record as evidence was not the way to proceed.

In addition, the presiding judge often shut down Milošević when he attempted to cross-examine some of the witnesses on extremely relevant issues. When he was allowed to cross-examine, he raised good points and quite often did an excellent job. From my perspective, there was far too much inquisitorial influence in the trial.

Many people cheer with their hearts the convictions of men and women who commit heinous crimes, and we are all fortunate that humanity has whittled away the impunity that human rights violators enjoyed for so long. But in the name of human rights, I also believe that we should seek to improve the process for the sake of justice and the rule of law. Witnesses should be subject to thorough direct and cross-examination, and criminal defendants should be fully heard.

Undoubtedly, it is difficult to balance these rights against a disruptive defendant, but no matter how noble the cause, I am still left troubled. I am troubled not so much by the admissibility of hearsay and the heavy leading of witness testimony on direct examination as I am by the true level of the sufficiency of the evidence required for a conviction, the lack of a jury trial, and, worst yet, the prosecutor's right to appeal a lower case judgment based on a finding of not guilty or the appropriateness of the sentence. The latter is something that would surely constitute double jeopardy in the criminal justice system to which I have grown accustomed.

To be clear, these comments are directed toward the process. In no way am I criticizing the brilliant prosecutors who did the best they could to work in a new venue, an international criminal court that was by no means flawless.

Having said this, I must note that Milošević's death did not close the book on crimes against humanity or on the contemporary methods of investigation and prosecution of these horrific crimes. It was only the beginning. The theory of the joint criminal enterprise and the practice of aligning the investigative plan with this specific prosecution theory have since been used at the tribunal and in other international and domestic courts that try crimes of this magnitude, ranging from war crimes to acts of terrorism. In addition, many of the coperpetrators identified in Milošević's indictment for crimes alleged to have been committed throughout Croatia have since been indicted themselves.

I must reiterate what I said at the outset of this book: All suspects and accused are presumed innocent unless and until they are proven guilty. But there is no way to write a book about my experiences without outlining these alleged offenses and the individuals who are suspected of having committed them. In the end, however, the Trial Chamber and the Appeals Chamber will determine the individual criminal responsibility of any given defendant. Indeed, the tribunal has acquitted several individuals who were accused.

MILOŠEVIĆ'S INNER CIRCLE AND COPERPETRATORS

On November 17, 2003, the tribunal formally indicted Milan Babić, the former president of the RSK, on one count of crimes against humanity involving persecution based upon political, racial, and religious grounds. He also was charged with four counts of violations of the laws or customs of war: murder; cruel treatment; wanton destruction of villages, or devastation not justified by military necessity; and destruction or willful damage done to institutions dedicated to education or religion. These were the crimes investigated by Team Four, and they included the murder and extermination of Croats and other non-Serb minorities in Dubica, Cerovljani, Baćin, Saborsko, Poljanak, Lipovača, and other areas in the Krajina region of Croatia.

The lead prosecutor on the trial was Hildegard Uertz-Retzlaff. Her expertise resulted in Babić entering into a plea agreement and cooperating with the OTP. The value of Babić's cooperation cannot be understated; nor can the heavy burden that fell upon Uertz-Retzlaff in methodically presenting Team Four's case to the court.

Babić testified against Milošević and provided an inside look at the joint criminal enterprise and Milošević's authority over the JNA, the DB, and other Serb forces. In 2004 he pleaded guilty to the crime of persecution and subsequently was sentenced to thirteen years in prison. Babić made this statement to the court:

> I come before this Tribunal with a deep sense of shame and remorse. I have allowed myself to take part in the worst kind of persecution of people simply because they were Croats and not Serbs. Innocent people were persecuted; innocent people were evicted forcibly from their houses; and innocent people were killed. Even [when] I learned what had happened, I kept silent. Even worse, I continued in my office, and I became personally responsible for the inhumane treatment of innocent people.
>
> The regret that I feel is the pain that I have to live [with] for the rest of my life. These crimes and my participation therein can never be justified. I'm speechless when I have to express the depth of my remorse for what I have done and for the effect that my sins have had on the others. I can only hope that by expressing the truth, by admitting to my guilt, and expressing the remorse [I] can serve as an example to those who still

mistakenly believe that such inhumane acts can ever be justified. Only truth can give the opportunity for the Serbian people to relieve itself of its collective burden of guilt. Only an admission of guilt on my part makes it possible for me to take responsibility for all the wrongs that I have done.

I hope that the remorse that I expressed will make it easier for the others to bear their pain and suffering. I have come to understand that enmity and division can never make it easier for us to live. I have come to understand that our—the fact that we all belong to the same human race is more important than any differences, and I have come to understand that only through friendship and confidence can we live together in peace and friendship, and thus make it possible for our children to live in a better world.

I have asked help from God to make it easier for me to repent, and I am thankful to God for making it possible for me to express my repentance. I ask from my brothers, Croats, to forgive us, their brother Serbs, and I pray for the Serb people to turn to the future and to achieve the kind of compassion that will make it possible to forgive the crimes. And lastly, I place myself at the full disposal of this Tribunal and international justice.[1]

Babić suffered deeply, but in spite of his remorse, he could not handle the ghastly horror of his deeds. On March 5, 2006, at The Hague, UN officials found Babić dead. He was alone in his locked cell. A plastic bag was over his head, secured tightly by a leather belt. Medical personnel could not determine a precise cause of death because the pathological examination indicated that he had suffered both a heart attack and asphyxiation from hanging. Some investigators noted that the width of the belt found around his neck did not match the ligature marks, and thus was conceived another conspiracy theory that stretched from the Balkans to The Hague. After all, Babić had testified against Milošević, and he was expected to testify against Martić the next day.

However, investigators found a note in Babić's handwriting. The note was in his Bible inside the cell.

My beloved,

Find peace for yourself and don't mourn for me. I need peace.

Your Milan.
On Sunday, 5 March 2006. Let the God forgive.

The coroner determined that the manner of death was suicide.

A few weeks later the media reported that according to the secretary general of the SRS, political leader Vojislav Šešelj had reliable information that Babić's suicide note said the tribunal had pressured him to testify against Serbs. The investigating judge found the accusation completely baseless.[2]

At the time of Babić's death, Šešelj also was lodged at the prison. On February 14, 2003, St. Valentine's Day, the ICTY had indicted him on charges that included persecution based on political, racial, or religious grounds; deportation; and murder, torture, and cruel treatment. These charges included the murders of Croats and other non-Serb minorities in Vukovar; prolonged confinement of non-Serbs in detention facilities and prison camps in Croatia; and torture, beatings, and sexual assaults.

Nine days after he was indicted, Šešelj surrendered to the war crimes tribunal. His trial is ongoing, and like Milošević did, he is representing himself. So far, his explosive conduct has led to several charges of contempt before the Trial Chamber.

Nine months before Šešelj's surrender, Babić's successor as president was taken into custody. I supervised the arrest of Milan Martić, the former police inspector turned president, on May 15, 2002. The tribunal had indicted him in 1995 for the Orkan rocket attacks in Croatia, which included attacks on the capital city of Zagreb. On at least two separate occasions, Martić had given the order to fire deadly rockets fitted with aviation "cluster bomb" warheads at the civilian population in the city center. The 262 mm rocket launchers fired M-87 missiles that released hundreds of thousands of deadly pellets, killing and maiming innocent noncombatants, including women and children. These shameful attacks gave an entirely new perspective to Abu Bakr's seventh-century orders to his commanders that "the blood of women, children, and old people shall not stain your victory."

At the time of his arrest, the mustachioed Martić looked me straight in the face with his ardent, burning eyes, as though we were mortal enemies. I could smell his arrogance. His stone-cold gaze showed subtle signs of fear, but he didn't look much different than he had in the many photographs I'd viewed throughout our investigation.

On December 18, 2002, the chief prosecutor amended the indictment of Martić to include some of the crimes investigated by Team Four.

These ferocious acts were war crimes and crimes against humanity that formed part of the joint criminal enterprise; they included the extermination, murder, unlawful confinement, torture, and sexual assaults of Croats and other non-Serb minorities throughout the Krajina region of Croatia. With brutal, willful blindness toward humanity, the deadly members of Martić's Police had repeatedly murdered and terrorized innocent civilians, including residents of Dubica, Baćin, and Cerovljani who were abducted and executed. Their bloody bodies were dumped into the river.

On June 12, 2007, Martić was sentenced to thirty-five years' imprisonment. Two years later he was transferred to Estonia to carry out his sentence. He now sits in a prison cell not far from a remote location where I once interviewed a foreign mercenary.

Jovica Stanišić and Frenki Simatović were arrested by Serb authorities on March 13, 2003. Less than two months later both were indicted by the tribunal and subsequently transferred to The Hague. They have been charged with participation in the joint criminal enterprise in relation to the murders, tortures, forced deportations, and other crimes against humanity that were committed throughout Croatia, including those committed in Vukovar, Western Slavonia, and the Krajina. These crimes were physically perpetrated by members of the special operations component of the DB.

Dermot Groome, the brilliant lawyer with whom I worked to develop the theory of the joint criminal enterprise, is the STA prosecuting the Stanišić-Simatović case. The prosecution rested its case on April 5, 2011, and two months later the defense case commenced. From what I can see from the parts of the trial I have watched, the two accused have maintained their dignity throughout the proceedings. Considering their training and discipline, this comes as no surprise to me.

One key person who helped Stanišić and Simatović in Croatia is fighting for his own freedom. Captain Dragan has engaged in protracted legal proceedings in Australia in an effort to prevent his extradition to Croatia, where he would be tried for crimes he allegedly committed during the war. Captain Dragan has been in prison for a number of years. He was released once, but he went on the lam, only to be captured before long by Australian police and once again placed behind bars. Recently, the Australian federal court dismissed his appeal on the extradition.

Maj. Gen. Aleksandar Vasiljević, the former head of KOG, testified for the prosecution against Milošević. In spite of the several statements we obtained from his former brothers in arms in the JNA counterintelligence circle, the tribunal never indicted him for his alleged role in the joint criminal enterprise. His culpability for crimes, if any, was left to national governments. And in April 2011, Vasiljević was charged in Croatia with sending operatives to Serb-run detention facilities for the purpose of questioning and torturing Croatian detainees. It has been further alleged by the Croatian authorities that Vasiljević was aware of many deaths that resulted from the mistreatment.

Ratko Mladić and Goran Hadžić were the last two fugitives of the ICTY. On May 26, 2011, Serbian president Boris Tadić announced the arrest of Mladić, the former head of the Bosnian-Serb army. Acting on an "anonymous tip," a special MUP unit and members of Serbia's special war crimes prosecution unit, all wearing black uniforms and masks, captured Mladić in Serbia. A notorious fugitive who had been on the run for more than fifteen years, he was charged with, among other crimes, genocide in Bosnia relating to the massacre at Srebrenica and the siege of Sarajevo. Mladić also is alleged to have been involved in war crimes in Croatia, including those at Škabrnja, which Team Four investigated.

I recall a statement made by one of our witnesses who had captured a Yugoslav intelligence officer during the perpetration of criminal activities during the war. Defiant, the prisoner of war warned the Croatian defenders, "Mladić will certainly attack you. He will burn you down and destroy you, because you simply don't stand a chance." In the end, Mladić was tracked down and captured—and unlike his victims, he will be given a chance. He will have his day in court but, unfortunately, not for criminal acts at Škabrnja and the mad crimes allegedly committed by forces under his command. The chief prosecutor at The Hague decided that Mladić's indictment would not be amended to include the crimes he was alleged to have been involved with in Croatia. This didn't sit well with Croats, including Croatian president Ivo Josipović. But that is the nature of prosecutorial discretion.

Just four months after Mladić's capture, President Tadić again appeared on public television. This time he announced the arrest of Hadžić, the last remaining fugitive, who had been in hiding for eight years. On

July 20, 2011, a special operations team of the Serbian police arrested him in a mountainous region of northern Serbia.

Until 2004 Hadžić had lived in Novi Sad, the city that hosted the MP Royal. He went on the run when sources inside the secret police in Serbia alerted him to his international indictment—the culmination of the precise investigative work of Team Four. The charges against Hadžić include his involvement in war crimes and crimes against humanity committed against Croats and other non-Serbs, such as extermination and murder, unlawful imprisonment and confinement, torture and physical and psychological mistreatment, forced labor, robbery and looting, and deportation and forced transfer. The crimes charged incorporate the abductions, torture, and murders of hundreds of patients, staff members, and other occupants of Vukovar Hospital.

Although they were named as coperpetrators in the joint criminal enterprise headed by Milošević, the tribunal never indicted Adžić, Jović, Kostić, Bulatović, Simović, or Kadijević. As in the case of Vasiljević, these matters have been left for national jurisdictions. Kadijević ultimately was indicted in Croatia for war crimes against a civilian population. An active Interpol Red Notice exists for his arrest and extradition. Having acquired Russian citizenship, he is believed to be living somewhere near Moscow. Adžić also was charged in Croatia with the crime of genocide. He died in 2012 at the age of seventy-nine.

The last two named members of the joint criminal enterprise were conveniently dead before Milošević was indicted for his crimes in Croatia. Radovan "Badža" Stojičić, the former commander of the territorial defense in SAO SBWS, made his way to the powerful position of Serbia's acting minister of the interior. He reported to Milošević and used his position to further his criminal activities and ties to organized crime throughout the region.

During the early morning hours of April 11, 1997, an armed, masked man entered Mamma Mia's restaurant in downtown Belgrade. He ordered everyone to lie face down on the floor. Several shots were fired at close range, and Stojičić, forty-six, was killed. It was speculated that the assassin was a mobster or maybe a CIA operative. Undoubtedly, many people wanted Stojičić dead. At the top of the list was Slobodan Milošević, who knew that the war crimes tribunal was closing in.

Three years later, on January 15, 2000, it was Arkan's turn to die. Željko Ražnatović, forty-seven, was sitting in the lobby of Belgrade's

Intercontinental Hotel when an assassin approached and fired at nearly point-blank range, shooting him through the eye. As the triggerman fled the scene, one of Arkan's bodyguards shot him in the back. The killer fell to the ground and crawled toward the hotel entrance. Accomplices dragged him to a getaway car that was waiting just outside.

It wasn't long before Serb authorities apprehended the assassin and his accomplices. The killer, a former police officer who is now in a wheelchair, claimed he was just an innocent bystander. But that didn't explain the soft body armor he was wearing when the bullet struck him in the back and paralyzed him permanently from the waist down. He ultimately was sentenced to thirty years in prison. Seven accomplices, including the two who helped the assassin escape from the hotel, also were convicted.

Again, speculation about the murder abounds. Some believe the mafia ordered the hit, but perhaps the most widespread theory blames Milošević and his desire to silence those who would be best positioned to testify against him at The Hague.

Although the public didn't know it at the time, the tribunal had indicted Arkan in 1997. This was the work of Team Four, before I came to The Hague. It was a "sealed" indictment, and UN investigators and prosecutors kept its very existence secret. In March 1999 the tribunal partially lifted the seal: The indictment's existence was made public, but the allegations and charges remained protected from disclosure.

Ten months later Arkan was assassinated. His violent ambitions were stopped dead in their tracks, and the warlord took many of his secrets to the grave. I recall Milošević's words about Arkan, relayed to us by the secret police informer code-named "Blackjack": "We need people like this now, but no one should think that they are more powerful than the state."

Whether his assassination is called a sanction or a "hit," in the minds of many inside the secret world of espionage, treason, and corrupt power, Arkan was terminated not for what he had done, but for what he knew. Much like his pre–World War I compatriot, Col. Dragutin Dimitrijević, code-named "Apis," who masterminded the assassination of Archduke Franz Ferdinand, the former head of the ferocious Tigers was rewarded for his loyal service to Serbia with a barrage of fatal bullets.

Unbeknown to intelligence agencies throughout the world, and the international community in general, we had many of the answers behind this complex assassination. Some of the details have been disclosed during international and national prosecutions; others remain confidential to this day.

THE VUKOVAR THREE

On a sunny spring day in 2002, I took a small team of investigators to Schipol Airport. There Gen. Mile Mrkšić formally surrendered, and we took him into custody. Mrkšić looked like a gentleman, and he carried himself like the senior military officer he was. But I knew the man behind that shattered military mask. He was absolutely devoid of emotion. He was the man Witness X said had condemned to death 264 unarmed patients and other noncombatants at Vukovar Hospital, the man who ordered Šljivančanin to "kill those shits."

On September 27, 2007, the Trial Chamber sentenced Mrkšić to twenty years in prison for aiding and abetting the murders at Ovčara. However, the Trial Chamber ruled there was no evidence that Mrkšić had ordered the killings. Instead, it found that his order for the JNA to withdraw and leave the unarmed detainees at the mercy of the local TO was criminal. Mrkšić knew about the TO's hostile feelings toward the patients, the Trial Chamber held, and by withdrawing the security provided to the "prisoners" by the JNA military police, Mrkšić aided and abetted in their murders. Two years later the Appeals Chamber upheld the conviction and the sentence. In October 2012 the tribunal transferred Mrkšić to Portugal to serve out his sentence.

Serb authorities arrested Lt. Col. Veselin Šljivančanin on June 13, 2003, and turned him over to UN war crimes investigators about two weeks later. Once again, the Trial Chamber held there was no evidence of a joint criminal enterprise or common purpose in the killings of the unarmed hospital patients. It further held that Šljivančanin did not exercise any command authority over members of the TO. Accordingly, he could not be held individually criminally responsible under the doctrine of "command responsibility" for failing to prevent the killings, since the soldiers who committed the crime were not under his leadership.

However, the Trial Chamber did find that Šljivančanin, a JNA major at the time, had command authority over the JNA military police. Šljivančanin was present and observed the prisoners being mistreated by the TO, and he knew of previous instances of brutality by the unit, including the murder of Croats. The Trial Chamber held that Šljivančanin failed to take the necessary steps to ensure that the JNA military police protected the prisoners, and consequently the Trial Chamber convicted him of aiding and abetting torture. The Trial Chamber also ruled that once the JNA military police withdrew and the prisoners were in the sole custody of the TO, Šljivančanin's culpability ceased. In 2007 he was sentenced to a mere five years' imprisonment.

As I watched the verdict in Šljivančanin's case being broadcast live, I couldn't believe the words I was hearing. The sentence was disturbing, to say the least. Common sense would dictate that if Mrkšić bore criminal responsibility for aiding and abetting murder for withdrawing the JNA, then Šljivančanin would too. How could the Trial Chamber say that Šljivančanin's responsibility stopped once the JNA withdrew, when that was the very reason it had found Mrkšić guilty of aiding and abetting the murders? Decisions like this may justify suspending the notion of double jeopardy after all.

Fortunately, two years later the Appeals Chamber found Šljivančanin guilty of aiding and abetting in the murders, and his prison sentence was increased to seventeen years. Yet just one year after that, based on new evidence claiming that Šljivančanin didn't learn of the massacre until after it occurred, the court reduced his sentence to a mere ten years. A few months after that, the tribunal granted him early release.

The initial sentence of five years shocked the world. It equaled about seven days in jail for each murder victim—or about the same length of time someone in the United States might serve for a third drunk-driving conviction. Even ten years only elevated Šljivančanin's sentence to two weeks in prison for each unarmed person at Vukovar Hospital who was abducted, tortured, and brutally murdered. In the former Yugoslavia, you can get that much jail time for smuggling cigarettes or hijacking truckloads of merchandise. Something was definitely wrong.

If justice is going to be served, it must be meted out equitably. This is particularly true when judicial proceedings involve different ethnic groups, with members who were both victims and offenders. While the sentencing of a criminal defendant necessarily stands on its own merit and must take into consideration both aggravating and mitigating circumstances, what happened here cries out for justice. The convicted are both heroes and criminals, depending upon the eyes of the beholder, and they all must be treated as equally as possible if there is ever to be peace in the region.

Ultimately, the Trial Chamber acquitted the third alleged coperpetrator in the Vukovar massacre—Capt. Miroslav Radić, who surrendered to the tribunal on April 21, 2003. The prosecution appealed the verdict, but the Appeals Chamber upheld the decision of the lower court. The rationale for this finding of "not guilty" was as bizarre as Šljivančanin's sentence.

Boris Tadić, as president of Serbia, and Ivo Josipović, the president of Croatia, have since stood together at the memorial at Ovčara. This is a wonderful step in the right direction, but Josipović and the people of Croatia know that the international tribunal has done little to hold accountable those individuals most responsible for this massacre. Dr. Vesna Bosanac, who was there at Vukovar and ultimately testified before the tribunal, responded to the verdicts by saying there was "no justice for Vukovar and its citizens at the Hague tribunal."[3] In relation to this case, she is absolutely correct. In my opinion, it was a parody of justice.

Somehow the quest for rectitude ended in an unlikely place: Serbia. The Serbian criminal justice system handed out sentences appropriate for this heinous crime, notwithstanding the fact that the victims were Croats and the killers were Serbs. The Serb courts convicted numerous members of the TO, including three senior members who were investigated by Team Four. Stanko Vujanović, commander of the TO, was found guilty and sentenced to a twenty-year term. Deputy commander Miroljub Vujović received the same sentence, and Milan Vojnović was sentenced to fifteen years in prison. Although some lesser terms were imposed, most of the defendants in the case received prison sentences ranging from fifteen to twenty years. Finally, there was some justice for the victims of the Vukovar Hospital massacre and their families.

THE BATTLE OF DUBROVNIK

Lt. Gen. Pavle Strugar was the commander of the Second Operation Group, which the JNA formed to conduct the military campaign against the Dubrovnik region of Croatia. In October 2001 I received a telephone call from Strugar's attorney, Vladimir Petrović, concerning the possibility of his client's surrender. He made three simple requests: for Strugar's son to accompany him to The Hague; for Strugar not to be handcuffed in front of his son; and for Strugar to be given an immediate medical examination as soon as he entered the UN detention facility for processing.

Fair enough, I thought. I informed my immediate supervisor of the developments in the case, just to keep him in the loop.

"We don't negotiate with war criminals," I was told.

"You're absolutely correct. I agree 100 percent . . . ," I began, hoping to shift the conversation from the direction I saw it was heading. Then I read his face and decided to switch tactics altogether. "C'mon, man, let me handle this!"

He just smiled and silently acquiesced. I appreciated his deference.

Within days I was at a remote Royal Dutch Navy air base waiting for the private jet to land. General Strugar, tall and gray, debarked the plane with his son and his attorney, Petrović. I had already spoken with the Dutch police about Petrović's request concerning the handcuffs.

"We have our procedures," the officer in charge told me.

I politely filled in the background behind the surrender. "I gave my word as an investigator, and I am asking for your professional courtesy to honor my request."

From that point on, it was not a problem. That is how police officers from around the world work together. It's a brotherhood all its own.

At the naval air base, General Strugar comported himself with the utmost dignity and maintained his military bearing and professionalism. He was polite and 100 percent cooperative. He understood the gravity of the situation. I felt the pain as he and his son looked at each other and embraced one final time before he was taken away—without handcuffs.

I kept my word, but the same was not true for the detention facility. Part of the agreement for Strugar's surrender included a medical evaluation immediately upon his arrival at the prison. I happened to see Petrović a couple of days later. To my surprise, he informed me that Strugar still had not received his medical evaluation. This fact was promptly conveyed to the STA, who immediately informed the Trial Chamber. The matter was sorted out without further delay.

Strugar did have medical issues, and shortly thereafter the tribunal granted him a provisional release. I later traveled to his home in Montenegro to interview him. His attorney and his family were there, and they were as kind and as accommodating as anyone could expect.

General Strugar's case was the closest to a "fog of war" that I encountered during my time in the former Yugoslavia. In other words, he committed mistakes during the heat of battle that cost innocent civilians their lives, but he didn't have the intent to kill. In the end, the tribunal found him guilty of violating the laws and customs of war relating to the attacks on civilians and protected places and buildings. The Trial Chamber acquitted him on other charges and ruled that Strugar's individual criminal responsibility was not based upon any orders to commit these crimes. Instead, in his position as the highest-ranking military officer in theater, he had failed to prevent the crimes from taking place and failed to punish those responsible afterward, although he had reasonable notice prior to the crimes' occurrence and actual knowledge following their commission.

In terms of the deaths of civilians, the Trial Chamber focused only on two potential murder victims. This very well may have been a correct legal analysis based on the actual charges that were lodged by the OTP. The problem, as I see it, was that neither a joint criminal enterprise nor a crime against humanity was alleged. This was so even though much larger and broader indictments against other accused, such as Slobodan Milošević, actually included unlawful activities in relation to Dubrovnik in the alleged joint criminal enterprise and several counts of crimes against humanity. Had the indictment been formulated differently, all the civilian deaths might very well have been given the justice they deserved. And the laws and customs of war, which have little, if any, application to criminal enterprises or crimes against humanity, would have been rendered moot.

Nevertheless, Strugar was sentenced to eight years in prison, with credit given for time already served. Effective February 20, 2009, he was granted early release and returned to Montenegro.

I was away from The Hague on November 12, 2001, when Vice Adm. Miodrag Jokić was taken into custody. The specific nature of my post-9/11 mission entirely prevented me from returning to the Netherlands. I was, however, in contact with my second in command, who supervised the arrest operation. Jokić was vice admiral and commander of the Ninth (Boka Kotorska) Military Naval Sector (Ninth VPS). He pleaded guilty to all charges and was sentenced to seven years in prison for the crimes surrounding the siege, attack, and spoliation of Dubrovnik. He is the first naval commander convicted of war crimes after Adm. Takazumi Oka of the Imperial Japanese Navy and Adm. Karl Dönitz of the German Navy following the World War II.

On September 25, 2003, Vladimir "Rambo" Kovačević was arrested in Serbia and later transferred to The Hague to face charges based on our indictment. A captain first class and commander of the Third Battalion of the JNA, Trebinje Brigade, he was diagnosed as a paranoid psychotic. In March 2007 the Appeals Chamber upheld the decision of the Trial Chamber to transfer the criminal jurisdiction of the case to the Serbian criminal justice system.

It was the first case ceded by the ICTY to Serbia. In July 2007 the Office of the War Crimes Prosecutor in Serbia indicted Captain Kovačević for war crimes connected to ravaging and pillaging in the Dubrovnik region of Croatia. He subsequently was admitted to a Belgrade military hospital for further evaluation.

The fourth accused, Milan Zec, was a battleship captain and chief of staff of the Ninth VPS at the time of the attack on Dubrovnik. He later was promoted to rear admiral and then to commander of the Yugoslav Navy, with the rank of vice admiral. Based on further assessment of the evidence and the position held by Admiral Zec at the time of the attacks on civilians and civilian objects, the prosecutor withdrew the charges against him on July 26, 2001.

Once again, had a crime against humanity or a criminal enterprise been charged in relation to the so-called Battle of Dubrovnik, Admiral Zec may very well have been successfully brought to justice.

THE ASSASSINATION OF ZORAN ĐINĐIĆ

The man who was instrumental in turning over Slobodan Milošević to UN war crimes investigators immediately became a dead man walking. On March 12, 2003, Zoran Đinđić, the prime minister of Serbia, was shot through the chest with a high-powered rifle. The assassin's den was across the street from the main state governmental building in Belgrade.

Đinđić's murder caused chaos in Belgrade, across Serbia, and throughout the Balkans. In the months after his death, police questioned tens of thousands of suspects and witnesses. One of the largest dragnets in the history of the Balkans was under way.

The assassination was part of a complex conspiracy that incorporated a number of different groups, each with a different motive. The Zemun Clan, a Serbian-organized crime gang, was at the center. The mobsters were concerned about Đinđić's crackdown on organized crime. There also were political reasons for the assassination. Individuals who were closely aligned with Milošević feared they also might be transferred to The Hague to face war crimes trials. Some sources have said that Milošević himself sanctioned the assassination from inside his prison cell at The Hague. The lone gunman was a former deputy commander of the JSO. And the plot was masterminded by none other than Legija, the former commander of the JSO.

Shortly after the Đinđić assassination, Legija was convicted for his role in the assassination of Ivan Stambolić in 2000. The Stambolić trial had been under way at the time Đinđić was killed. Legija was ultimately also convicted in connection with the prime minister's assassination and sentenced to forty years in prison. He now has a cumulative 120-year sentence hanging over his head. I learned that by the time he was sent to prison, Legija and other members of the JSO had already compiled a dossier on me as the lead investigator on the Milošević case for war crimes perpetrated in Croatia.

In all, more than forty individuals have been indicted for playing various roles in the Đinđić assassination plot. Members of the prime minister's personal security team are among them. Also charged were Vojislav Šešelj, on trial at The Hague for war crimes; the security adviser for former Yugoslav president Vojislav Koštunica; the chief of army intelligence; and many members of Serbian organized crime.

At least three suspects remain on the run. The fugitives are a top priority of Interpol, since it is well known in law enforcement and intelligence circles that significant elements of Serbian organized crime operate from major cities and cells all over the world.

CRIMES IN AND AROUND MOSTAR

I left The Hague in 2002 fully aware that it would be some time before all the people I had investigated were indicted, captured, and put on trial. My two years of work on cases such as the wooden-rifles incident and the murder of Bosnian police officer Nenad Harmandžić eventually came to a successful close. My involvement in the arrests of both Tuta and Štela was almost surreal. But in reality these two men, leaders of the KB, were responsible for multiple war crimes and crimes against humanity.

After 161 days at trial, Tuta was found guilty and sentenced to twenty years' imprisonment. Štela received eighteen years. The Appeals Chamber upheld the convictions and sentences in 2006. Both men were sent to Italy to serve out their sentences. Štela was released on parole in January 2012, and Tuta was released on February 18, 2013.

In April 2004 the tribunal publicly indicted Jadranko Prlić, Bruno Stojić, Slobodan Praljak, Milivoj Petković, Valentin Ćorić, and Berislav Pušić on nine counts of grave breaches of the Geneva Conventions and eight counts of crimes against humanity. These were senior military and political leaders who, in one way or another, were involved with the HVO and the crimes alleged to have been committed by them, including the deaths of the Spanish peacekeepers, which formed part of the persecution count of the indictment.

It must be noted that at the time of this writing there has been no finding of guilt for the six men, and, legally speaking, they are innocent until proven guilty. In fact, to be clear, I was not involved in the investigation that may or may not have linked any of the accused in this particular indictment to the killings of the two Spanish lieutenants. My job in this particular instance related strictly to the immediate evidence surrounding the murders of Lieutenant Aguilar and Lieutenant Muñoz. Both officers, since their deaths, have been promoted to the rank of captain, and both received posthumous medals for their bravery and their ultimate sacrifice.

But that wasn't the end of my work in international criminal justice. I was still troubled by the fact that civilian deaths often were not included in criminal indictments because of the notion of "collateral damage," even if the killings took place within the context of a crime against humanity. And with the case involving the Spanish peacekeepers, although they were incorporated in the overall persecution count, charges specifically relating to their murders were not included.

With this legal quagmire in mind, my next endeavor took me to the University of Notre Dame. There, the aim of my doctoral research was to pierce the military veil of combatants who commit serious acts of violence during the perpetration of a criminal enterprise.

ACKNOWLEDGMENTS

It has been more than ten years since I completed my work at The Hague, and I have worked on this book on and off throughout this time period. It goes without saying that a project like this cannot be done in isolation, and I have many people to thank.

I must begin with my great-aunt Kay Cencich, who was instrumental in providing historical facts about my family. If not for her, I never would have known that my great-grandfather, Josip, walked to Philadelphia after leaving Ellis Island or that my grandfather and two of his siblings were survivors of the 1913 Massacre in Michigan's Upper Peninsula. She even gave me the first look at my great-grandfather and great-grandmother. Their wedding picture now hangs in my study.

Kay was born Kathryn Podnar in 1922 in the borough of McKees Rocks, Pennsylvania, a blue-collar town near Pittsburgh. Her parents had emigrated from Croatia, and as a young child Kay moved to Hamtramck, Michigan, and then to Detroit, where, after receiving her degree in education from Wayne State University, she had a long career as a schoolteacher. In Detroit she met and married my grandfather's brother, Joe. Kay fell asleep in the Lord before this book was finished. A memorial lunch was held in November 2011 at one of her favorite places, Lukich's Restaurant, just outside Detroit. It was truly fitting.

In addition, I am forever indebted to Mirjana Pleše, the principal of the local school in Lokve, Croatia. She and her family opened their arms and their home to me as I researched this book. Among many kindnesses, she showed me the school logbooks containing entries for my great-grandfather and took me inside the bunkers that had been used by the Nazis some fifty years before. She is truly a wonderful woman, and the people of Lokve are fortunate to have her as a neighbor and a friend. I feel blessed to know her.

My cousins Boris Cenčić and Nena Bogdanić were there for me, too. They dropped everything they were doing to ensure that I had informative and memorable visits to Croatia. I had not met them before my first trip to Croatia, but I soon felt as if I had known them all my life. Their father, Edo, was equally gracious. With his great sense of humor, he provided me with critical information about the occupation of Lokve during World War II, his clandestine activities as a member of the Partisan resistance, and his subsequent career with the Yugoslav State Security Service. He passed away just after my visit in 2007.

My four years working for the UN at The Hague were some of the best years of my life. I am thankful to the many staff members and friends at the ICTY. They are international civil servants and career criminal justice professionals committed to the highest principles of law and justice. I am honored to have served with them.

Patrick Picciarelli, a retired lieutenant with the New York City Police Department and a crime novelist, gave me advice on how to write my first book and negotiate the contract in a way that only Pat could. I am deeply appreciative to my colleagues Christine Kindl and Christian Chartier for their thoughtful comments on the manuscript. And I am truly fortunate to have worked on this project with Elizabeth Sherburn Demers, PhD, senior editor at Potomac Books. She believed this was a story that needed to be told, and she gave me the chance, as a first-time author, to do so.

My wife, Andrea, and my children, Jonathan, Catalina, and Sebastian, were always with me in one way or another as we moved to the Netherlands and as I traveled throughout the Balkans and the territory of the former Yugoslavia. In many ways their lives were upended, but as a family, we all felt privileged for the opportunity to serve at such a meaningful level. To them, most of all, I am forever grateful.

APPENDIX I
Cenčići Jerbićevi

The earliest traces of the Cenčić clan were in the Čapljina area of Herze-govina, a place that fell victim to the hideous war crimes I investigated. The Cenčić surname is said to have derived from the Proto-Slavic sobri-quet *cene*, likely meaning "dinner." Other versions have the name origi-nating from Latin and meaning "price" or "centurion." In any event, the clan members originally were part of the Slavic tribes that migrated to the region in the sixth century from an area north of the rugged Carpathian Mountains and flanked by both the Black and Baltic Seas—a region that now is considered Poland, Ukraine, and Belarus.

Eleven centuries later, these "South Slavs" turned around and went north again, this time to the Gorski Kotar region of what is now Croatia, near the Slovenian border, in order to avoid persecution by the Ottoman Turks. Like many other Christians, the Cenčić clan left Bosnia to escape the brutality of the Janissaries, who, operating under the Ottoman Em-pire, had two objectives: to convert Christians to Islam or to kill them. Their journey left only traces of memories behind.

Many of the Cenčić family documents I have been able to uncover are written in Latin, which made my journey all the more adventurous. With a magnifying glass and oblique lighting, I first smiled and then felt a chill as I read the old baptismal records. They eloquently referred to the act of *levantibus patrinis* (being raised to be baptized by the godparents) and listed the names, addresses, parents, and godparents of some of my ancestors. Just one ledger in the dead language gave life to thousands of words in my mind.

The records provided some fairly detailed information. In 1672, for example, Laurentius Cencich (Latin for Lovro Cenčić) moved to Čabar, which is not far from the small Gorski Kotar community of Loque (Latin for Lokve), which in English means "puddle." I learned that Lovro's father had been a servant of Petar Zrinski, the Croatian ban who had been beheaded by the Habsburgs after plotting to remove foreign influence from Croatian territory.

Lovro's great-great-grandson, Antonius (Anton), was born in Lokve in 1758. Anton fathered Jacobus (Jakov) in 1770. Jakov's son Michael (Mihovil) was born in 1806 and most likely was called just Miško. That was the year of the fall of the Holy Roman Empire.

Miško was the nephew of a man who had worked as a *sudski*, or court administrator, under Maria Theresa, the Holy Roman empress. When Miško was twenty-one years old, he fell in love and married Ursula Jerbić. Her father owned a café in the center of Lokve, where the local school now stands. The townspeople still talk about the café owner's legendary strength.

Thus the Cenčići Jerbićevi clan—that is, the Cenčić family members who are the direct descendents of this union—came into existence. Miško and Ursula Cenčić's first child was my great-grandfather Josip's father, Lovro.

Lovro grew up under serfdom. He was a farmer and a devout Catholic who eventually married Agnes Cenčić. Although also a Cenčić at birth, she was not a member of the Cenčići Jerbićevi clan. The couple had eight children: Vjenceslav, also called Vinko; Andrija; Božica; Pavle; Ivana; Margareta; Josip; and Marija.

One thing is certain: Lovro was a man with a clear vision for his children's future. I was able to discern from some of the records that when they didn't complete a particular level of schooling, he brought his children back to start over again the next year. He never gave up on them.

Josip Cenčić (Josephus Cencich as recorded at birth) was the couple's second-to-last child, born on March 2, 1874. He grew up in Lokve, a village with chickens and pigs in the yards and horses trotting through the muddy streets. Roosters heralded the dawn. There was no electricity or running water, but the town was spotless. Every morning the women donned their aprons and cleaned the outside of their homes. It was a busy place with a sense of purpose.

Through his childhood years, Josip enjoyed the many stories and legends that originated in and around Lokve and Gorski Kotar. The tales were passed on from generation to generation. There was the story of the *demon goranskih šuma* (the demon of Goranske woods), and there was the tale of the "Freehunters" who went out and killed bears with only their hands and a knife.

On one occasion, the story goes, a father and son went hunting, and a bear killed the father. The son set out on a journey of retribution and justice, hunting the bear for nearly two years. Finally, he found the very animal that had killed his father. He took vengeance at last. The story ends as the boy, a young man by then, stands and watches as the bear melts the red snow beneath its body.

When Josip was sixteen years old, he heard of the amazing opportunities in America. These undoubtedly were exaggerated tales about the wealth and success immigrants would achieve. Such stories filled the newspapers, and unscrupulous agents of steamship companies who had returned to Europe also spread tales about the high wages a worker could earn. Many ethnic Croats sold everything they owned just to buy a ticket for the biggest show on Earth.[1]

It took Josip two years to save enough money—about thirty U.S. dollars' worth of Kronen, called Krune in Croatian, the new currency of the Austro-Hungarian Empire, which went into effect the year Josip emigrated. By 1892 he needed to make a decision about where in America he would settle.

For Josip, there were only two choices that guaranteed a steady income, at least in his mind: hard work in the copper mines of Michigan's Upper Peninsula, the area colloquially known as the UP, or the equally backbreaking and dangerous labor in the coal mines of Pittsburgh, Pennsylvania. There were stories all around Gorski Kotar about both places—the money that could be made and the happiness that could be found. Later, some of Josip's cousins from Lokve would choose Pittsburgh, but Josip's love of the water made him select the barren land along Lake Superior.

Shortly before Josip left for America, on April 15, 1892—Good Friday—he and his family took part in the Procession of the Cross. More than a century later, I imagined him passing by as I stood in front of Sveta Katarina's Church. In my mind's eye, I could see the priest and the procession of faithful Croats slowly making their way down the dirt road, saying their rosaries. I pictured them climbing the steep hillside to the site of the cross and then making their way to the small village cemetery where the members of the Cenčić family had been laid to rest.

By May 7, 1892, Josip was ready to depart. His parents came to see him off, and surely many other family members and friends were there as well. His Uncle Miha and Aunt Katarina came to say good-bye. His godparents, Augustin Mihelčić and Margareta Majnarić, likely were there too. And Josip's siblings were with him: Andrija, Pavle, Vinko, and sisters Ivana and Božica. What a beautiful name, Božica. It's the diminutive of "Christmas."

Two family members were absent. Josip was only two years old when his sister Margareta died at age five on a brisk September morning at Lokve 100, the Cenčić house. Lovro waited until Agnes finished nursing Marija, only ten days old, before he entered their bedroom with the bad news. Margareta had lost her battle with a serious illness; they didn't even know its name. Baby Marija's death soon followed.

But now a new life was beginning. Josip, the family's youngest living child, would be the first to leave for the New World.

There were many reasons why his older brothers stayed behind. For one, with Josip in America, the family household wouldn't have to be divided up further when it was passed on from Lovro to his remaining sons. The house eventually wound up with Vinko, and it remained in his family.

Excited and anxious, Josip climbed aboard the train in Lokve. His first stop was Naples, where he was placed in quarantine for a number of days before he was allowed to board the SS *Belgravia*. Built in Scotland, the massive ship was designed to accommodate almost two thousand passengers, but hundreds more were crammed in. The *Belgravia* made a number of trips between Europe and New York before it eventually sank off the east coast of Canada in 1896.

This was the first year that Ellis Island was open to immigrants from around the world. And as the *Belgravia* entered Upper New York Bay on June 24, 1892, the Statue of Liberty welcomed all the souls aboard. Those who hadn't survived the voyage were taken off first. As he began to disembark with the other surviving passengers, Josip most likely heard music playing and saw the ship's mast proudly displaying the Stars and Stripes. He had made it to America.

Solid at 5 feet, 10 inches (nearly 178 centimeters), Josip passed the medical exam, the first stop for immigrants at Ellis Island. Next he went to the Great Hall for a legal inspection. The stone-cold immigration inspector held the ship's manifest and asked a number of background questions. He must have passed. He was soon a legal alien in the United States.

Josip exchanged the few Kronen in his pocket for U.S. dollars. A rail agent sold him the train ticket he needed to travel from Philadelphia to Michigan, but he still had to make his way to Philadelphia. So he and some friends—Croats, Serbs, and Italians he met on the *Belgravia* and at Ellis Island—walked the nearly seventy miles to Philadelphia, where they climbed aboard a train heading for northern Michigan.

Josip's final stop was the settlement of Red Jacket, later renamed the village of Calumet. He went to work for the Ahmeek Mining Company, just five miles away in neighboring Keweenaw County, Michigan. Keweenaw is a Chippewa Indian name meaning "crossing place." Copper had been mined in the area since the Native Americans had first dug it from the ground with hand tools.

Life was hard in the UP. The weather was harsh and the working conditions were even worse. Many cultures intersected here, and in many ways it represented the people who built America.

Josip's hard work paid off. He was making money, and he decided to return to Lokve to find a wife. Four years after he first stepped into the New World, he was on a ship headed back to the old country.

Back home, Josip found work in Gorski Kotar. One day he and a couple of friends met three young women who were on their way to work at a tobacco factory near the neighboring town of Delnice. Among them was Paulina Sanković, a twenty-two-year-old from Škrljevo, a small Croatian village near the Adriatic Sea. Paulina was beautiful, with a dark complexion, fair hair, and deep blue eyes. Josip immediately began courting her.

Paulina had been born Geneva "Fafa" Sanković. Her father, Šime, was a gendarme for Austria-Hungary who, along with Paulina's mother, Lucija nee Frančisković, died early. Paulina and her siblings were separated, and Paulina was eventually taken in by an Italian couple and given the name Paola, after their natural daughter who had died at birth.

Josip and Paulina were married on July 17, 1897, in Sveta Katarina's Church in Lokve. Not quite a year later, Josip was on his way back to America, alone. He had money to earn and a wife to bring to the States.

He traveled aboard the SS *Friesland* out of Antwerp, and he arrived back in New York on June 14, 1898, with just four dollars in his pocket.

After two long, lonely winters of grimy work in the mines, Josip was more than ready to see his wife and family again. He sailed to Croatia expecting to fetch Paulina, but he returned to America alone because of a lack of funds, leaving his homeland for the last time on November 3, 1901. This time he traveled to America via Le Havre, in Normandy, where he boarded the SS *La Gascogne*.

Josip may have come back to Michigan alone, but he left more than his wife in Croatia. Their first son, Pavle, was born in 1902. Two years later, Paulina made the long-awaited journey to America to join her husband. Ten months after arriving in Michigan, she gave birth to their second child, Marija. And nearly two years later, on July 10, 1906, my grandfather Ivan was born.

Then, quite unexpectedly, during the summer of 1907, Paulina packed up, boarded a ship for Europe, and took the young children back to Croatia. I was never able to learn the precise reasons for her abrupt decision. She was only thirty-two when she left the United States. Paulina was pregnant, but she didn't know it yet. Apparently, Josip could do nothing to stop her. Their daughter Jožica was born later that year in Croatia.

With no need to pay rent for an entire house, Josip moved to Ahmeek Village, where he lived as a boarder in the home of John and Mary Kanolerich and their daughters, Josepha and Mary. Eleven other boarders also lived there; among them were Jakob Cencic and John Cencich, both from Lokve, but from different Cenčić clans.

Eventually, Paulina decided to reunite the family. In April 1913, after more than five years of separation from her husband, she boarded the RMS *Saxonia* in Fiume, which is now Rijeka in Croatia. Built in Scotland in 1900, the steamship later would hold prisoners of war during World War I.

Paulina returned to Michigan with all four children. Young Ivan became ill crossing the Atlantic; he lost weight, and Paulina feared he would not survive. The three-week voyage must have seemed longer than the five years the couple was apart.

The family arrived at Ellis Island on April 21, 1913, and Josip eagerly awaited their return. He had wanted to accompany his family on the journey from Croatia, but he could not afford it. Little Ivan was still ill when the ship docked, but it wasn't long before he was on the mend. And for the first time, Josip set eyes on his daughter Jožica. The Cenčić family was together again, and they would remain committed to one another for the rest of their lives.

Eventually the family members took new names. The Cenčić surname was Anglicized by adding an "h" and dropping the diacritics. Ironically, the new surname "Cencich" was the same as the Latin spelling that had been imposed on the ethnic Croats under the rule of Hedervary, the ban of Hungary. Josip was now Joseph, or Joe, and Paulina became Pauline. The children's names changed too. Pavle, named after Josip's brother, was now called Paul. Marija, one year younger than Paul, was Mary. My grandfather, Ivan, became John, and Jožica, one year younger than John, became Josephine but went by Rose. The story goes that when Jožica first went to school in the UP, she didn't speak English. When the teacher asked her name, she just stood there silently. The cute little girl's cheeks were bright red, so the teacher called her Rose and the nickname stuck.

Josip continued to work under harsh conditions in the copper mines off and on for twenty-one grueling years. Then, on July 14, 1913, the workers went on strike. The strike wasn't just about money; the working conditions had forced the miners' hands. The men were working a thousand feet underground for twelve hours a day. They didn't want to strike, but they felt they had no choice.

Things got worse, and the Cencich family faced a number of crises. The first came about because of the strike. By and large, the public supported the striking miners. But as they had in Pittsburgh in 1892, the mining companies brought in hired guns. Poor families were even poorer with their breadwinners out of work, and now they also had to suffer gunshots and bloodshed on the streets.

In spite of the hard times and the violence, "Big Annie" Clemenc, the wife of a Croatian miner and a local heroine, arranged for a holiday celebration. On Christmas Eve 1913 about seven hundred people, including my grandfather and his siblings Paul, Mary, and Rose, gathered at the Italian Hall in Calumet. Suddenly, a man believed to be a strikebreaker working for the mining company yelled, "Fire!"

The joyous holiday spirit changed quickly to panic. The crowd broke up and attempted to escape. Children were screaming, adults were pushing, and everyone fled toward the main exit, a pair of double doors. But the doors had been intentionally blocked from the outside. There was complete pandemonium as adults and children fell on top of one another and bodies rolled down the stairs. Soon the children's cries and screams ended, and their bodies went cold. Firemen did their best to rescue those they could.

There never was a fire. The 1913 Massacre, as it came to be known, took seventy-three lives. The oldest victim was sixty-six; the youngest was just two. Somehow, my grandfather and his brothers and sisters survived.

Some four years later, when Josip's and Paulina's newest addition to the family, Joe, was less than a year old, their house caught fire. It was another extremely cold night in the UP, and the family had stoked the woodstove for the night. Presumably, a random spark started the fire. Fortunately, baby Joey's cries alerted the family as they slept, and miraculously, they all escaped. The poorly built house, however, burned to the ground.

Outside in the bitter cold, Pauline dropped to her knees and cried. Josip took her hand and the hands of the children. Standing in the snow, they said the Lord's Prayer, beginning with the Sign of the Cross: *U ime Oca I Sina I Duha Svetoga.* When they were finished, Josip looked at each of them, his gaze lingering on Pauline.

"We will make it!"

Nothing else was said. The family believed in him. They would eventually rebuild their lives in Detroit.

Before they made that move, however, World War I brought many changes to the Cencich family.

It is worth remembering that many Croats in America were still citizens of Austria. As such, they didn't want the United States to go to war with Austria-Hungary.[2] That's not to say they weren't loyal to the United States; they were. But who wants to go to war against his cousins?

During the war years, Josip had little communication with his family in Europe. Mail from America was slow going in or out of the Royal Post Office in Lokve, and eventually all correspondence was cut off. Sometimes the only way Croats in America learned the fate of their loved ones from the old country was from lists of Croatian war dead that were published by the Austro-Hungarian army and sold by the Croatian newspaper, the *Narodni List.*[3]

On September 12, 1918, unaware that the war would soon be over, Josip and his son, Paul, walked through the front door of the draft registrar's office in Mohawk, Michigan. They both registered for the draft, but in the end, they never bore arms.

Back in Lokve, it was a different story altogether. Josip's nephew Vinko was an officer in the Kaiserliche und Königliche Kriegsmarine, also called the k.u.k. Kriegsmarine—the Austro-Hungarian navy. But Vinko would never lift a finger against the Americans or other Allied forces.

Vinko deserted from the navy—and he knew where to go. He had visited his Uncle Josip almost ten years earlier. So he made his way to Michigan, where he met up with Josip. What a dilemma he faced. America was at war with the Germans and Austro-Hungarians, and Vinko's wife and children were still in a Croatian enclave that lay within Austria-Hungary.

Josip and Vinko discussed the delicate situation. In the end, Vinko knew what he had to do: He turned around and traveled across the Atlantic and through the Strait of Sicily, heading to a North African refugee camp just outside the heavily French-influenced city of Bizerte, Tunisia. There, Vinko joined a Serb volunteer unit that had recently been mustered up. Soon he would be fighting on the side of the Entente and against his former brothers in arms.

From there Vinko was taken to the Greek port of Salonika, where the Salonika front had been established. Summer turned to winter, and the brave soldiers on both sides faced harsh conditions. The powerful Vardar winds blowing down from the mountains brought in gales and heavy snows. By winter's end, hundreds of thousands of soldiers had perished.[4]

Vinko fought as long as he could on the front. Then he lay down on the snow-covered ground. What few clothes that covered his shivering body were frozen solid. He was severely frostbitten, and gangrene had begun to set in. His comrades eventually carried his near-dead body to a train. Somehow he ended up in Budapest, where he was hospitalized for a while. He died from tuberculosis some years later.

Vinko's medals for gallantry during the war went to the grave with him. Years later, in remembrance of the bravery of those who fought at the Salonika front, Marshal Tito himself paid a state visit to the area of the entrenchment camp that once had been called the Bird Cage because of the barbed wire that encircled the area.[5] Vinko's son Edo, by then a member of the Yugoslav security service, accompanied the former Partisan leader at the ceremony.

With the Great War over in Europe, Josip's eldest son, Paul, left the UP. My grandfather, John, was next. He was just thirteen and had gone to school only as far as the sixth grade. But the automobile industry was paying good wages, and he was looking for work and a life of his own. He found a job in Detroit and spent his lifetime working at the Chrysler plant there. Josip, Pauline, and the younger siblings followed; by 1921 they were all in Detroit. Josip took a job working for "Fords," as the Ford Motor Company is still colloquially called.

Before they had left the UP, Josip and Pauline had had three more children—Albina; Antonjia, who everyone simply called Nettie; and Lawrence, who was named after Josip's father, Lovro.

In Detroit my grandfather met Agnes Sučić, whose parents had come to America some years after Josip. Her father, Ivan Sučić, entered Ellis Island aboard the RMS *Carpathia*, one of the future *Titantic* rescue ships, via Trieste after an eighteen-day voyage across the Atlantic. He had left the beautiful Croatian island of Krk, the largest island in the Adriatic. It had a mild Mediterranean climate and beautiful coves, birds, and beaches. But there was no work.

Ivan's father, Jozo, and his mother, the former Lucija Barbarić, were from a town known as Castelmuschio in Italian and Omišalj in Croatian. The oldest town on Krk, it was built by the Romans on a cliff overlooking the sea, and it dates back to a time before the Croats arrived in the sixth century.

In New York, Ivan met Katarina, also a Croat. She was only fifteen when they married. They lived not far from Ellis Island, in a one-time tenement house at 129 Washington Street that still stands, now completely encircled by modern buildings. The World Financial Center is just a few blocks to the west, and the New York Stock Exchange just a bit farther to the east.

On a cold winter day I stood on the corner of Washington and Albany Streets in south Manhattan with my wife and children, and I let my imagination take me away. I pictured what life must have been like for my ancestors living in this neighborhood at the turn of the century, and I recalled a more recent horror. The former tenement house at 129 Washington Street sat in the shadow of the Twin Towers of the World Trade Center, just one block away. As my family and I stood there in 2004, rebuilding was still under way.

Agnes and her brother, Eli, had both been born in New York City. Ivan Sučić did his best to support his family by working odd jobs anywhere from the streets of the Battery to the slaughterhouses of Hell's Kitchen. It was 1907. The neighborhoods were tough, and gangs ruled the streets. It was the same year that Salvatore Luciana, a.k.a. Charles "Lucky" Luciano, came to New York. And going from his crowded living quarters to work was often dangerous. An Irish gang known as the Gophers was known for fights, strong-arm robberies, and other street crimes. And there was the threat of another Black Hand, La Mano Nera.

Ivan did his best to avoid trouble, but New York simply wasn't the place for the couple who had become known as John and Katherine Sucich. In 1919 they left for Chicago. Like many Croats before him, John found work in the steel industry. In Chicago, there were enough Croats to support five Croatian parishes, including St. Jerome's of Chicago and Sacred Heart.

The couple's children, John, Peter, and Carl, were born while they lived on the Near Southwest Side of Chicago. But it seemed as though the problems they'd left behind in New York City had followed them west. Al Capone had come to Chicago, and crime was rampant in the Windy City.

Katherine was afraid of the violence, and John was betting on the horses. Katherine convinced her husband that it was time to move again. While many of John Sucich's cousins eventually settled in Pittsburgh, this Sucich family chose Detroit.

So there they were: John Sucich and his family on one Detroit city block, and Josip Cencich and his family on another. Both Croatian-American families were trying to get by. Eventually, they met.

In 1929—the heart of Prohibition, with Detroit's Purple Gang in full swing—John and Katherine's daughter Agnes married my grandfather. The bride was fifteen, and her new husband was twenty-three.

The families tried to keep life simple. When they weren't working or attending Mass at St. Jerome's, on the corner of Melbourne and Oakland, Josip and his sons would sit together listening to "Ty" Tyson broadcasting Detroit Tigers baseball games on the radio.

One day, quite mysteriously, John Sucich went missing. As far as his family knew, he simply disappeared. Katherine didn't know whether he was dead or alive. With Agnes's help, she took care of her younger children. For years the family told everyone, including me, that John had died.

During my research for this book, however, I found records showing that John Sucich had actually outlived his wife. Had he gambled too much and then fled from the loan sharks? Had he run off with another woman? Or had he truly died, as we were led to believe, and had his identity stolen? No one will ever know.

Back in Lokve, World War II was looming, and the people of Josip's village were caught completely off guard. The occupiers arrived in 1941, mostly in tarp-covered cargo trucks. Benito Mussolini's troops quickly overtook the undefended town of just under fifteen hundred inhabitants. Soon Lokve was surrounded by handmade concertina wire, and mines were laid around the outskirts to keep people from escaping. The Italian flag flew in the center of town.

Most Lokve residents were members of the local Communist Party. To avoid capture and execution, many Partisans hid in the mountains just outside the town. Brave members of the underground resistance attacked the occupying forces from strategic points as best they could. They planted bombs on trains used by fascists and Nazis, and under cover of night they positioned themselves for the next day's activities.

They traveled throughout the Gorski Kotar region on snow skis, wearing red stars on their caps, ready to fire their rifles. They were good fighters, but they also needed to pass information in and out of Lokve.

The Italian soldiers knew there were spies among them, and to collect relevant information, the soldiers coerced neighbors to identify neighbors. The identities of the informers were kept secret. Italian soldiers carried one woman into St. Katarina's church on a stretcher, her body covered by a white sheet. Lokve's residents filled the pews. One by one they were forced to walk in front of the altar, where the reluctant collaborator stood behind a red curtain with just a small peephole between her and her neighbors. The words *si* or *no*, uttered by the informer, let the Italian occupiers know who belonged to the underground resistance. Summary executions quickly followed.

In town, help came from an unlikely source. Darinka Puškarić was a local schoolteacher who taught the children living in the forest. As the war went from winter to winter, she undertook dangerous missions, passing intelligence back and forth between a number of secret "operatives." One of them was Edo Cenčić, Josip's nephew.

Edo had been a student in Zagreb, but he returned home to Lokve in January 1942. A Partisan, he did his job, and he did it well. He also fell in love with the schoolteacher-turned-spy.

The Italian forces took a different view of Puškarić altogether. The senior officer issued an order for the courageous woman, who undoubtedly had saved many lives, to be arrested and executed. Fortunately, a local hero and leader in the resistance, code-named "Chimney Sweeper," found a way for her to escape just minutes before she would have been captured. The vicious occupiers would soon be gone as well.

As they fled during the capitulation of 1943, the Italian soldiers destroyed property in Lokve. They burned homes and set fire to a pile of books from the school. Seizing the moment, a brave woman from Lokve saved as many of the books as she could. One volume that escaped the torch contained the school records of Josip Cenčić and many of his brothers and sisters. This was the same book I examined in awe some sixty-four years later, when Mirjana Pleše pulled it off of a dusty shelf in the local schoolhouse.

Soon the Nazis replaced the Italians in Lokve. They were even more brutal than their predecessors. They slit people's throats and tortured innocent, unarmed civilians. They burned homes. Lokve 100, the new residence of the Cenčić family, was shelled. Townspeople tried to save the innocent. They even took in young German soldiers—teenagers who were caught in a war they did not understand.

Edo was in Šibenik on April 17, 1945, when Lokve was liberated completely, and he told me what life was like during the liberation. The residents had been fighting too. In fact, a local Lokve woman had captured the top-ranking German general and hanged him as he pleaded for mercy. His body and those of the other Germans who were killed during the final hours of their occupation were buried in a nearby pit.

With the war over, Edo put the clandestine skills he had developed to good use. He became a member of the Yugoslav Security Service. He was no different than any other patriot; he joined his country's secret service with a vision of serving the people. He started in the department of UDBA that was concerned principally with political analysis, but during his career he worked his way to the upper echelons of the organization. He also was elected twice to the Croatian parliament.

Puškarić, the schoolteacher-turned-spy, eventually returned to Lokve, and the romance that had developed during the clandestine operations continued. She and Edo were married in Zagreb's city hall. Edo was able to provide me with these details just before he died, after my visit to Croatia in 2007.

By the end of the war, Josip was retired, and just nine days after the Germans surrendered to Allied forces, Pauline died. For the next six years Josip lived alone at his humble Newbern Street home in Detroit. Today, all that remains is an empty lot. Not far away, Josip and Pauline are buried side by side in Detroit's Mt. Olivet Cemetery.

On a Sunday morning one early autumn, my wife and children joined me as I tidied the gravesite and placed flowers at their final resting place. I was reminded of the passage in John 12:24: "Truly, truly, I say to you, unless a grain of wheat falls into the earth and dies, it remains alone; but if it dies, it bears much fruit."

Josip and Pauline had a fruitful life, indeed. And in the end the members of the Cenčići Jerbićevi clan found the peace their souls desired. Like the story of the young Freehunter from Josip's boyhood, they faced many bears. But even when complete strangers tried to pervert the very essence of their ethnic upbringing, they clung to their love of God and placed family and friends above all else. They didn't merely tolerate the ethnic differences among their neighbors; they celebrated them.

These courageous, hardworking men and women proved themselves in the forests of Gorski Kotar, in the copper mines of Michigan's UP, in Detroit's auto factories, and in the coal mines and steel mills of Pittsburgh. From the small Croatian enclave in the once-vast Austro-Hungarian Empire to the working-class neighborhoods of America, they left a legacy as ordinary people who faced extraordinary challenges.

APPENDIX II
Cases and Related Legal Documents

Biographies of suspects, details of crimes, and dialogue with witnesses, suspects, and accused were drawn directly from the following cases and related public documents. They can be found at www.icty.org.

Prosecutor v. Babić, ICTY Case No. IT-03–72 (Transcripts, November 26, 2003–July 18, 2005).

Prosecutor v. Dokmanović, ICTY Case No. IT-95–13a (Amended Indictment, December 2, 1997).

Prosecutor v. Dokmanović, ICTY Case No. IT-95–13a (Transcripts, July 4, 1997–June 25, 1998).

Prosecutor v. Martić, ICTY Case No. IT-95–11 (Amended Indictment, December 18, 2002).

Prosecutor v. Martić, ICTY Case No. IT-95–11 (Transcripts, January 1, 2001–December 13, 2005).

Prosecutor v. Milošević, ICTY Case No. IT-01–50 (Original Indictment, October 23, 2002).

Prosecutor v. Milošević, ICTY Case No. IT-01–50 (Transcripts, July 3, 2001–March 14, 2006).

Prosecutor v. Mladić, ICTY Case No. IT-09–92 (Fourth Amended Indictment, December 16, 2011).

Prosecutor v. Mrkšić et al., ICTY Case No. IT-95–13/1 (Second Amended Indictment, December 2, 1997).

Prosecutor v. Mrkšić et al., ICTY Case No. IT-95–13/1 (Transcripts, May 16, 2002–December 8, 2010).

Prosecutor v. Naletilić and Martinović, ICTY Case No. IT-98–34 (Appeal Chamber Judgment, May 3, 2006).

Prosecutor v. Naletilić and Martinović, ICTY Case No. IT-98–34 (Second Amended Indictment, September 28, 2001).

Prosecutor v. Naletilić and Martinović, ICTY Case No. IT-98–34 (Transcripts, August 12, 1999–May 3, 2006).

Prosecutor v. Naletilić and Martinović, ICTY Case No. IT-98–34 (Trial Chamber Judgment, March 31, 2003).

Prosecutor v. Prlić et al., ICTY Case No. IT-04–74 (Indictment, March 2, 2004).

Prosecutor v. Prlić et al., ICTY Case No. IT-04–74 (Transcripts, April 6, 2004–March 2, 2011).

Prosecutor v. Ražnatović, ICTY Case No. IT-97–27 (Indictment, September 23, 1997).

Prosecutor v. Strugar et al., ICTY Case No. IT-01–42 (Appeal Chamber Judgment, July 17, 2008).

Prosecutor v. Strugar et al., ICTY Case No. IT-01–42 (Indictment, February 22, 2001).

Prosecutor v. Strugar et al., ICTY Case No. IT-01–42 (Transcripts, October 25, 2001–July 17, 2008).

Prosecutor v. Strugar et al., ICTY Case No. IT-01–42 (Trial Chamber Judgment, January 31, 2005).

Prosecutor v. Tadić, ICTY Case No. IT-94–1 (Appeal Chamber Judgment, July 15, 1999).

Prosecutor v. Tadić, ICTY Case No. IT-94–1 (Trial Chamber Judgment, May 7, 1997).

NOTES

1. THE HAGUE

1. Michael Smith, *Killer Elite: The Inside Story of America's Most Secret Special Operations Team* (New York: St. Martin's Press, 2008), 202.
2. Ibid.
3. Ibid., 191–201.
4. Ibid., 191, 197.
5. Gordan Malić, "In the Convicts Battalion, Tuta Was the Ideologist, and I Was the Commander: We Were Accountable Only to Šušak and Boban!," *Globus*, March 17, 2000.
6. Ibid.
7. Ibid.
8. Ibid.
9. Ibid.
10. Ibid. See also Gordan Malić, "Terorista sa Pavelicevog praga," *BH Dani*, September 22, 2000.
11. Malić, "In the Convicts Battalion."

3. WOODEN RIFLES

1. John Steele and Michael Smith, "MI6 Grenade Fired from Public Park," *Telegraph*, September 22, 2000; BBC, "MI6 Attack Weapon Identified," September 22, 2000.
2. Henry McDonald, "Croat General Armed Real IRA," *Observer*, September 24, 2000.
3. Neil Mackay and Pero Jurisin, "Croatian War Criminal Linked to Real IRA Gun-Running," *Sunday Tribune*, September 17, 2000.
4. McDonald, "Croat General Armed Real IRA."

4. A POLICEMAN'S MURDER

1. Prosecutor v. Naletilić and Martinović, ICTY Case No. IT-98–34 (Trial Chamber Judgment, March 31, 2003), 178, 180.

5. TWO SPANISH LEGIONNAIRES

1. Prosecutor v. Prlić et al., ICTY Case No. IT-04–74 (Transcript, January 25, 2007).

8. THE CONSPIRATORS

1. Biographic information for all suspects and accused persons was taken directly from public indictments.

10. INDICTMENT OF A PRESIDENT

1. Richard Overy, *Interrogations: The Nazi Elite in Allied Hands, 1945* (New York: Viking, 2001), 48.
2. Stanley Pomorski, "Conspiracy and Criminal Organization," in *The Nuremberg Trial and International Law*, ed. George Ginsburgs and Vladimir Kudriavtsev (Dordrecht: Martinus Nijhoff Publishers, 1990), 219.
3. Carla Del Ponte, *Madame Prosecutor: Confrontations with Humanity's Worst Criminals and the Culture of Impunity* (New York: Other Press, 2009), 140.

11. MALA JASKA

1. Gregory Freeman, *The Forgotten 500: The Untold Story of the Men Who Risked All for the Greatest Rescue Mission of World War II* (New York: NAL Caliber, 2007), xi, 82.
2. Ibid., 81.
3. Ibid., 203.
4. Ibid., 209.
5. Ibid., 245–47.
6. Ibid., 85.
7. Ibid., 139.
8. Diana Nelson Jones, "North Side's 'Mala Jaska' Deteriorates as Route 28 Grows," *Pittsburgh Post-Gazette*, May 20, 2009.
9. George Prpic, *The Croatian Immigrants in America* (New York: Philosophical Library, 1971), 125.

EPILOGUE: THE HAGUE CRUCIBLE

1. Prosecutor v. Babić (Transcript, January 27, 2004).
2. Kevin Parker, *Report to the President: Death of Milan Babić* (The Hague: International Criminal Tribunal for the Former Yugoslavia, June 8, 2006), 6.
3. "Hague Court Cuts Serb Major's Murder Sentence," *International Business Times*, December 9, 2010.

APPENDIX 1: CENČIĆI JERBIĆEVI

1. Prpic, *Croatian Immigrants in America*, 211.
2. Ibid., 239.
3. Ibid., 236.
4. Alan Wakefield and Simon Moody, *Under the Devil's Eye: Britain's Forgotten Army at Salonika 1915–1918* (Stroud, UK: Sutton Publishing, 2004), 13–31, 166.
5. Ibid., 32–46.

BIBLIOGRAPHY

Bassiouni, M. Cherif. *Crimes against Humanity in International Criminal Law.* The Hague: Kluwer Law International, 1999.

Bower, Tom. *Blind Eye to Murder: Britain, America and the Purging of Nazi Germany—A Pledge Betrayed.* London: Granada Publishing, 1981.

Burgwyn, H. James. *Empire on the Adriatic: Mussolini's Conquest of Yugoslavia, 1941–1943.* New York: Enigma Books, 2005.

Del Ponte, Carla. *Madame Prosecutor: Confrontations with Humanity's Worst Criminals and the Culture of Impunity.* New York: Other Press, 2009.

Emsley, Clive. *Gendarmes and the State in Nineteenth-Century Europe.* Oxford: Oxford University Press, 1999.

Freeman, Gregory. *The Forgotten 500: The Untold Story of the Men Who Risked All for the Greatest Rescue Mission of World War II.* New York: NAL Caliber, 2007.

Ginsburgs, George, and Vladimir Kudriavtsev, eds. *The Nuremberg Trial and International Law.* Dordrecht: Martinus Nijhoff Publishers, 1990.

Goñi, Uki. *The Real Odessa: How Perón Brought the Nazi War Criminals to Argentina.* London: Granta Books, 2002.

Herwig, Holger. *The First World War: Germany and Austria-Hungary, 1914–1918.* London: Arnold Publishing, 1997.

Hupchick, Dennis P., and Harold E. Cox. *The Palgrave Concise Historical Atlas of the Balkans.* New York: Palgrave, 2001.

International Committee for the Red Cross. *The Geneva Conventions of August 12, 1949.* Geneva: International Committee for the Red Cross, 1949.

International Committee for the Red Cross. *Protocols Additional to the Geneva Conventions of 12 August 1949.* Geneva: International Committee for the Red Cross, 1977.

International Criminal Court. *Elements of Crimes*, UN Doc. PCNICC/2000/1/Add.2. Geneva: United Nations, 2000.

International Criminal Tribunal for the Former Yugoslavia. *Basic Documents—Documents de Réferénce.* The Hague: International Criminal Tribunal for the Former Yugoslavia, 1998.

Ipsen, Knut. "Combatants and Non-combatants." In *Handbook of Humanitarian Law in Armed Conflicts*. Edited by D. Fleck. Oxford: Oxford University Press, 1995.

Kinross, Patrick Balfour. *The Ottoman Centuries: The Rise and Fall of the Turkish Empire.* New York: Morrow, 1977.

Laughland, John. *Travesty: The Trial of Slobodan Milošević and the Corruption of International Justice.* New York: Pluto Press, 2007.

Overy, Richard. *Interrogations: The Nazi Elite in Allied Hands, 1945.* New York: Viking, 2001.

Parker, Kevin. *Report to the President: Death of Milan Babic.* The Hague: International Criminal Tribunal for the Former Yugoslavia, June 8, 2006.

Pictet, Jean S., ed. *Geneva Conventions of 1949: Commentary.* Vol. 3, *Relative to the Treatment of Prisoners of War.* Geneva: International Committee of the Red Cross, 1960.

———. *Geneva Conventions of 1949: Commentary.* Vol. 4, *Relative to the Protection of Civilian Persons in Time of War.* Geneva: International Committee of the Red Cross, 1958.

Pomorski, Stanley. "Conspiracy and Criminal Organizations." In Ginsburgs and Kudriavtsev, *Nuremberg Trial and International Law*, 213–46.

Pozzi, Henri. *Black Hand over Europe.* Zagreb: Croatian Information Centre, 1994.

Prpic, George. *The Croatian Immigrants in America.* New York: Philosophical Library, 1971.

Smith, Michael. *Killer Elite: The Inside Story of America's Most Secret Special Operations Team.* New York: St. Martin's Press, 2008.

Wakefield, Alan, and Simon Moody. *Under the Devil's Eye: Britain's Forgotten Army at Salonika 1915–1918.* Gloustershire, UK: Sutton Publishing, 2004.

INDEX

abbreviations, xxi–xxvi

ABiH (Army of Bosnia and Herzegovina), 29–31, 33–34

Achilles, 89

Adžić, Blagoje, xxvii, 116, 154, 179

Agotić, Imra, 140

Aguilar Fernandez, Francisco, 60–61, 66, 188

Ahmet, 16–17

AID (Agency for Information and Documentation, Bosnian), 16

al Qaeda, 77

Albanians, 70–71, 73, 76–77, 115, 123, 126

Albright, Madeleine, xiii

Amanpour, Christiane, 71

Amber Star, 7

Andabak, Ivan, xxvii, 12, 21–22, 39–43

antiterrorist groups (ATG), 20, 26, 69, 101, 133–34

AOS (American Group), 131

Apple-1, 90–91, 92

Arbour, Louise, xxvii, 8

Arkan (Željko Ražnatović)
    about, xxix, 72, 120–21, 126, 131
    crimes, 102–3, 121, 127–28, 138
    death, 154, 179–81
    indictment, 154, 180

Arkan's Tigers, 100–103, 119, 120–21, 127, 130, 135

Army of Bosnia and Herzegovina (ABiH), 29–31, 33–34

Arshad, Azim, xxvii, 91, 92, 105

Babić, Milan, xxvii, 118–19, 130, 140–41, 154, 174–76

Babylon-on-Thames attack, 41–42

Bačić, Mirjana, 170

Bačić family, 170

Baćin, 91, 93, 112, 169–70, 174, 177

Bačka Palanka Lobby, 124, 127

Barbarić, Lucija, 202

baseball, 22

BBC News, 41, 157

Belgravia, SS, 196, 197

Beli Orlovi (White Eagles), 96, 108, 127, 131, 155

Berlin, 5–6

bin Laden, Osama, 77

Bird Cage, 201

Black Sea mercenary, 17, 36

Blackjack, 124–26, 128, 180

Blair, Tony, 71

Blakey, G. Robert, 149

Blewitt, Graham, xxvii, 8, 146

Bogdanović, Radmilo, 137–38

Borovo Selo, 104, 112, 128

Bosanac, Vesna, 183

Bosanska Dubica, 92

Bosnia, about, 13, 16–19, 39, 70

Bosniaks
    about, 15, 18–19
    KB attack in Sovici, 19–22
    Srebrenica, 83
    war in Mostar, 8, 23–24, 48, 63–64
    wooden rifle incident, 29–34

Bosnian-Croats, 15, 19–20, 30

Bosnian-Muslims. *See* Bosniaks

Boston Globe, 42

Brajdić brothers, 133

British Secret Intelligence Service (MI6), 41–42

British Special Air Service (SAS), 6–7

Bruška, 84–85, 112

Bulatović, Momir, xxvii, 120, 126–27, 154, 179

Bulevar street, 23, 29, 37, 62

Bureau of Law Enforcement for the Department of Alcoholic Beverage Control, 9
Bush administration, xiv
Byzantine Ruthenians, 107

C-017, 131
California University of Pennsylvania, 165
Calumet (Michigan), 197, 199
Čandić, Mustafa, 139
Capone, Al, 203
Captain Dragan, 85, 129–32, 177
Carabinieri, 23, 29, 45, 66
Carlos, a.k.a. Carlos the Jackal. See Sánchez, Ilich Ramírez
Carpathia, RMS, 202
Ćelija, 102, 127
Cenčić, Agnes, 194, 196
Cenčić, Anton, 194
Cenčić, Boris, 2
Cenčić, Edo, 201, 204–6
Cenčić, Ivan (John), 198, 199, 202
Cenčić, Jakov, 194
Cencic, John, 168
Cenčić, Josip (Joseph), xxvii, 1–3, 13
    childhood, 194–96
    in Detroit, 202, 203, 206
    marriage through WWI, 197–201
    as young adult in America, 196–97
Cenčić, Jožica (Rose), 198, 199
Cenčić, Lovro, 193–94, 196
Cenčić, Margareta, 194, 196
Cenčić, Marija (Josip's sister), 194, 196
Cenčić, Marija (Mary) (Josip's daughter), 198, 199
Cenčić, Paulina Sanković (Pauline), 197–99, 200, 202, 206
Cenčić, Pavle (Paul), 198, 199, 200–201, 202
Cenčić, Stevo, 169
Cenčić, Vinko, 194, 196, 201
Cenčić clan, 1–2, 13, 47, 193–94. See also Cenčići Jerbićevi clan; specific members
Cenčić names, Anglicization of, 199
Cenčići Jerbićevi clan, 194, 196, 197–99, 201–6. See also specific members
Cerovljani, 91, 93, 112, 174, 177
Cetingrad, 133
Četniks, 108, 115, 163–64

Chimney Sweeper, 205
Chinese embassy bombing in Kosovo, 72
CIA, 10, 77, 109, 124
Cindrić family, 89, 169
Cindrich family, 169
Clausewitz, Carl von, 79
Clemenc, "Big Annie," 199
Clinton, Bill, 71, 72
Čolaković, Aziz, 30
Čolaković, Hamdija, 30
collateral damage, 106, 188
command responsibility, 35–36, 158, 181
common purpose doctrine (CPD), 148, 150–51, 155–56. See also joint criminal enterprise
conspiracy laws, 150–51
Convicts Battalion (KB). See KB
coperpetrators, naming of in Milošević indictment, 154, 156, 159
Corić, Valentin, 188
Covió, Mijo, 169
Covich, Marko, 169
Croatia, about, 18, 109–10
Croatian Fraternal Union (CFU), 167
Croatian Intelligence Service (HIS), 38
Croatian Party of Rights (HOS), 57
Croatian Presidential Archives, 38–39
Croatian Union of the United States, 167
Curtis, Kevin, xxviii, 144

Dalj, 99, 102, 112, 120, 121
Dalj Planina, 102, 112, 120, 121
Daljski Atar, 104
Dayton Agreement, 29, 46
DB (Serbia State Security Service)
    Blackjack, 124–26
    crimes in Grabovac and Krajina, 82, 112
    JATD/JSO, 108, 130, 143, 187
    MP Royal, 123–24
    as part of joint criminal enterprise, 110, 112, 121, 134, 136, 174, 177
    Red Berets, 70, 85, 103, 108, 117, 128–32, 155
    senior officers, 117–18
Death Cell 601, 5
Del Ponte, Carla, xxviii, 146, 152, 159
Delta Force, xix, xxiii, xxv, 7
demon of Goranske woods, 195

Dimitrijević, Dragutin, 180
Đinđić, Zoran, xxviii, 144, 186–87
Dinko, 52
Dokmanović, Slavko, 100
Doljani, 19, 20–22, 24, 31
Driguet, Catherine, xxviii, 15, 16, 34, 58
Dubica, 90–94, 112, 174, 177
Dubrovnik
    arrests and convictions for crimes in,
        183–86
    crimes in, 104–6, 112, 120, 126–27
Dušan Silni, 96, 108, 127, 155
Dzuro, Vladimir, xxviii, 95

Ellis Island, 196–97, 198, 202
Erdut, crimes in, 100–101, 102–4, 120, 121
Erdut Planina, 102, 121
Escobar, Pablo, 7
exhumations of human remains, 54–55,
    73–75, 91, 99, 169

Falcon, 49, 51–52, 54
FBI (Federal Bureau of Investigation), 72
Ferdinand, Franz, 15, 180
forced labor, 25, 32, 48, 179
forensic accounting, 87
forensic evidence, 10, 54, 74, 87, 155
Frančisković, Lucija, 197
Friesland, SS, 198
Fruška Gora, 113
FRY (Federal Republic of Yugoslavia),
    about, xxiii, 70, 143
Fugitive Investigative Support Team (FIST),
    100
funding of joint criminal enterprise, 77, 87,
    110, 112, 118, 134–35, 138

Galbraith, Peter, 136
Garrod, Martin, 37
Gendarmerie, 23, 66, 81, 197
Geneva Conventions, 10, 31, 35, 57, 188
German army, 73–74
Glock-1, 25–27
Gophers, the, 203
Gorski Kotar region, xi, 1–3, 193–95, 197,
    204–5
government, conspirators control of, 94,
    110, 112, 118, 119

Grabovac, 103, 112
Greater Serbia concept, 81–82, 105, 109,
    115, 127, 158
Groome, Dermot, xxviii, 149, 150–51, 152,
    177
Grujić, Ivan, 103–4

Habsburgs, 194
Hadžić, Goran
    about, xxviii, 119, 124
    arrest and indictment, 178–79
    crimes, 99, 119–20
    as part of joint criminal enterprise, 126,
        136, 138, 154
Hague, The, about, 5, 7
Hardin, Bill, xxvii, 81, 82, 84, 85, 88
Harmandžić, Nenad, 45, 48–55, 57, 58
Heliodrom Detention Center, 24–26, 31–32,
    49, 51–52
Herzegovina mafia, 45, 57
Hitler, Adolf, 12, 167
Hrvatska Kostajnica, 92, 112
human shields, 30, 32–34, 37, 80, 92, 96
Humo, Esad, 62
Hungarians as victims, 100–103, 107, 110,
    121, 127
HVO
    background, 8, 19
    crimes in Mostar, 19, 22, 24, 188
    headquarters search warrant, 45–48
    Spanish legionnaires attacks, 60–65
    wooden rifles incident, 29–34, 37

ICRC (International Committee for the Red
    Cross), 60–61, 62, 65, 98
ICTY (International Criminal Tribunal for
    the former Yugoslavia), about, xiii–xv,
    10, 145
indictment of Milošević, 146–61
    case presentation, review and signature,
        158–59
    investigative plan, 146–48, 152
    prosecution theory, 148–52, 160–61
    tribunal judge confirmation, 159–60
    writing of, 152–57
Intelligence Support Activity, 7, 100
International Committee for the Red Cross
    (ICRC), 60–61, 62, 65, 98

International Criminal Tribunal for the former Yugoslavia (ICTY), about, xiii–xv, 10, 145
international law, 9, 35, 56, 59, 63, 145
International Police Task Force (IPTF), 45
Interpol, 100, 123, 179, 187
interpreters, about, 41
interrogation, about, 26, 40, 41
investigations of Yugoslav war crimes, about
    background, xvii, 7–8, 9–10
    process, 18, 35, 86, 111, 145–46
IPTF (International Police Task Force), 45
Iranian Revolutionary Guard, 19
Irish Republican Army (IRA), 11, 12, 37, 41–42
Israeli State Secret Service, 138
Italian mafia, 77

JA (Yugoslav Army), 82
Jackson, Robert H., 165
Janša, Janez, 116
JATD, 108, 130. *See also* Red Berets
Jerbić, Ursula, 194
JNA (Yugoslav People's Army)
    about, 18, 108, 110, 136
    antiterrorist groups, 133–34
    Babić, 118
    counterintelligence, 140
    crimes in Croatia, 79–80, 82–84, 88–92, 94, 97–100, 104–5
    Milošević, 112, 117
    Presidency of the SFRY, 113–14
    senior officers, 115–17
Johnstown (Pennsylvania), 166
joint criminal enterprise. *See also specific members*
    indictments, 148–57
    overview of operations, control, and strategies, 109–12, 115
    precedence setting for future indictments, 160–61, 173
Joint Special Operations Command (JSOC), 7
Jokić, Miodrag, xxviii, 185–86
Josipović, Ivo, 178, 183
Jović, Borisav, xxviii, 113–14, 154, 179
JSO, 108, 130, 143, 187. *See also* Red Berets

Jump Rope, 84–85
jurisdiction of ICTY, 10, 145

K-2, 130–31
Kadijević, Veljko, xxvii, 115–16, 154, 179
Kanolerich, John and Mary, 198
KB (Convicts Battalion)
    background, 8–9, 11–12
    Bosnia attacks, 19–22, 23, 24, 26
    wooden rifle incident, 29–34, 36–37
Kertes, Mihalj, 124, 126, 127, 128, 137
key characters, xxvii–xxx
KGB (Soviet Committee for State Security), 16, 109
KLA (Kosovo Liberation Army), 70–71, 77–78
Klisa, 102
KOG (Counterintelligence Group of UB), 108, 116–17, 139, 140
KOS (Counterintelligence Service of Yugoslav's People's Army), 132, 134, 167
Kosovo
    about, 76–77
    investigation in, 72–76
    overview of Serb criminal activities in, 69–72
Kosovo Force (KFOR), 72
Kosovo Liberation Army (KLA), 70–71, 77–78
Kostić, Branko, xxviii, 114, 154, 179
Koštunica, Vojislav, 143, 144, 187
Kovačević, Vladimir, xxviii, 186
Krajina
    conspirators' control, 112, 118, 119
    crimes, 81–85, 87–93, 130
    Log Revolution, 133
Krajina Milicija (Martić's Police). *See* Martić's Police
Krk, 202

La Cosa Nostra, 167
La Gascogne, SS, 198
La Mano Nera, 203
Lady-O, 137–39
land mines, 5, 15, 74, 86, 96
las Canarias, 23, 62
law of war, 63, 106, 107

League of Communists, 111, 118, 119
Legat, 125
Legija, xxx, 70, 131, 187
Leutar, Jozo, 39
Lipovačka, 169
Lipovačka Dreznica, 88–89, 169
local territorial defense units (TO). *See* TO
Log Revolution, 133
Lokve, xi, 1–2, 163, 194, 196–97, 204–5
Lovas, 96–97, 112, 127
Luciano, Salvatore, 203
Luković, Milorad "Brazil." *See* Ulemek, Milorad "Legija."

Macedonia, 71, 75
Magdić, Martin, 170
Magdić, Mile, 170
Majnarić, Margareta, 196
Mala Jaska, 166–70
maps, vii–xi
Marechaussee, 56, 57
Maria Theresa, 194
Marinović clan, 85
Marinovići, 84–85, 112
Martić, Milan
  about, xxix, 82, 119, 135
  arrest, indictment and trial, 154, 176–77
  Babić, 118, 175
  Red Berets, 129–31
Martić's Police
  about, 82, 118, 119
  crimes, 82, 84–85, 88, 89, 92, 169
Martinović, Vinko (Štela). *See* Štela
Massacre of 1913, 199–200
Međugorje, 62
mercenaries, foreign, 8–9, 21–22, 25–27, 36–37
Mesić, Stjepan, 115–16
MI5 (British Security Service), xxiv, 42, 100
MI6 (British Secret Intelligence Service), 41–42
Michigan's Upper Peninsula, 195, 197
Mihailović, Draža, 163–64
Mihelčić, Augustin, 196
Milošević, Slobodan
  Arkan, 121, 126, 154, 180
  arrest, custody and charges, 143–45
  background, xxix, 70, 80, 111–13, 136

death, 171–72
Đinđić, 187
funding, 87, 112, 126
Greater Serbia goal, 81–82, 125, 127–28
indictment (*See* indictment of Milošević)
joint criminal enterprise, 125–28, 130, 135–39, 179
Kosovo, 71–72
MP Royal, 124
Presidency, 114
Red Berets, 130, 132
trial, 77, 171–72, 174, 175, 178
Ministry of Defense, Serbia, 117
Mladić, Ratko, xxix, 82–83, 85, 178
Montenegro, 105, 114, 120, 126
Mostar, x
  arrests and convictions for crimes in, 188–89
  investigation in, 16, 19–20
  Spanish legionnaires murders, 59–67
  war in, 19, 22–24
  wooden rifles incident, 29–37
Mount Hum, 63
Mount Srđ, 104
MP Royal, 123–25, 128
Mrkšić, Mile, xxix, 98, 100, 137, 181–82
Muñoz Castellanos, Arturo, 62–63, 64–66, 188
MUP (Ministry of Internal Affairs), 55, 69, 117, 120, 155, 178
Murugan, Rajie, xxix, 91, 92, 105
Muslims
  Bosniaks (*See* Bosniaks)
  Croatia, 107, 110
Mussolini, Benito, 12, 167, 204
Musulin, George, 164, 166
My Gorski Kotar (Gordana Brkić Žagar), 2–3

Nadin, 82, 83, 112
Naletilić, Mladen (Tuta). *See* Tuta
narcotics trafficking, 77, 126
Narodni List, 200
NATO (North Atlantic Treaty Organization), 19, 24, 71–72
Nice, Geoffrey, 161
Niemann, Grant, 100
Nuremberg trials, 149, 151, 163

Observer, 42
October 5 Overthrow, 143
O'Donnell, Bernie, xxix, 144
Office of Special Investigations (U.S. Air Force), xxv, 9, 77, 124, 157
On War (Clausewitz), 79
108th Special Operations Corps (Commando Troepen), 7
Operation Ensue, 6
Operation Goshawk, 38–39
Operation Halyard, 163–64, 166
Operation Labrador, 139
Operation Opera, 139
Operation Storm, 118
Orkan rocket attacks, 176
Oscar, 96
OSCE, 86
OSS (Office of Strategic Services), 163–64, 166
Ovčara, 98–99, 170, 181, 183
Overy, Richard, 151

Pajo, Enis, 30
Palestine Liberation Organization (PLO), 11
Panić, Milan, 127
Pap, Juliana, 100–101, 104
Pavelić, Ante, 12, 40, 167
Petković, Milivoj, 188
Petrovci, 107
Petrović, Vladimir, 184
Pfundheller, Brent, xxix, 81, 82–84, 85, 88
Pittsburgh, 165–70, 195
Pittsburgh Steelers, 166
Pleše, Mirjana, 2–3, 205
Praljak, Slobodan, 188
Predore, 94
Presidency of SFRY, 110, 113–14, 115–16, 117
presidents of republics, 118–20
prison at The Hague, 5
Prizren, 72–76
Prlić, Jadranko, 188
Proboj-1, 139
Proboj-2, 139
Procession of the Cross, 195–96
pronunciations, xxi
propaganda, 110, 117
prosecution theory, 148–52, 159, 160–61, 173

Prosecutor v. Tadić, 148, 150, 151
Provisional IRA, 37
Purple Gang, 203
Pušić, Berislav, 188
Puškarić, Darinka, 204–6

Radić, Miroslav, xxix, 100, 183
Rakin, Natalija, 104
Ralston, John, xxix, 8, 9
Raštani, x, 19, 24, 31
Ražnatović, Željko (Arkan). *See* Arkan
Real IRA, 41–42
Red Berets, 70, 85, 103, 108, 117, 128–32, 155. *See also* JSO
Red Faction Army, 11
Red Jacket, 197
Red Notices, Interpol, 123, 179
refugees, war, 133, 169
Republic of Croatia, about, 18, 109–10
Republic of Serbia, about, 112, 125
Republic of Serbian Krajina (RSK), 112, 118, 119
RICO Act, 149
Rodrigues, Almiro, 160
Royal Canadian Mounted Police, 15, 72, 105
Royal Casino, 123–25, 128
Royal Marines, 37
RSK (Republic of Serbian Krajina), 112, 118, 119
Rubin, James, 71
Rump Presidency, 114
Ruthenians, 107, 110, 166

Saborsko, 88–90, 112, 174
SAJ, 69, 101
Salonika, 201
Sánchez, Ilich Ramírez, 11
Sanković, Paulina. *See* Cenčić, Paulina Sanković
Sanković, Šime, 81, 197
SANU Memorandum, 70
Šar Mountains, 76
Sarajevo, about, 15, 39, 132
SAS (British Special Air Service), 6–7
Saxonia, RMS, 198
SBWS (Slavonia, Baranja and Western Srem), 95–104, 112, 119, 130, 153

Scheveningen
   Carlton Beach Hotel, 6
   Prison, 5, 7, 57, 100, 171
SČP (Serbian Četnik Movement), 115, 119
SDG (Serbian Volunteer Guard), 100–103,
   119, 120–21, 130, 135
SDS (Serbian Democratic Party), 118, 119
SEALs, Navy, 7
Second Operation Group, 183
security clearance of war crime
   investigators, 7
security for war crime investigators, 29, 34
Senasi, Marija, 101–2, 104
September 11 attacks, 157
Serbia, Republic of, about, 112, 125
State Security Service, Serbia. *See* DB
Serbian Četnik Movement (SČP), 115, 119
Serbian Democratic Party (SDS), 118, 119
Serbian Freedom Movement, 115
Serbian National Renewal Party, 115
Serbian National Security (SNB), 101, 108,
   119, 130, 155
Serbian Radical Party (SRS), 115, 176
Serbian Volunteer Guards (SDG), 100–103,
   119, 120–21, 127, 130, 135
Šešelj, Vojislav, xxix, 114–15, 154, 176, 187
Šešelj's Men, 95, 108, 127, 131, 138, 155
SFRY (Socialist Federal Republic of
   Yugoslavia)
   about, 18, 70
   Presidency, 110, 113–14, 115–16, 117
Shea, Jamie, 71
Shin Bet, 109
Simatović, Franko
   about, xxx, 117–18, 124, 126, 154
   arrest, indictment, and trial, 154, 177
   crimes, 127–28
   Red Berets, 128–32
Simović, Tomislav, xxx, 117, 137–38, 154,
   179
Škabrnja, crimes in, 79–80, 82–85, 112, 178
Skater, 87–88
Škrljevo, 197
Slavonia, Baranja and Western Srem
   (SBWS), 95–104, 112, 119, 130, 153
Šljivančanin, Veselin, xxx, 98, 100, 137,
   181–83
Slovenia, about, 18, 70, 116

Smith, Bradley F., 151
SNB (Serbian National Security), 101, 108,
   119, 130, 155
Socialist Alliance of Working People of
   Serbia, 111
Socialist Federal Republic of Yugoslavia
   (SFRY). *See* SFRY
Socialist Party of Serbia (SPS), 111, 113
Socialist Republic of Serbia, 112
Soldier of Fortune Magazine, 26, 36
sovereignty, national, 7, 18, 38
Sovići, x, 19–22, 24
Spanish Battalion (SPABAT), 60–66
Spanish legionnaires, murder of, 59–67,
   188–89
SPS (Socialist Party of Serbia), 111, 113
Srebrenica, 83
SRS (Serbian Radical Party), 115, 176
St. Katarina's Church, 2, 195-197, 204
St. Nicholas Cemetery, 169–70
St. Nicholas Church, 167, 168
Stabilization Force (SFOR), 19, 29, 66
Stambolić, Ivan, xxx, 111, 113, 187
Stanišić, Jovica
   about, xxx, 117, 124, 134, 135
   arrest, indictment, and trial, 154, 177
   crimes, 126, 127–28, 130
   Red Berets, 132
Štela (Vinko Martinović)
   about, xxix, 11–12
   arrest and conviction, 37–38,
      55–57, 188
   crimes, 23, 25, 32–33, 35–36, 48, 49–53
Stempf brothers, 49
Stojić, Bruno, 188
Stojičić, Radovan, xxx, 101, 120, 154, 179
Strinović, Davor, 103–4
Strugar, Pavle, xxx, 183–85
Sučić, Agnes, 202, 203
Sučić, Ivan (John), 202, 203–4
Sučić, Jozo, 202
Sučić, Katarina (Katherine), 202–3
Sucich, Agnes, 203
Sucich, John, 203
Sunday Tribune, 42
superior orders, 59
Switzerland, 17–18
Szent-Gyorgyi, Albert, 147

Tadić, Boris, 148, 150, 151, 178, 183
Takač, Ernest, 32–33, 50, 52–53
Team Eleven, 131, 144–45
Team Five, 129, 145, 147, 149
Team Four. *See also specific team members*
  about, 80–81, 85–87, 145
  Babić investigation, 174
  Dubrovnik investigations, 105, 106
  Krajina investigations, 91–92, 93
  Milošević indictment and
    prosecution, 146–48, 158–59,
    161
  overview of Croatia investigations,
    107–8, 111
  Slavonia, Baranja and Western Srem
    investigations, 104
  Western Slavonia investigations, 94–95
Team Ten, 39
Tito, Josip Broz, 18, 164, 167, 201
TO (local territorial defense units)
  about, 115–17
  conspirators' control of, 110, 118, 119,
    120–21
  Dubrovnik crimes, 104–5
  Krajina crimes, 82, 88–90
  Red Berets, 130
  Slavonia, Baranja and Western Srem
    crimes, 96, 98, 102–3
  trials and convictions of members,
    181–82, 183
  Western Slavonia crimes, 94
Todorović, Stevan, 6–7
Torkildsen, Morten, xxx, 87
Torn Victor, 7
Tuta (Mladen Naletilić)
  about, xxix, 11–12
  arrest and conviction, 37–38, 55–56,
    57–58, 188
  crimes, 21–22, 25, 35–36

UB (Yugoslav People's Army Security
  Administration), 108, 116–17, 139,
  140
UDBA (State Security Administration of
  SFRY), 167, 205
Uertz-Retzlaff, Hildegard, xxx, 156–57, 159,
  160, 174

Ulemek, Milorad "Legija," xxx, 70, 131,
  187
UN Educational, Scientific, and Cultural
  Organization (UNESCO), 104, 105
UN peacekeepers, 59–67, 136, 188–89
UN Security Council, xiii, 10, 18, 71
Upper Peninsula of Michigan, 195,
  197
Ustaše, 12, 40, 84, 93, 96, 125, 138

Van Hecke, Jan, xxx, 11, 15, 16, 48,
  56, 58
Vasiljević, Aleksandar, xxx, 116, 138, 140,
  154, 178, 179
Vasiljović, Dragan, xxx, 85, 129–32,
  177
Virginmost mayor assassination, 134
Voćin, 94–95, 112, 127, 170
Vojvodina, 117, 125
VRS (Bosnian-Serb Army), 83, 178
Vujanović, Stanko, 183
Vujnovich, George and Mirjana, 163–64,
  165–66
Vujović, Miroljub, 183
Vukovar Hospital massacre
  arrests, trials, and convictions of those
    responsible, 99–100, 181–83
  description, 97–99, 107, 115, 120,
    137–39, 170
Vukovar Three, 100
Vuković, Mate, 169
Vuković, Pero, 169–70
Vukovići, 87–88, 112

Western Slavonia, 94–95, 112, 127, 153
White Eagles (Beli Orlovi), 96, 108, 127,
  131, 155
Williamson, Clint, xxx, 100
Witness X, 132–37, 140
wooden rifles incident, 27, 29–37, 57
World War I, 15, 198, 200–201
World War II, 2, 5, 12, 93, 163–64,
  204–5

Yugoslav Army (JA), 82
Yugoslav Navy, 104, 186
Yugoslav People's Army (JNA). *See* JNA

Yugoslav People's Army Security
 Administration (UB), 108, 116–17,
 139–40
Yugoslavs in America, 165–70, 196–204,
 206

Žagar, Gordana Brkić, 3
Zagreb, 38, 40, 119, 126, 139, 166, 176
Zec, Milan, xxx, 186
Zemun Clan, 187
Zrinski, Petar, 194

ABOUT THE AUTHOR

John Robert Cencich was born in St. John's, Newfoundland, and moved to the United States with his family as a young boy. He lived outside Detroit, Michigan, until he graduated from high school at the age of seventeen and enlisted in the U.S. Air Force. He subsequently enjoyed a long and successful career in law enforcement. Trained by the FBI and Scotland Yard, he served for more than twenty-five years as a police officer, investigator, and special agent with the U.S. Air Force Office of Special Investigations. His experiences include national security and counterintelligence investigations, protective service operations, violent crimes, undercover work, and traditional and nontraditional organized crime investigations. He also served a special attachment with the London Metropolitan Police.

In 1998 he began a four-year appointment with the UN War Crimes Tribunal at The Hague. There he led one of the largest international criminal investigations in history, involving crimes against humanity such as murder, extermination, rape, torture, and persecution.

Dr. Cencich is a tenured professor of justice studies at California University of Pennsylvania. He also serves as the director of the Pennsylvania Institute of Criminological and Forensic Sciences. He served previous appointments on the Organized Crime Committee of the International Association of Chiefs of Police and the Pennsylvania State Advisory Committee on Wrongful Convictions. The results of his work led to more than fifty commendations, including the Police Meritorious Service Award with Bronze "V" device, the Meritorious Service Medal from the U.S. government, and a formal resolution passed by the Senate of Virginia.

He earned a doctorate in juridical science from the University of Notre Dame and an advanced law degree from the University of Kent at Canterbury. He also holds a master's degree in criminal justice and a bachelor's degree in organizational management.